1984

KARLHANS MÜLLER

The Architecture of Transport in the Federal Republic of Germany

INTER NATIONES   BONN

The Author:

Karlhans Müller was born in Frankfurt/Main in 1938. By profession and vocation he is a journalist, having worked, for many years, for the "Frankfurter Neue Presse" and "Frankfurter Allgemeine Zeitung" before being appointed head of the press and information division of an eminent firm in the transport industry. He is editor-in-chief of a magazine and has written several books dealing with transport and energy problems.

Cover page 1: With its 23 metres lifting height and 185 metres chamber length, the shaft lock on the lateral canal of the Elbe near Uelzen is Europe's largest lock.

Cover page 2: With its eleven commercial airports the Federal Republic of Germany and West-Berlin benefit from an excellent air traffic infrastructure.

Picture opposite title: In large cities, traffic systems take up an increasing amount of space. In Nuremberg, several Federal roads and railroads form a junction.

Cover page 3: Long-distance railway network in the Federal Republic of Germany and West-Berlin. The dotted areas indicate the metropolitan railway either in operation or under construction, as well as rapid local traffic on existing track.

Translation by Karen Roux-Nielsen

ISBN 3–7879–0196–5

© 1981 by Heinz Moos Verlag, Munich
Overall production in co-operation with Inter Nationes · Bonn

Printed in the Federal Republic of Germany

PREFACE

We are living in times of extreme mobility marked to a great extent by the technical achievements in the field of transport and their global application. Motorisation has changed our lives, but then it has also changed the image of our cities and even entire landscapes. Occasionally, one recognises signs of the freedom which the motor vehicle has given us threatening to turn into the opposite. In a country such as the Federal Republic of Germany which, owing to its geographical position in the heartland of Central Europe, is a transit country between North and South, East and West, several dozen billion Deutschmarks are spent annually in order to keep pace, middling at least, with the evolution of traffic and to cope with the ensuing problems. For Federal trunk roads alone, between 600 and 700 bridges are built every year. Throughout the Federal Republic of Germany, modern buildings have come into existence for the purpose of road, rail, nautical and air traffic.

It is these buildings and their design that this book is about. It provides an introduction not only to traffic constructions of the past three decades, but also to those dating back to much earlier times, inasfar as they still serve their purpose today, or bear special significance for the history of transport architecture. Due to limited space, communications traffic, i. e. postal and telecommunications, had to be excluded, and neither have pipelines and cableways been taken into account. Special emphasis is on the intramunicipal traffic and its problems. Aspects of areal economy and town planning could, therefore, only be dealt with briefly.

The enormous volume of construction resulting from war destruction and, in particular, from the soaring development of road traffic, could not fail, in many cases, to the quality of design being neglected. Nevertheless, many traffic constructions of high technical and architectural value have been erected already during the early post-war years. Often, traffic constructions built in the last decades give evidence that technical constructions, whilst bearing in mind constructive and material-related prerequisites, can be conceived in such a way that they enrich rural and urban landscape.

Contrary to the habitual art of building, transport architecture – as Friedrich Tamms sees it – is strictly linked to functionalism, to the laws of building statics and to the principle of economy. Transport constructions are the works of engineers. Is their design, then, not a foregone conclusion, making the contribution of an architect superfluous?

Today, this question is of the past. It has meantime generally been accepted that traffic constructions also – and very much so – require artistic designing. Here, too, the exception proves the rule. Says Friedrich Tamms: "Technical buildings should and can be designed without elements or materials alien to the construction so as to comply with aesthetic, i. e., non-technical, laws." And Gerd Lohmer who is an equally experienced architect in the field of bridges and transport construction, remarks: "Concepts such as composition, rythm, counterpoint and harmony are equally well used in architecture as in music."

A prerequisite for a convincing design both from a technical and an aesthetic point of view is the very close and trusting co-operation between engineer and architect. This aspect is scrutinised especially in the context of the construction of bridges. It is amazing to see the restraint exercised by the departments of architecture vis-a-vis transport architecture among the great variety of which, as a rule, only certain sections are dealt with. It is in a bulky world history of architecture, published by Pier Luigi Nervi, of all places, that you will find only one single picture of a bridge among 700 other illustrations in the volume on contemporary architecture. This picture shows the viaduct erected in 1967 over the river Pelcevera in Genoa, giving a brutal image of a bridge in an urban landscape – a good example of construction in disrespect of man.

According to Fritz Leonhardt, civil engineers "should remember and take into account, first and foremost, the effect on man and on man's well-being when planning and designing their constructions. The civil engineer can and must contribute essentially to achieving this aim, also through co-operation with an architect." This is particularly

5

true for transport constructions, for they are to blame to a considerable extent for the uneasiness the ugly and uniform looks of our cities have created. Although most people, today, will have to do without a "School of Seeing", every single one is affected by deformity. Even though this may not come to the surface of our consciousness, it still affects us subconsciously. Ignoring the necessity of design ultimately means to aid and abet intellectual and spiritual atrophy in man. Generations and generations will have to live with what we place amidst the landscape today, or with what is being built as short-distance public transport amenities under the surface of large cities. Those responsible must not restrict themselves solely to a technical solution, but should not rest ere a design commensurate with the constructional task has been achieved.

In view of the volume of material, transport architecture can only be portrayed in examples, and all the more so since one should not forego to point out developments and causes. At times, the selection of the objects is a matter of chance, due to the rather considerable difference in co-operativeness on the part of authorities, construction firms and architects.

The author is indebted to a great number of people. Gratitude is expressed particularly to Ministerialrat Dipl.-Ing. Günter Bergbrede, Prof. Dr.-Ing. Walter Druth, Prof. Dr.-Ing. Dr.-Ing. h.c. Fritz Leonhardt, Dr.-Ing. Dipl.-Ing. Gerd Lohmer, Ministerialdirektor Dipl.-Ing. Burkart Rümelin, Head Construction Director Dipl.-Ing. Klaus Scheelhaase, Ministerialdirigent Dipl.-Ing. Walter Stoll and Prof. Dr. Friedrich Tamms.

Dreieich, March 1980

KARLHANS MÜLLER

TABLE OF CONTENTS

PREFACE   5

CHAPTER I   Motorways, Roads and Bridges   9

CHAPTER II   Waterways and Ports   45

CHAPTER III   Rail Transport Installations   71

CHAPTER IV   Urban Transport and Relevant Constructions   91

CHAPTER V   Air Transport Buildings   133

ANNEX   Bibliography   170

      Photographs and Illustrations   171

CHAPTER I Motorways, Roads and Bridges

The extremely high density of traffic in the Federal Republic of Germany is the combined result of a very dense population, the economic circumstances and the position of this country in the heart of Central Europe. 61.4 million people live on an area of 248 600 square kilometres (including West-Berlin), corresponding to 247 inhabitants per square kilometre. The number of motor vehicles registered has increased from 12.2 million in 1965 to 24.6 million in mid-1978. The trend is for these numbers to increase further. Over the past years, an average of 17 thousand million Deutschmarks have been spent annually for the construction and maintenance of roads. The network of public roads boasts an overall length of approximately 467 000 kilometres of which more than 170 000 kilometres are classified roads, mainly district or state, i.e. "land" roads (more than 65 000 each). The network of Federal motorways or "autobahns" extends over 6711 kilometres (early 1978). Then, there are another 32 290 kilometres of Federal roads.

The Roman and Napoleonic heritage

In the South and West of the Federal Republic of Germany there are a number of roads which today still follow the road routing of the Romans who were the most eminent road builders of antiquity. Within their empire, they had created a road network of more than 250 000 kilometres in length, 75 000 kilometres of which were highly sophisticated, solid trunk roads which were maintained by them throughout the centuries. These lifelines of Roman supremacy had been laid out as straight as was at all possible, without any consideration for the landscape. Natural obstacles were overcome by the Romans by building dams and bridges, by levelling off rocks, by building serpentines leading to mountain passes, or by driving tunnels into the rock. Whilst the overland roads would generally be 4 to 5 metres wide, the heavily frequented connection between Mainz (Mogontia-

cum) and Cologne (Colonia Agrippinensis) measured 6 metres in width. The Via Appia, the road leading from Rome to the South, was even double that width.

During the Middle Ages, the Roman road and route network was restored and complemented in particular with East-West connections between the Rhine and Weichsel rivers. Contrary to the road constructions of the Romans, however, these were mainly simple earth tracks which turned into morasses after rainfall and after the thaw set in in spring. The roads deteriorated more and more, and nowhere could one, even remotely, speak of any road management. Only with the advent of mercantilism and the era of industrialisation did these conditions change. The increased production of goods demanded an efficient distribution system. Earth tracks had to be turned into solid highways, "Chausseen", which could be used all year round. Particularly France showed commendable achievements in the generous development of trade routes. It was Napoleon I (1769–1821) who, though being led primarily by military considerations, initiated the construction of these paved roads in the countries conquered by him. Thus, the fast road links between Wesel and Bremen and Hamburg via Münster and Osnabrück, and between Paris and Mainz via Metz were built, the route of the latter being planned to carry on as far as Kassel.

Many routes, and especially those in the occupied German territory on the left of the Rhine date back to that time. Their route reflects the centralism which even today is a characteristic of France's network of national roads. As in Roman times, trunk roads under Napoleon were built with long straight stretches. Whenever a change in direction became necessary between two destinations, a connecting curve with a small radius which could easily be passed by vehicles was taken to be sufficient. Little attention was given to villages when drawing up these routes, but military considerations took absolute priority. Also, the road's cross-section revealed its purpose: On a strengthened stretch of about 3 metres wide, artillery as well as supply columns could be moved. Next to it, there was the so-called "summer path" for cavalry and foot soldiers which was a stretch of lawn lined with poplars providing shade.

The Nuremberg-Regensburg motorway near the Beratzhausen connection point.

Over the past decades, these avenues were cleared, because in the course of road enlargements the edge was moved too close to the tree trunks. For today, the regulations issued by the Federal Ministry of Transport stipulate that trees along a road have to be removed once the trunk has exceeded the circumference of a beer bottle – a measure easily visualized by road maintenance staff. When building new or extending old country roads, the distance between the trees should be 4.5 metres, if there are no guard rails.

Unlike France, nationalist particularism in Germany obstructed any road planning for a long time. It is true that as early as 1779 the transport engineer Christian F. von Lüder submitted his "General Road Plan" for the "Traversing of Germany with Paved Roads" which today appears like an anticipation of the "autobahn" network, but his futuristic ideas met with little response. In the German states, road planning remained piecemeal, perhaps with the exception of Bavaria and Prussia. As a rule, the trace would follow the borders of properties leading without fail to deviations. Bends in the course of district and state roads, and even in federal roads indicate even today medieval cross-country and cattle trails.

The additional distances resulting from the zig-zag course of the routes are now avoided by using a curve with a radius as long as possible, wherever this is feasible.

From "Avus" to "Autobahn"

The roads which the first motorists were faced with were absolutely inadequate. For a long time after World War I, when the production rates in the motor vehicle industry soared, the condition of the road network was catastrophic. Often, cars travelled with long clouds of dust in their wake. At times, water splashes in the pavement were carefully maintained so as to force motorists to slow down.

One of the first milestones in modern road making is the "Avus" in Berlin. This first automobile race track in Germany simultaneously served as a highway for motor vehicles free of intersections. The carriageways in both directions were separated by a wide central reserve. In 1909, private entrepreneurs founded in Berlin the Automobil-Verkehr- und Übungs-Straße GmbH (Motor Vehicle Transport and Test Road Ltd.) for the purpose of building the "Avus". Construction began in 1912, but could not be finished until 1921 due to the first World War. The "Avus" was open to the general motor vehicle traffic, but there was a fee for its use. The race track consisted of two straights of approximately 9 kilometres length which had initially been linked by strongly superelevated curves. When testing the possibilities of superelevation, one went as far as the vertical wall in order to gain relevant experience. As a testing ground for modern road surfacings and construction equipment, the "Avus" attracted the attention of experts from all over the world. Already in 1928, tests were conducted there – based especially on findings arrived at in the U.S.A. – with concrete pavements which became of essential value for the construction of the motorways later. The results were satisfactory enough for 90% of all sections of "Autobahn" completed until the mid-Fifties to be given concrete surfaces. The transverse drop

was drastically reduced in 1971, when reconstructing the northern curve of the "Avus". Today, the "Avus" forms part of the Federal motorway system and is linked, without any intersections, to the Berlin orbital motorway system.

A novelty in German road construction was the "Kraftwagenbahn" (Motor vehicle path) between Cologne and Bonn begun in 1929. This was a rapid traffic road exclusively used by motor vehicles which had no level intersections. The roadway of this "Exclusively Cars" road comprised four lanes of 3 metres width each. The lanes in opposite direction were not only spatially, but also optically separated by a 30 centimetre wide centre line of a distinct colour which, however, was constantly ignored, thus leading to frequent hazardous situations with the oncoming traffic.

The "Verein zur Vorbereitung der Autostraße *Ha*nsestädte – *Frank*furt – *Ba*sel" *(HAFRABA)* (Society for the Preparation of the Trunk Road Linking the Hanseatic Cities, Frankfurt and Basle) which was founded at Frankfurt City Hall on 6 November 1926 after a lengthy preparatory period and which was carried by private initiative, has made international road construction history. It was the society's purpose to undertake all technical, economic, financial, transport policy-related and propagandistic preparations for the construction of a North-South traffic axis from Hamburg (as well as Lübeck and Bremen) via Frankfurt/Main to Basle. In order to save on construction costs the original HAFRABA draft submitted in 1927 provided for different widths of carriageways with two, three or four lanes of 3 metres width each – depending on traffic density in the individual sections. At this point in time, there were half a million of motor cars in Germany.

In summer 1931, the HAFRABA society submitted a set of new guidelines for the technical layout of motorways which were to become an important basis for the design of the national motorways, "Reichsautobahnen", built after 1933.

Map, drawn in 1927, of a German motorway network.

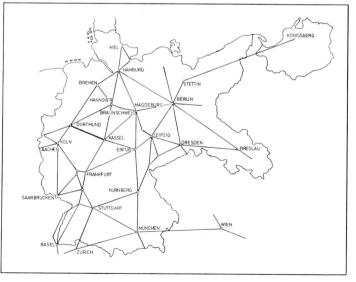

The first sections of "Reichsautobahn" were laid out straight, the routing principles having been drawn from railroad building.

The Berlin "Avus", the first car racing track in Germany which was started in 1912, but only finished in 1921, was, at the same time, an intersection-free road for motor car traffic. This picture of a car race was taken in 1931.

This is how the "Avus" looked like in 1956. The concrete surfaces tested here in 1928 revealed important principles for the subsequent construction of motorways.

The "Kraftwagenbahn" between Cologne and Bonn, started in 1929, was a novelty as a "Cars Only" road without level intersections. The photograph dated back to 1955. Later, this rapid traffic road was extended into a motor-way with a wide reserve in the middle.

The motorway connection point Zehlendorf near the border of Berlin (West). The abrupt bend behind the bridge does not live up to modern principles of routing.

By making perspective drawings, optical errors in routing can be avoided. This drawing of the Main crossing near Randersacker on the Frankfurt-Nuremberg motorway was made in 1953.

The Hamburg – Frankfurt – Basle motorway near the Frankfurt motorway intersection. It was here that the first spade was dug for the construction of national motorways, owing to the pilot work of HAFRABA e.V. The trace is as straight as can be. In the Fifties, the Federal Motorway from Cologne to Nuremberg was built over it. This aerial view was taken in 1956. Towards the end of the Seventies, the North-South route was enlarged to comprise four lanes in both directions.

The course of the motorway of this section near Kassel built in the Thirties is rather unmethodical. Unexpected curves behind hill tops are dangerous.

Embedding the road well into the landscape can be achieved by giving it a stepped cross-section.

These new guidelines provided for a central reserve of 3 metres width between the 7 metre-wide carriageways comprising two lanes of 3.5 metres each. (The lane width was only brought up later by 0.25 to 3.75 metres, a dimension which is still valid today.) Already then, a clover shape was proposed for the rectangular intersection of two motorways. As soon as 1927, the HAFRABA society had presented the plan of a German motorway network. In the early Thirties, several studies on a European motorway system had been prepared. The work and the publications of HAFRABA e.V. had led to motorway projects being vividly discussed in many European countries, the first blue-prints of these projects dating back partly to almost a decade earlier. The Milan road engineer and entrepreneur Piero Puricelli had pushed hard, as early as 1922, for the construction of an "autostrada" between Milan and the Northern Italian lakes. Already in 1924 it was opened to traffic. Up till 1935, private companies constructed 478 kilometres of motorways mainly in Northern Italy which, however, did not consist of separated carriageways and which, on an average, were only 10 metres wide including the verges. In order to push the HAFRABA project ahead, the society decided to accelerate planning work for the section from Frankfurt/Main to Mannheim/Heidelberg. But owing to legal difficulties and due to prejudices and the political atmosphere in Germany, the go-ahead for the financing by way of levying a road toll dragged on.

On 23 September 1933, the first spade was dug near Frankfurt/Main in the construction of the national motorway. This had only been possible thanks to the preparatory work of seven years of HAFRABA and their planning of the Main to Neckar section up to the very last stage. The National Socialists who had meantime come to power suppressed this achievement of HAFRABA e.V. in word and deed: The national motorways were supposed to become "Adolf Hitler's roads". Kurt Kaftan who was HAFRABA e.V.'s press relations officer before 1933, points out in his book, "Der Kampf um die Autobahnen" (The struggle for the motorways), which was published in 1955, that the Nazies, before assuming power, had been opposed to the HAFRABA plans, and had even gone as far as to fight them. In mid-1933 events suddenly overtook one another. By a law decreed on 27 June of same year an enterprise, the "Reichsautobahnen" (National Motorways) was founded for the purpose of "building and operating an efficient network of roads for motor vehicles" which was to be a subsidiary of the Deutsche Reichsbahn-Gesellschaft (German National Railways), a state-controlled enterprise. Few days later only, Fritz Todt was appointed "General inspector of roads and road management". Not only did he determine the location and the design of these motor vehicle roads; it also was him who had final decisive power over all interests affected by the planning. Even before the proclamation of the law on the national motorways, the "Reichsbahn" had set up in Frankfurt/Main, which was the seat of HAFRABA e.V., a "Superior Supervisory Board for the Construction of the Motorways" with the aim to put the blue-prints for the section Frankfurt to Mannheim/Heidelberg into practice. In August 1933 the HAFRABA society was converted into a "Society for the Preparation of the National Motorways", (abbreviated in German GEZU-VOR), which had its seat in Berlin. Its principal purpose was to lay down the lineation of the national motorways.

The development of the autobahn system was seen by Hitler as a tool for Germany to regain its military power. In May 1935 the first motorway section between Frankfurt and Darmstadt was opened to traffic. By 1942, 3859 kilometres of motorways had come into operation of which 2110 kilometres are in territory of what is today the Federal Republic of Germany. It was not until 1952 that the construction work on the Hamburg-Frankfurt-Basle motorway could be taken up again. Ten years later, this 820 kilometre-long section was practicable all the way through.

At that time, Ministerialdirektor H. Koester, who had been involved in the project from the very start, wrote: "It required the road engineers' entire professional skills to adapt the motorway over so long a distance to the extreme changes in landscape and terrain, and to create, through the art of routing, the preconditions for an economic operation and free flow of the ever increasing volume of traffic."

The art of routing

Wherever the terrain permitted, the first sections of national motorway had been laid out straight through the landscape. The principles of routing were derived from railway construction, all the more since many experts came from the "Reichsbahn" and the street constructors had acquired hardly any experience with rapid traffic roads. Originally, the Frankfurt-Darmstadt motorway – over recent years, it has been enlarged to four lanes in each direction – had been laid out in straight sections only. Wherever a change in direction was needed, curves of a radius of 200 metres were introduced, without providing for a transitional curve. Later, this proved to be of great disadvantage. No one is capable, after driving a long straight stretch at high speed, to abruptly turn the steering wheel in the angle of the curve radius. The driver needs to be given a certain lapse of time – if only the fraction of a second – to bring the steering wheel from zero-position into the curve position. This is why a straight and a curve are linked by a transitional bow. To this end, one calculated twice the radius of the actual curve. However, in order to arrive at a gradual transition, one used the comparatively flat initial portion of transition spirals, i.e., mathematically defined spiral curves with an ever decreasing radius of curvature. Since these transition spirals are very difficult to be computed by hand, they were only applied in isolated cases, until special rulers had been developed to this end. The spiral was not a regular method in the building of Federal and State roads until after the Second World War. Today, road designing is assisted by EDP programmes.

But the old principles of routing still had other disadvantages: Thus, it became apparent that a straigth extending over a great many kilometres had a tiring effect on the driver of a motor car. Again and again, cars and lorries veered off the pavement because their drivers fell asleep. Furthermore, the original routing method often presented a drastic interference with the landscape. Sudden curves of a comparatively small radius for directional changes appeared rather unharmonious.

Amalgamation of the rest areas into Stuttgart–Singen Federal motorway.

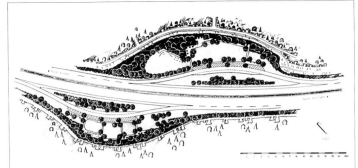

Staggered carriageways, Munich–Berlin motorway near the valley of Alt-mühl.

The interference by the construction of the motorway in this forest of oak trees near Aschaffenburg was mitigated by laying out the carriageways separately. Also, the middle reserve was considerably enlarged in other places for reasons of landscaping.

Modified clover intersection of the motorway and the new B 16 Federal trunk road south of Regensburg.

In the Thirties still, and even more so after World War II, it was tried to arrive at a generous and softly swinging lineation. Thus, e.g., the old route south of Baden-Baden designed by HAFRABA was completely re-designed, using with very few exceptions radii of between 5000 and 20000 metres with long spiral transitions. Only occasionally a short straight was included, particularly in the vicinity of connection points.

Straights are a taboo in modern road building because they "offer more advantages to the person who plans and builds them than to the actual user" (Hans Lorenz). "A straight nearly always heads in the wrong direction. Apart from anything else, the next curve will demonstrate that". Today, road builders are using straights only in their routing when there is a convincing reason to do so. In the meantime, widely recognized guidelines exist for the length of a straight depending on the design speed of the road. For instance, a road which can be used without any danger with wet, yet clean pavement at a speed of 120 k/h, should not have straigths exceeding 2400 metres in length. Also, a lengthy straigth cannot be justified, in most cases, from a landscaping point of view either. However, when building single carriageway Federal and State roads, sufficient sighting distances in view of oncoming traffic must be provided for overtaking manoeuvres. Because this was not always sufficiently borne in mind, a section of the 505 Federal trunk road called the "Bamberg tributary" was popularly known as the "Bamberg cemetary".

The traditional fields of application in road building have come to add new ones over the past decades. More and more, questions relating to the optical aspects of the road, to terrain design and planting, driving dynamics and psychology as well as aesthetics are taken into account. For the aim, as formulated by Hans Lorenz, is to "create roads and motorways which everyone likes to use and which provide a feeling of safety, evoking the wish to use them more often. If they do not have these properties, they are not good quality roads". Also, aspects of environmental control, such as the preservation of nature and noise control gain increasing importance in the planning process. In view of growing significance of the environment, the building of roads and motorways increasingly meets with the opposition of the population living in the affected areas. In spring 1979, the project to build a motorway from Olpe to the area of Bad Hersfeld through a nature reserve almost triggered off a Cabinet crisis in the "Land" of North Rhine-Westfalia.

By clever routing and skillfull designing, roads can become an asset to the landscape, but bad routing and improper design may cause the opposite. One of the sins of youth of modern road building are not only completely straight stretches of the road leading into the horizon, but also straights which feature an overhead construction over the top of the route. Such phenomena, known among experts as "heavenly gates", can give the driver of a motor car a feeling of anxiety. Still worse are optical delusions. A driver must be able to judge falling and rising gradients correctly and to recognize bends and see where roads branch off or join. Particularly dangerous are unexpected curves behind hilltops. Such hazardous surprises are ruled out if the transitional bow leading into the curve begins before the hilltop.

The course of a road becomes unintelligible if the road reappears laterally staggered on a series of hilltops, a phenomenon called "jumping" by professionals. Such mistakes can be detected and avoided in time by perspective investigations in the planning stage. Today, road builders avail themselves of the most modern procedures, such as, e.g., stereography and periscope photography applied to models. Also, a widely used technique is photogrammetry to obtain a geometrical survey of the terrain.

As previously mentioned, it was attempted, even before the Second World War, to make the motorways blend into the landscape as harmoniously as possible. During the excavation and ground work, attention was given to the levelling of the slopes and, in the case of incisions, to the rounding off of edges in the terrain. Planting, which followed immediately in the wake of the construction works, served to create special visual attractions. Even then, landscape gardeners were called upon for these tasks. It was with great energy that they pushed for the routing to be adapted to the environment to the greatest possible extent. They invented a multitude of possibilities to cover up human interference in the landscape. On both sides of the route the landscape was being changed in order to adjust differences in relief. Only a few years after the completion of the road line between natural and artificial landscape often could no longer be determined. Thus, on slopes the carriageway on the near side of the hill was sometimes built in a higher position than the one nearer the valley. In several places along the Federal motorways, e.g., in the heathland of the Lüneburger Heide, in the Spessart forest and in the Rhine valley, the road route was blended into the landscape by enlarging the middle reserve by several times leaving natural vegetation found there untouched.

At first, after the Second World War, economy was the premise most adhered to. The acquisition of property was limited to what was absolutely inevitable and necessary, to the extent that there was no opportunity left for planting also the farther surroundings along the route. New plantings had to do with the small strips on either side of the road which had been used during construction. During the advent of environmental preservation, however, things changed a great deal in favour of the landscape gardeners. The guidelines for the design in road construction published in 1966 require, parallel to the lineation planning, that a landscaping plan be set up in which new plantings play an important part. On principle, each road construction project has to be screened for a possible interference in the landscape. This fundamental scrutiny is followed by a concomitant landscape preservation plan to neutralize any blots that have occured. Furthermore, there is a planting plan which even indicates the location of the individual bushes and trees.

With a clever layout, a new entity of landscape and space emerges, with a new emphasis, which offers more variety to the eye of the driver. The planning experts, e.g., endeavour to lay out the route through a forest in such manner that the end of the woodlands is not immediately visible upon entering this stretch since this would optically stress the interference in nature.

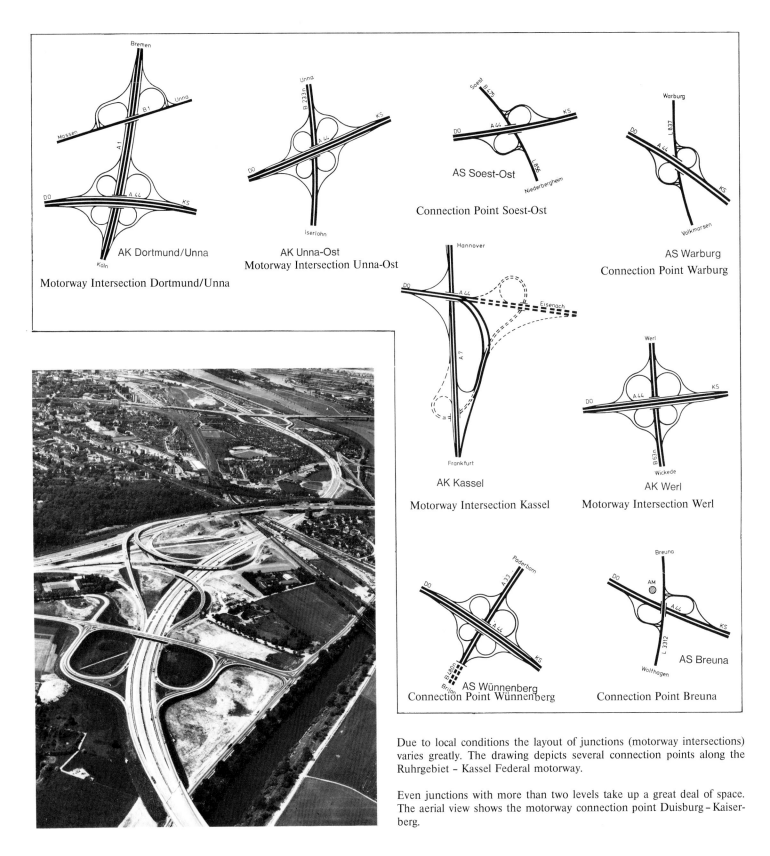

AK Dortmund/Unna
Motorway Intersection Dortmund/Unna

AK Unna-Ost
Motorway Intersection Unna-Ost

AS Soest-Ost
Connection Point Soest-Ost

AS Warburg
Connection Point Warburg

AK Kassel
Motorway Intersection Kassel

AK Werl
Motorway Intersection Werl

AS Wünnenberg
Connection Point Wünnenberg

AS Breuna
Connection Point Breuna

Due to local conditions the layout of junctions (motorway intersections) varies greatly. The drawing depicts several connection points along the Ruhrgebiet – Kassel Federal motorway.

Even junctions with more than two levels take up a great deal of space. The aerial view shows the motorway connection point Duisburg – Kaiserberg.

Today, the construction of motorways in the Federal Republic of Germany is based on a design speed of 140 k/h in flat areas and 120 k/h or 100 k/h in mountainous country, if they are downright thoroughfares covering long distances. Hans Lorenz defines this concept as follows: The design speed "means that each vehicle which does not exceed that particular speed, is guaranteed that at every point the bend will not be too sharp, the transverse drop not too little and the sighting distance for braking sufficient".

With a design speed of 140 k/h, the curve radius is at least 1400 metres, but the ideal would be 5000 metres. In mountainous country, the minimum radius is laid down with 1000, respectively, 600 metres. In the case of Federal motorways, ascending gradients of more than 4% are avoided wherever possible. According to a stipulation by the Federal Ministry of Transport, additional lanes for slow traffic should be built whenever the speed of a truck on this section drops below 50–60 k/h. Because frequent lane changes are detrimental to traffic safety, the additional slow-traffic lanes which are also built where there are slopes are carried on uninterruptedly over several slow sections.

Along the outer edges of the motorway, stopping lanes are built where to leave vehicles which have broken down, as stopping on the pavement of a rapid traffic road might be perilous. But even there, stopping without there being a real need for it is prohibited. There are proper rest areas for parking. Because of the traffic noise, they are often at some distance from the route.

As early as 1937, superelevated curves had been made a rule for all roads in Germany. The transverse drop has its limits where stationary or slow moving vehicles, and in particular heavy lorries, threaten to slide to the inside of the bend, e.g., with icy roads, which, in the case of single carriageways, would mean them coming into head-on collision with the oncoming traffic. Until recently, the transverse drop was restricted to 5%. Since, however, solid rubber and steel tires have been out of use now for a long time, road engineers have been conceded to go up to 7% superelevation.

The distances between the connection points of the motorways differ; on an average they amount to 8 kilometres. On principle, when laying out the route, it has to be taken into account that exits and entries must be seen in good time, so as to enable the driver to adapt himself to conditions as early as possible. The most clearly arranged connection points and junctions are those located in so-called basins, such topographical conditions, however, being relatively rare. Junctions, exits and branch-offs on hilltops should be avoided for the sake of traffic safety.

Standard solutions for the layout of junctions are the clover shape for intersections and the trumpet where motorways join. The triangle with direct ramps, however, is more advantageous for a freely flowing traffic, since this concept does not have any small radii. In the case of the clover, the growing tendency is not to expose the stronger flows of traffic to intertwining – which is a problem in the clover shape – because the joining flow of traffic has to intercross on a short section of the parallel lane with exiting cars. By way of direct ramps, which are coming more and more into use, these difficulties can be avoided and the efficiency of junctions increased. In doing so, the topography as well as the character of the landscape have to be taken into account. If in very steep terrain there is very little surface available, the junction can be designed in the form of a Maltese cross which, with its four levels, however, would constitute a strong interference in the building plan and the image of urban areas. In this case, direct underground ramps are recommended. In order to prevent vehicles from swerving into the oncoming traffic lane, the middle reserve is reinforced throughout by steel guard rails. The same goes for the outer motorway edges if there are dam slopes of over 2 metres in height. Railguards which were then still made of wood were installed as early as 1937 at particularly dangerous spots, e.g., at the outer edges of high dams in the Hamburg region. Because crossing game may cause serious accidents, it is kept away from motorways by a variety of measures. Game protection fences which are designed in such a way that overpasses and subways can serve as game passages have proved most successful so far. With the high speeds at which vehicles move along on the motorway, gusts of wind from the flank can force a vehicle off the pavement or into the neighbouring lane. A lateral shift can be expected, in particular, on high dams or on bridges across a valley. There are traffic signs and, in places, wind sleeves to warn against this danger. Often, however, more can be done: Thus, it is possible to protect dam sections by arranging the planting on the weather side. Also, on the edge of a forest, a gradual change in the wind pressure can be brought about by means of wind protection planting and, similarly, the once commonplace fences erected as a protection against snow drifts can now be replaced through designed earth works and plantings.

Particularly in urban pressure areas, noise protection has become increasingly important. By directing the road in a cleft in the terrain and by means of protective mounds and reflecting or absorbing breast walls, it is tried to shield off closeby residential areas. In the early days of motorway building, petrol stations were erected in the triangular refuge of the connection points between the access and exit ramps. This principle was eventually given up because of interruptions of traffic and the lack of room for expansion. Petrol station facilities were completely separated from the connection points. Passenger vehicles will find the pumps facing the route, whereas trucks fill up at the back of the station. On principle, all pumps were roofed. Great importance is attached to a uniform layout of station facilities so as to enable the driver to orient himself immediately and not be confronted with changing layouts all the time. In order to reduce queues to a minimum during the peak travel season, additional pumps are installed which in some places are approached diagonally. As a rule, there is a petrol station along the motorway every 25 kilometres, although the basic installations planned for new sections are initially based on twice that distance.

The motorway traveller will find a service area, on an average, at every 50 kilometres. Even today, they are still laid out after the old principle "First the horse and then the rider". The driver who bran-

It requires a generous layout so as to avoid congestion at the frontier – as here between Belgium and the Federal Republic of Germany, near Aachen.

ches off from the main carriageway first approaches the filling station, behind which there will be an extended parklike area. Part of this will always be reserved for lorries and trailers as well as coaches. The architectural design of the service area restaurants and the selection of construction materials should always reflect the building style of the landscape. In some instances, a hotel or a motel form part of the complex, and for reasons of noise reduction these are situated as remotely from the motorway as possible. Services areas are, as a rule, built as double-sided installations, as are petrol stations. In the Federal Republic of Germany there are only few examples for brigde restaurants which are so highly popular on the Italian "autostrada". Although only one facility is required for traffic in both directions, they are more expensive to build.

At approximately every 50 kilometres, there are motorway maintenance depots in charge of the upkeep of the road and clearing duties in winter. The buildings are grouped around a rectangular yard. Opposite the administration building facing the entrance there is the hall for the vehicles as well as the workshop. For the depot which contains the gritting material, wood is the preferred construction material, road salt reacting agressively to concrete and brickwork. For aesthetic reasons, no silos are built. The motorway maintenance depot will also receive the calls from the emergency help phones installed along the carriageway edge at intervals of 2 kilometres.

The Belgo-German frontier-crossing at Lichtenbusch near Aachen.

The first motorway bridge restaurant in the Federal Republic of Germany was opended in 1969 on the Munich–Berlin motorway, a short distance from the German Democratic Republic frontier.

On the history of bridge building

From the very start, bridges have always played an important part in people's life. Terms like "bridging a gap", e.g., reflect even today the strong symbolic value attached to these buildings. The history of bridge building is closely connected to the development of technical sciences, but also very much so with the degree of political will for organisation.

The Romans, who were masters also as far as bridge building was concerned, had constructed a series of bridges in Germany. Probably the most important one of all spanning the Rhine river, according to Hans Hitzer, must have been the wooden bridge near Mainz which rested on 26 stone pillars. The pillar substructure consisted of dozens of oak trunks with enormous iron pile shoes. The last remains of these foundations were removed from the river bed at the end of the 19th century, because they obstructed navigation. Most likely the Roman bridge was destroyed in the 3rd century by the Teutons. In the subsequent centuries, it was mainly fords – apart from ferries – which served for crossing rivers, some of these even being cobbled. Quite often it was here that settlements were founded. Town names, such as Frankfurt (ford of the Franks) and Schweinfurt testify to this. However, both ferries and fords could not, or only with great difficulty, be used in the event of floods or drift ice. Only bridges could ensure an at all times safe and rapid crossing of a river. During the reign of Charlemagne (747–814), bridge building was revived. On his instructions, the Rhine was bridged over again near Mainz in the early 9th century, whilst making use of the foundations of the former Roman bridge. However, the bridge did not last for long, as the wooden structure soon burnt down.

It was only in the 12th century that stone constructions were added to the timberwork – which testified to the masterly skills of the carpenters. The bridge builders of the middle Ages, known as Fratres Pontifices, also used very flat arches in addition to the semicircle taken over from Roman times. The oldest evidence still existing today are the "Stone Bridge" spanning the Danube at Regensburg and the bridge over the Main river at Würzburg which both date back to the middle of the 12th century. The main bridge at Frankfurt which initially was made of wood and later was reconstructed in stone, also was of outstanding importance for the North-South traffic.

Architects kept on building bridges according to long-standing traditional rules, until the advent of railway and navigation in the mid-19th century confronted them with completely new tasks. Now, entire valleys and sea arms had to be spanned with bridges. Apart from larger stone viaducts, huge steel constructions arose, the engineer's bold designs.

As bridge architect Gerd Lohmer explains, this resulted in the splitting up of the master-builder's profession into architecture, on one hand, and civil engineering on the other, with either branch heading into a direction totally different from the other's and becoming more and more estranged. If, in the 14th century, large bridges were to be given a dignified look, an architect was called upon who designed portal buildings with gates and turrets in the spirit of the epoch, and who added statues and other ornamental elements which had not the least bit in common with the technical construction of the bridge. The fact that the relationship between engineer and architect gradually improved, is owed to men like Paul Bonatz and their work. They recognised the engineer as an equal partner and were at pains to give a building an attractive form without violating any constructive principles. In doing so, the architects – as Bonatz pupil Gerd Lohmer recounts – came to respect very highly and understand the responsible work of the engineer, whilst the engineer gained an insight in "how a sober engineering work can be turned into a perfectly shaped piece of art".

It is true, though, that this is also an epoch marked by a profound change in style. No longer is it the architect's task to allegedly "embellish" a bridge by some garnishings or other, but to design it on the basis of the given statical and technical conditions in a formally attractive way. Above anything else, it was attempted to blend bridges into the landscape so that they were perceived as a natural part of it. At the same time, construction techniques have made great progress. The era of concrete had long since dawned. As early as 1882, the Dyckerhoff & Widmann company had built near Seifersdorf a bridge for the Saxony state railway which was made of stamped concrete and spanned 10 metres. The world's longest-spanning stamped concrete bridge was conceived in 1904–6, with an effective span of 64.5 metres. It bridged the Iller river near Kempten and still exists today. It was only at the beginning of the 20th century that steel concrete took over from stamped concrete. In 1907, the Baden railway company ordered the first steel concrete bridge leading across the Lörrach river.

Between the two world wars, bridges were built mainly from steel or reinforced concrete. The time of unreinforced stamped concrete was definitely of the past, and the time of prestressed concrete had not yet come, although the idea of prestressing was already being toyed with and the first plans were being put into practice. Following the proposals of Franz Dischinger, the arched bridge built across the Saale river in 1927/28, which had a span of 68 metres, had for the very first time an artificially prestressed tieback so as to exert a favourable influence on the stress condition of the arch, the pavement deck being held free of any tensile stress by the dead weight horizontal thrust. The possibilities of reinforced concrete were limited, in the case of girder bridges, to 50 metres because of the dead weight increasing with the span, whereas with arched bridges this limit could be considerably exceeded. The bridge across the Mosel near Koblenz which was built after several years' preparation in 1932-34, with three arches of up to 118 metres inner width, was in its days a rare technical achievement. Franz Dischinger, who had directed the statical and constructial work on the superstructure, proudly spoke of the boldest massive arch bridge in the world. In saying so, he referred to the ratio of the square of the span to the rise, for, the greater this ratio, the greater the horizontal thrust and the forces which have to be absorbed by the construction. In other words: the flatter the arch, the more difficult it becomes to build the bridge.

Construction work on the national motorways took such a rapid start in 1933, that at first one did not concern oneself a great deal with design questions. At that time, approximately seven million people were out of work. In order to provide a maximum number of people with a job, the excavation of the building sites was done by hand in the early days of motorway construction.Only in exceptional cases, dredgers were allowed to be used for the construction of bridges, as was also the case for the construction of motorway sections.

The first bridges were built by the railway engineers as purely function-orientated buildings, basing themselves on longstanding plans from the national railways. Overpasses, in most cases, would be built as a two-span girder bridge with solid abutments and pillars. But already after the opening of the first section of motorway between Frankfurt and Heidelberg, the demand for an attractive design and amalgamation with the landscape was voiced along with the need for better constructive solutions. This resulted in a very fruitful "coercive marriage" between civil engineers, architects and landscape designers. Consultants were called upon to prevent lapses against good design or the laws of aesthetics.

Apart from Paul Bonatz, it was Friedrich Tamms who played an exemplary part in Berlin in the designing of motorway bridges. Tamms, who was then chief architect of the national motorway company, writes on this issue: "In order not to demonstrate our plans on paper only, but also in reality, we built some important parts of the envisaged bridges on a 1 : 1 scale with real material, i.e., in ashlar, brick, concrete, steel, etc. on the grounds of the motorway maintenance depot Wilhelmshagen, east of Berlin. Thus, the types for subsequent buildings on all motorways were created. This collection of sample buildings was shown, after completion of all details including also the freestone-like treatment of concrete, painting of the steel, connection with the earth bank, etc., to general inspector Todt and his staff, one of which was Paul Bonatz, and was in every respect and detail given the full consent of all those present". All authorities had to submit blue-prints for national motorway bridges to Tamms and Bonatz for examination, revision and further development. Even completed bridges were sometimes subjected to corrections. The concrete surfaces at the abutments and the wing walls were given stone masonry treatment. By adding Main gravel, a reddish surface effect was achieved, and a yellow-white one when using Rhine gravel. Cornices would be drove finished (surface treatment of stone with a masonry tool).

The use of natural stone was promoted, giving preference to local material so as to underline the landscape-related character of the building. Job creation also played an important part in utilizing hewn stone. Soon, close-by quarries could no longer meet the demand, so that the boom in the natural stone industry spread as far as the Riesengebirge region.

During the first years of motorway construction, many bridges had been built as brick arches or arched viaducts. From an aesthetical point of view, these are quite acceptable. Some of these viaducts consisted entirely of natural stone, whilst others are faced concrete constructions.

In the 19th century, it was very popular to ornate bridges with gates and turrets, such as is the case of the Moselle bridge near Traben-Trarbach.

With 64.5 metres, the bridge across the Iller near Kempten built in 1904–06 is the longest-spanning stamped concrete bridge.

The arched bridge across the Saale near Alsleben (with a span of 68 metres) built in 1927/28 featured for the first time a prestressed tieback.

The pillars of the Limburg motorway viaduct were tapered, thus, appearing very slim. This bridge was blown up as the war drew to an end. In the background, there is Limburg Cathedral.

Above and below: In the early Sixties, the destroyed viaduct over the Lahn river was replaced by this filigree-like girder bridge.

Todburg bridge, a 340 metre long viaduct on the Stuttgart–Munich motorway where it ascends to the Alb plateau, was completed in 1957.

For the Holledau viaduct on the Munich–Berlin motorway, a separate bridge was built for the carriageways in each of the two directions.

Contrary to former times, when the lineation of a road was generally guided by the technical principles of bridge building, bridges are today included into the modern location principles. The 70 metre-high and 700 metre-long Haslochbach bridge on the Frankfurt–Nuremberg motorway is built in the shape of an S. It was opened to traffic in 1961.

In making a decision for one type of construction or the other, technical and ideological reasons played as important a part as did job creation programmes and the necessity to save steel. Almost all of these viaducts were blown up towards the end of the war. Inasfar as they were rebuilt in their former shape, the necessity to make the most economical use of the limited funds available required the constructions of arches with reinforced concrete. As a rule, the facing had to be limited to the front parts. The high level of wages no longer permitted the construction of new viaducts with arches of hewn stone.

When designing the 513 metre-long Limburg motorway bridge at the end of the Thirties, Paul Bonatz, as the chief artistic adviser to the "General inspector for roads", tried to give his very best. Limburg, with its medieval town centre largely intact and over-shadowed by the late romanesque cathedral, lies only at one kilometre's distance from the motorway route which crosses the Lahn valley at a height of 57 metres. The prevailing opinion, then, was that long arch openings, be it in form of girders or arches, would reduce cathedral as well as castle to toy size. This is why the decision was in favour of a viaduct with thirteen arch openings of 29.5 metres internal diameter each. On to the piers semicircle arches were set which were stretched to form a parabolic curve. The columns tapered off from 6 to 4.5 metres so as to give a very slim impression. The entire structure, including the arches, were built in natural stone and filled in with stamped backing concrete. The high-level arches, the natural masonry and the accentuated cornices were used by Bonatz as constructive elements similar to those of the cathedral. The construction supervisors took great care to ensure that the stone material produced from a great number of quarries was mixed in a similar manner as had been done for Limburg Cathedral. The bridge looked like a transom in the deep incision of the valley, but nevertheless brought about a direct relationship between bridge and cathedral. The harmony was such that the cathedral was photographed, in most cases, through one of the bridge arches. – At the beginning of the Sixties, the long discussions as to whether or not to reconstruct the blown-up bridge ended with the intentional option for substituting it by a girder bridge which rests on six slim pairs of concrete pillars. This bridge, made of prestressed concrete, which, compared to the previous construction, appears like filigree, is not meant to adapt itself to but rather to contrast with the cathedral dating back to the early 13th century.

Further examples of viaducts from pre-war motorway construction times are the bridge spanning the Saale valley near Jena designed by Friedrich Tamms, with its 17 arches built in shell limestone, which still exists today, and the 500 metre-long Theiß Valley bridge in the Taunus region which is a 40 metre-high arched bridge with numerous arches in natural stone filled in with backing concrete. A particular successful design is the one of the suite of hillside bridges on the Cologne – Hanover motorway in the Weserbergland region. The main bridge on the Arensburger Hang, with 28 openings over a length of 620 metres, is built entirely in red sandstone masonry. The supports are interrupted by spar-arches. The entire construction is in itself curved and twisted. Nearby, three other bridges have been built from the same material, measuring between 250 and 320 metres in length.

In the early days of motorway building, steel construction was not yet acquainted with the technique of welded bridges, but made use of rolled steel girders or rivetted constructions. With wider effective spans, the main girders consisted of trusses linked to each other by cross girders. On top of these cross girders rested the carriageway deck with a concrete pavement which constituted a dead weight. In addition, truss bridges are very expensive to build and maintain, and are not particularly considered to improve the landscape.

Today, there are hardly any truss bridges to be found any longer in the road system. But this also means that the relevant technical know-how is gradually lost. When the repair work on one of these bridges required extensive rivetting work because the use of high-strength bolts could not be considered because of their different looks, German steel construction firms had to "throw the sponge" and call in experts from England. Technical and economical reasons, but also the influence of the "Bauhaus" which had a strong preference for concrete, have contributed to old crafts and skills no longer being mastered today. Thus, there are hardly any wooden bridges left, although this building method could still be attractively applied to pedestrian passovers. The art of carpentry lies waste, and carpenters have turned into "form builders" for concrete constructions.

Prestressed concrete – a revolution in bridge building

After the Second World War, almost all bridges in Germany lay destroyed. Having to start from scratch, on one hand, was a heavy burden, but on the other hand, it also offered the chance to make use of new building techniques on a large scale and to do technical pioneering work in many a respect. Soon, the provisional solutions of the early post-war years were followed by final ones often excelling in a boldness and elegance which previously have passed as Utopian. The network of motorways and Federal roads in the Federal Republic of Germany alone counts 25000 bridges of a total length of 832 kilometres and a total bridge surface of more than 15 million square metres (1977). Every year, another 600 to 700 bridges are added to the Federal trunk road system. In proportion to the network length, the number of bridges is constantly increasing. This is due to the topographical structure of the landscape in areas where new road sections are being built, and to the restrictions to which routing is subject in pressure areas. The length and number of viaducts has increased on new motorway sections so as to ensure a more flowing lineation. In more densely populated areas the development of trunk roads for the purpose of unravelling traffic makes elevated highways and flyovers necessary; today, approximately a third of the total road building costs are spent on bridges, tunnels and retaining walls.

Whilst formerly the technical aspects of bridge building determined the location of larger bridges and, the lineation of a road section, it is the traffic requirements today which are preponderant. Modern routing principles take bridges into account. This is why they are built also with oblique-angled junctions, curved, tilted or twisted. Many of the bridges built during the last decades are located in a bend, and, at times, the carriageway of the construction may even be found to be forming an S.

Often, the driver will no longer notice bridges on the motorway, so much have they become part of the road. It is due to this development, which is closely connected with the progress of construction techniques, that bridges have constantly increased in length and height. The highest motorway bridge crosses the Kocher valley at 185 metre's elevation. It is part of the new section of motorway between Weinsberg and Nuremberg. This prestressed concrete struc-

The Kocher Valley bridge which is part of the new Weinsberg–Nuremberg motorway, spans more than a kilometre. It was built after the cantilever building technique (with auxiliary girder, an advance building carriage at the bottom and – for subsequent finishing of the full sectional area – a trailer carriage).

A comparison of size: The Munster of Ulm, with 161 metres the world's tallest church tower, is clearly outstripped by this 178 metre high pillar of the Kocher Valley bridge.

The superstructure of the 380 metre-long bridge across the Elz in the Eifel region was built with this advancing frame. The prestressed concrete deck measured 30 metres in width. In the field area, it is only 50 to 65 centimetres thick but expands mushroomlike to 2.45 metres at the middle supports. The octagonal piers are hollow and up to 100 metres tall.

The double-storeyed Mangfall bridge on the Munich–Salzburg motorway which was built in 1958/59 after the cantilever building technique is an exception, the main girders being of the truss type.

One of the most remarkable achievements in bridge building is the Bendorf
motorway bridge spanning the Rhine river near Koblenz.

The arch of the Blombach Valley bridge, completed in 1959, was built
with reinforced concrete and spans over 150 metres.

Viaduct on the Stuttgart–Singen Federal motorway near Neckarburg.

25

ture is 1128 metres long, and rests on eight piers the tallest one of which outstrips the world's tallest church tower, the Munster of Ulm (161 metres) by a good many metres.

Approximately 60 p.c. of bridge constructions belonging to the Federal trunk road system are solid stone, concrete or reinforced concrete bridges. The 6800 prestressed concrete bridges take a 27 p.c. share, whilst steel and steel compound constructions take up only 13 p.c. However, the picture changes drastically, if the different building methods are broken down according to bridge surface. Whereas stone, steel and reinforced concrete experienced a limited growth only, the bridge surface of prestressed concrete bridges has quadrupled from 1966 to 1976. Their still growing share exceeded 60 p.c. in 1976.

Over the past decades, bridge building has been marked by a well-nigh rapturous development of technical possibilities. From the end of the Forties considerable improvement on concrete quality and the production of high-quality prestressing steels allowed for the construction of prestressed concrete bridges with, in some instances, a captivating and bold design. Prestressed concrete brought about a revolution in bridge building. Thanks to it, the building height can be reduced considerably in comparison to reinforced concrete design. Thus, it is possible to create bridge structures so unobtrusive as was hardly conceivable in former days.

Because one had not yet mastered complicated statical examinations, architects and engineers depended on dividing bridge constructions into clearly separated building sections each of which had one function only. In doing so, a great deal of material was wasted. Furthermore, the constructive reserves were not used to the full and one had to put up also with other drawbacks. Modern civil engineering now regards every bridge in its entirety, a whole in which each individual part is to serve as many purposes as possible at the same time. Frequently, it is only by means of a computer that the complicated statical calculations required by such an approach can be coped with.

A great step ahead was the development of the cantilever building technique without wasteful scaffoldings which, in addition, would obstruct navigation. By way of the repetition method the cantilevered supporting unit is advanced. It was Ulrich Finsterwalder who contributed substantially to the development of this concrete building technique which was used, for the first time, in 1950 on the site of the Lahn bridge at Balduinstein. Quite a stir was caused at home and abroad, when in 1952 the Nibelungen bridge in Worms was built after the cantilever technique. With this Rhine bridge, the three main openings of which measure up to 114 metres in length, the lower reveal of the girder is slightly curved. Technically speaking, these are cantilever beams fixed into the pier the free ends of which are linked together by a shear force hinge.

Thus, cantilever building made its way on an international scale in the construction of large bridges. Licences for German patents for prestressing methods and cantilever building were awarded to foreign countries. By way of further methods, such as, e.g., the use of travelling scaffolds, building was mechanized to an extent hitherto inconceivable. The ratio between material and labour cost has almost reversed. Today, bridges are built at a much lower cost than previously, taking into account the decline in currency value.

In 1958/59, when the Munich – Salzburg motorway was under construction, a concrete bridge was erected at the place of the destroyed Mangfall bridge. This bridge is remarkable in many respects. Since the surviving columns were to be reemployed, the individual spans were fixed at 90, 108 and 90 metres. The double-storeyed superstructure carries, on a second deck situated at bottom boom level, the pedestrian and bicycle traffic. Although the main girders are not of the solid wall type but of the truss type with crossed diagonals, it was possible here, too, to employ the principle of cantilever building. As the bridge is more than 60 metres above the bottom of the valley, this proved very practical but so expensive that this construction was not repeated.

The middle section of the Bendorf motorway bridge built in the Sixties which crosses the Rhine river to the North of Koblenz, spans over 208 metres. This bridge, too – for a long period of time it was the world's widest spanning concrete girder bridge – was built using the cantilever technique. In spite of its enormous proportions (total length 1030 metres, overall width almost 31 metres), it distinguishes itself by unusually slim pillars and a narrow super-structure, particularly in the field centre, which makes the bridge appear very light and, thus, blending in harmoniously with the landscape.

Although prestressed concrete dominates bridge building, the reinforced concrete building method is still being employed. This is particularly true for smaller bridges, but also for arched bridges. One example is the bridge across the Blombach Valley which was opened to traffic in 1959. It spans 150 metres with an overall length of 328 metres. With its elegant arches and slim support piers it is quite attractive to look at. The only large arched bridge built in recent years is situated near Neckarburg where it bridges the Neckar river. Its arches were constructed after the cantilever technique, whereas the carriageway which rests on elevated supports was built by the incremental launching method.

The incremental launching method which, over the past nine years, has proven particularly economical in the construction of about 130 big bridges, was developed under the direction of Willi Baur in the engineering partnership firm "Stuttgarter Ingenieurgemeinschaft" founded by Fritz Leonhardt. According to this procedure, sections of the superstructure are repetitively manufactured one after the other immediately in a stationary formwork behind the abutment. After the hardening of the concrete the bridge section is advanced on slide bearings by means of hydraulic presses. In order to reach the next pier without too big cantilever moments, there is a light cantilevering steel nose projecting from the first section.

Progress also in steel bridge construction

In the building of steel bridges, two methods have taken the lead after the Second World War, i.e., composite constructions and light pavements with a so-called orthotropic deck (abbreviation for orthogonal – anisotropic: this is a plane bearing structure used particularly in bridge building which has different elastic properties in two vertically opposed directions). Both these systems distinguish themselves by their considerable material economy as well as high load reserves. In composite construction, the steel construction and the reinforced concrete deck interact as a compound. The orthotropic deck consists of a plane cover plate which has the main supports, cross girder and the longitudinal ribs welded on to it so as to make all building elements form a complete entity.

The Werra Valley bridge on the Hamburg – Frankfurt motorway near Hedemünden which measures a good 500 metres in length, had been built in 1937 on 50 metre-high brick pillars with a parallel boom steel truss superstructure. After it had been destroyed, the progress in construction techniques was put to account in choosing for one of the directional carriageways a steel compound construction and, for the other one, an orthotropic deck. When reconstructing the bridge, it did no longer stretch over the valley like a board, but was adapted – as is usual nowadays – to the swing of the gradient (the line of inclination determined by the drop) in a sag curve. Thus, one could speak of the bridge swinging from one crest of the valley to the other. In 1937, by the way, 3900 tons of steel were needed for the superstructure against only 2500 tons in 1952, although the latter construction was based on higher load assumptions.

One of the first bridges to come into existence after the Second World War was the Rhine bridge built in 1947/48 at Deutz near Cologne. It was designed with a solid wall box girder in which the upper and the bottom booms were joined in a shear-resisting way by a closed sheet of metal. The Deutz bridge, the structural height of which is only 3.2 metres in the middle section spanning the 184 metre-long main opening, is a particularly successful solution. Says designer Fritz Leonhardt: "It was only possible to achieve this image of slimness because there was no authority at the time to supervise me. Under the given regulations, no permission would have been granted to build it". The bridge in the Cologne Zoo, too, is a success. The asymmetrical beam (it is a box girder) spans 259 metres and reaches 10 metres in height above the river pier.

The motorway bridge near Hedemünden built in 1937 which spans the Werra valley looked like a board *(left)*. During reconstruction, the superstructure was adapted to the gradient of the road section *(right)*.

The Cologne Zoo bridge could almost be called elegant with its asymmetrical girder.

The arches of the Kaiserlei bridge connecting Frankfurt/Main and Offenbach, consists of double tubes.

One of the first bridges to be built after the Second World War was the Rhine bridge in Cologne–Deutz.

This suspension bridge with a main span of 500 metres was built in 1965 across the Rhine river near Emmerich.

Two carriageways and a railway track are part of the "Vogelfluglinie" (The bird's flight line) leading across the Fehmarnsund and linking the Federal Republic of Germany and Scandinavia.

In order to improve the transverse rigidity, the arches of the bridge across the Fehmarnsund are leaning laterally so as to support each other in the vertex.

Due to the slightly swinging lineation of the bottom boom and the long stretched foil-like superstructure, the bridge gives the impression of hovering lightly above the water. One of the arched bridges with a suspended carriageway deck is the Kaiserlei bridge between Frankfurt and Offenbach. Its arches span 220 metres across the Main river. Each of the lateral arches consists of a double tube of twice 2 metres in diameter. The hangers which carry the 36 metre wide pavement appear almost graceful. The arches of the Fehmarnsund bridge, completed in 1963, are leaning laterally so as to touch in the vertex and support each other, in order to improve transverse rigidity. With its two lanes and a railroad track on one side, the bridge spans 250 metres.

With spans becoming increasingly wider, suspension bridges were built with considerably more light-weight superstructures. This technique was first conceived in England, France and the U.S.A. In the Federal Republic of Germany, too, there are a few suspension bridges which, owing to the small width of the rivers, are, however, of very modest dimensions. The oldest such suspension bridge on German territory still in existence was built in 1896/97 near Langenargen on Lake Constance. Two supporting pillars, or pylons, of this suspension bridge in hewn stone each carry the steel cable over a span of 72 metres. The middle section of the Rodenkirchen motorway bridge which was jointly designed by Fritz Leonhardt and Paul Bonatz, spans 378 metres. The bridge was completed in 1941, but then destroyed in the war and rebuilt in 1954. The suspension bridge across the Rhine near Emmerich has a span, in the main opening, of 500 metres.

For the Rhine bridge near Emmerich, Fritz Leonhardt had designed, in co-operation with Gerd Lohmer, a monocable system. At the pylons, the cable was to split into two strands which lead to the stayings located in the secondary opening sections of the bridge, next to the carriageway. Although the binding offer of the tendering partnership would have saved several millions in cost, the authorities refused to accept the project. With a span of 500 metres and a 23 metre wide pavement, the steel superstructure was designed to measure only 1.2 metres in height.

Truss bridges – a typical design for the railroad

Truss bridges are typical for railroad bridge building. In flat country, the carriageway deck is usually located at the bottom of the structure, whereas in mountainous areas it is at the top. Over the past decades, the German Federal Railways have built a number of bridges which when seen from below, could be taken for road and not rail transport constructions, were it not for the overhead line masts. In some cases, truss bridges have been substituted by box girder bridges, costs being the reason for giving up the openwork construction. However, with new constructions with spans from 50 to 60 metres, the truss bridge is more economical, as a rule, in particular if the bridge consists of several openings.

Even today, truss bridges are a typical feature of railway bridge building. In the mountains, the track deck is usually at the top, and at the bottom in flat country.

Today, the German Federal Railways, as Hans Siebke from administrative headquarters puts it, tends to give preference to truss again, "Especially because girder bridges for the railways have never fully satisfied expectations from architecture's point of view." The box girder bridge's advantage of low maintenance costs which is due to a smaller surface, is largely set off by the careful designing of constructive details of truss bridges, so that the cost aspect hardly matters any longer when it comes to a decision on what type to choose. "From a certain length of span, truss bridges are simply more attractive", says Siebke. Contrary to the old traditional truss which often appeared to lack harmony in its strutting, great importance is nowadays attached to a quiet strutting design in truss constructions. Here, the Federal railways prefer strutting truss without any posts, and their people in charge of bridge building make a great effort to couple in their construction bar statics and the mechanics of continuity.

Bar reinforced arched bridges add attractive touches to the landscape, and have become fashionable again. One such example is the railway bridge across the Lahn river near Lahnstein which was built in 1968 to replace a truss superstructure dating from 1901. The hollow box type arch is joined bend-proof with the stiffening girders above the support. The 100 millimetre strong suspenders are welded together with the upper and lower suspender heads.

For the purpose of testing and evaluating constructive elements for new track sections, the German Federal Railways have built at Uhlerborn on the Main a series of life-size models of bridges, tunnels and other technical constructions. The engineers are not only after the constructive presentation of details, but also want to find out about the co-ordination of equipment – e.g. the overhead line – and solve questions of aesthetical design. The aim is to find widely applicable standardized types, so that in case of a tender, the specifications can be produced in computer print-out form.

In 1954/55, this bridge with parallel boom triangle truss girders replaced the Kaiser bridge North of Mainz which had been erected in 1904 and destroyed in 1945.

The truss girders of this girder bridge across the Rhine to the North of Koblenz has a system height of 12 metres.

Bar reinforced arched bridges such as this one situated near Kücknitz, have become fashionable again.

In 1968, the bar reinforced arched bridge built across the Lahn near Lahnstein replaced a truss superstructure dating from 1901. The effective span is nearly 80 metres.

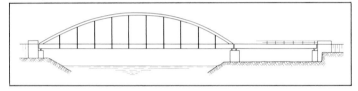

Cable stayed bridges

With the advent of cable stayed bridges, a new bridge type was created in which the orthotropic bridge deck was suspended directly from tightly stretched ropes which are supported by pylons towering high above the carriageway. Franz Dischinger who, as early as 1938, had worked on a project for a cable stayed bridge with a 750 metre span for two railway tracks across the Elbe river near Hamburg, was the one who gave the impulse for a series of cable stayed bridge drafts by publishing very important studies in 1949. Fritz Leonhardt and his staff who had done some fundamental research work on the aerodynamic stability of long-span cable bridges, designed the cable stayed bridges which were to form the "Düsseldorf Bridge Family" the first of which was built from 1951–54 – a major breakthrough in the construction of large bridges.

The design of the pylons and the routing of cables for cable stayed bridges can be quite different. Instead of the usual cable planes located on the outside, one will more frequently find a centre rope wall which is run over individual pylons in the central reserve of the carriageway. Already in 1935, the German engineer Haupt had taken out a patent for this type of centre girder bridges. For the first time in the Federal Republic of Germany, the pylons were arranged in the central reserve on the bridge across the Northern Elbe near Hamburg which was opened to traffic in 1962. The building headroom of the bridge deck is only 3 metres. The 172 metre span middle opening is joined with two lateral openings of 64 metres each and end spans. Although the rope layers are run through the pylons at 17 and 23 metres height, empty sheet metal dummies which look like graceful needles, project 53 metres above the pavement. This was meant by the architect to enhance the optical effect.

When building the Severin bridge in Cologne which was completed in 1959 (main span 302 metres), only one pylon was erected in an asymmetrical position, in spite of the considerable additional expenses; on the right bank of the Rhine, it constitutes a "counterpoint" (Lohmer) to the cathedral whose towers rise high above the city. A second pylon on the left bank would have been a sharp interference in the image of the city and its landmark. Both rope walls connected laterally to the girder of the Severin bridge are joined at the top of the A-shaped pylon, thus increasing the spacious image of the bridge.

The stayed centre girder bridges which span the Rhine at Duisburg – Neuenkamp (1970) and Düsseldorf – Flehe (1979) are, to date, the bridges with the longest main span (350, resp. 368 metres). The Köhlbrand bridge in Hamburg, built between 1970 and 1974, is very impressive, too. The clear height of the carriageway is 53.8 metres above the 325 metre-long middle opening, enough even for a 200 000 t supertanker to pass beneath the structure unloaded. Both pylons erected on high pillars tower over the port landscape with 130 metres. The pavement (with four lanes) of the 520 metre long river bridge is suspended on 88 steel ropes with a thickness of between 54 and 104 millimetres and weighing approximately 400 tons in total. The cable forces are constantly monitored by pressure gauges developed especially for this bridge. The construction of the Köhlbrand bridge had been preceded by intensive wind tunnel tests at the Technical University of Munich. In order to shield off traffic from wind effects, a speed limit of 50 k/h was established on the bridge. At night, drivers are warned by illuminated wind sacks. Including the ramps whose maximum gradient is 4 % the bridge is 3940 metres long. Building costs amounted to 113 million Deutschmarks. The entire structure rests on 75 piers and abutments for the foundation for which 1700 piles had to be rammed down 18 metres deep. The actual river bridge is made of steel, the ramps having been constructed with traveling scaffolds in prestressed concrete.

With the construction of the Rhine bridge near Düsseldorf – Flehe, the longest cantilevering construction of the world was put into practice. The 41.7 metre wide carriageway of this steel bridge was drafted as a orthogonal – anisotropic (= orthotropic) deck. On both sides of the 16.3 metre wide hollow steel box it protrudes approximately by 12.7 metres. At intervals of 9 metres, inclined struts support the cantilever. The bridge weighs 8000 tons, including its stayings. Seven rope strands each transfer the said weight to the top of the pres-

The pylon of the Severin bridge on the right bank of the Rhine constitutes a counterpoint to Cologne Cathedral. In the centre background there is Deutz bridge and in the rear Hohenzollern bridge.

33

As early as 1959, Severin bridge, a cable stayed bridge of a main span of 302 metres, was completed.

In the late Seventies, the Rhine bridge in Düsseldorf–Flehe was built as the world's longest cantilevering structure. The 1147 metre-long bridge consists of a 779 metre-long shore span of prestressed concrete and a 368 metre long centre girder cable stayed bridge of the steel box type. The pylon, however, was made of prestressed concrete.

The pylons of the Köhlbrand bridge in Hamburg (1970–74) were erected on high piers and rise to a height of 130 metres.

Owing to difficult geological conditions, the end spans of the bridge across the Neckar Valley near Weitingen were not equipped with piers, but with a sub-tensioning rope wiring with interspersed "air supports".

tressed concrete pylon reaching 129 metres above the carriageway. As part of the new motorway between Stuttgart and Lake Constance, work is presently being conducted since 1978 to bridge the Neckar valley near Weitingen at 127 metres height by a 900 m long bridge with a steel superstructure (design by Fritz Leonhardt and staff). Due to difficult geological conditions (strongly fissured and unsettled shell limestone), no piers were planned for the slopes of the valley. The bridge's end spans of 234 and 263 metres respectively were equipped with a sub-tensioning rope wiring with interspersed "air supports". The 31.5 metre wide carriageway cross-section consists of a torsionally rigid (distortion-resistant) hollow box of 6 metres height and 10 metres width, and a light steel carriageway deck which is protruding and supported on both sides. A further novelty are the extremely slim piers with point bearings for the box girder. Whilst steel construction has largely lost the territory to reinforced concrete construction, as regards medium span bridges, it could nevertheless keep its predominance in respect of large bridges thanks to rope designs. Paramount for this development are costing aspects only, as bridge building has become, over the past decades, strictly economically orientated. By now, cable stayed bridges of a span of up to 700 metres can be built cheaper in prestressed concrete than in steel, says Fritz Leonhardt.

On the design of civil engineering constructions

Bridges are civil engineering structures the shape of which necessarily follows from the construction. Does this thesis hold true?
In the days of the Bauhaus, the contention was voiced that engineering or technology in itself was a beautiful thing. Even today, there are still people in civil engineering who cherish this opinion and – what's worse – act accordingly in that they neglect the design. According to Friedrich Tamms, this testifies to their lack of artistic talent or comprehension of aesthetic's laws. All those engineers who have great achievements in bridge building to their credit have been and are at pains to arrive at a good design. For it was more often than not that the desire to build formally perfect bridges instigated the development of new constructions, to span the arch even farther and create an even more light-weight superstructure.
Today, the art of bridge building consist in creating structures with the smallest possible financial means which do not only live up to their purpose, but are also aesthetically attractive because they blend into one technical construction and form. However, this requires the will for artistic design. Engineering and art must join forces so as to avoid that structures are erected which merely serve their purpose but which, other than that, are like foreign bodies in their environment and put man ill at ease.
Purposefulness, construction type and choice of material, says Friedrich Tamms, are the three components of the elementary form. The bridge architect and municipal architect draws from an experience acquired over many decades: "The designer of engineering constructions is well advised to restrain himself from exerting too much influ-

ence on the so-called preliminary questions so that he may fulfill his actual task, which is designing the technical structure, all the more effectively." This is where "the ability to think in constructive terms and the feeling for statical ratios" counts. The architect must be absolutely aware of the flow of forces, and this is why architects of engineering constructions must learn to understand the language of engineers, designers and draughtsmen, for the shape must never deny the technical basis from which it evolves. "Engineering constructions should and can be designed, without introducing any elements or materials foreign to the construction, in such a way that they can also satisfy aesthetical, i.e., non-technical laws" (Tamms). A purposeful handling of the material must go hand in hand with a convincing attention to detail. This task ranges from the junction points of individual construction elements such as, e.g., the rivet graphs in a steel building, to the design of face areas where the construction is in reinforced concrete.
Designer Herbert Schambeck draws attention to the fact that there are no patent solutions for bridge building waiting in a drawer ready for application. When thinking through his design, the engineer must ask himself whether the constructive solution he has in mind will blend unobtrusively into the environment, or whether it will force a new dimension on the same which he will then have to be able to defend. Schambeck views the draughtsman's task of the engineer "as as combination of free design and the control of the same design procedure by a sense for statics and the calculation . . . The very first thing for an engineer to realise is his obligation that there is such a task to design, to want a particular shape, and that this task will require a lot of time and the effort to think." Either the engineer will try to come to a solution on his own, fully aware of his responsibilities, or he will tackle this task jointly with an architect, in which case the co-operation between the two partners whose capabilities complement each other, is not only to the benefit of the structure, but also to the benefit of all parties involved. It is the dialogue which counts. There is no way that the engineer can simply delegate the designer's task. According to Schambeck, a well-shaped bridge distinguishes itself by its "integration in the landscape, entity of form and bearing properties, unity of form and construction method and, finally, by the manifest expression of a distinct creative will".
The famous engineer David B. Steinmann attacks many a colleague by saying: "No bridge builder is worthy of that name until he is filled with passion and desire to make his buildings look beautiful". Comment Paul Bonatz and Fritz Leonhardt: "Beauty is not in the accessories, it is in the genuine, sensible and true elementary form, in what is simple, it is in leaving out and avoiding everything arbitrary, fortuitous and fashionable." Both of them stress the fact that the abstract rational mind of the calculating engineer comes hardly ever associated with an artistic sense of form. "To be beautiful, to be final, however, is something a work does not acquire by itself or by chance, but only if a conscious and well-trained will leads it to this point". And to achieve just this, it requires the appreciative co-operation of talents trained accordingly.

A crossing angle of 45° and navigation requirements stipulated a main span of 290 metres for the motorway bridge across the Danube near Deggenau. The landmark of this bridge which was opened to traffic in 1975 is its characteristic pylon shaped like a Y closed at the top.

Above the original design, and *below* the design that was ultimately put into practice for the Fehmarnsund bridge. Out of nine openings on one side, only five remained, and on the other side they were even reduced from five to two. Asks the architect: "Was it really worthwhile to save money?"

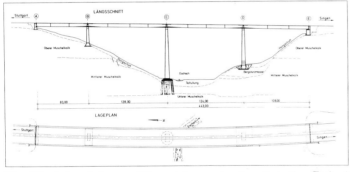

The difficult foundation conditions at the construction site in the Eschach valley led to the following solution during the construction of the Stuttgart–Singen motorway.

This prestressed light-weight pedestrian bridge near Wiesbaden–Schierstein looks like plastic art in the Rhine landscape.

This prestressed concrete light-weight bridge in the vicinity of Osnabrück captivates by its flowing lineation.

Krahnenberg bridge near Andernach on the Rhine.

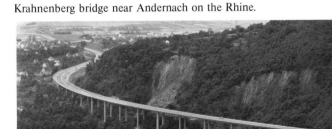

Already at the turn of the century, MAN – Maschinenfabrik Augsburg–Nürnberg AG – had sent architects to work as partners with their steel construction engineers at their Gustavsburg plant. Under the direction of Wilhelm Härter, the architectural department contributed substantially to the successes of the enterprise. This secured the company a lead over all its competitors.

"In recognition of his great services to the co-operation between architect and engineer", Härter was awarded the title of Honorary Doctor of the Braunschweig Polytechnic in 1953.

Ulrich Finsterwalder points out that the constructive possibilities of prestressed concrete construction have led to new forms which cannot claim any common roots with the former shapes of stone or concrete bridges. The well-known designer and bridge builder thinks it imperative for an engineer or architect to be wanting and striving to create a work of art. "Each one of them must seek to further, from his own position, the partner's work to the best of his abilities. Thus, they will jointly create something better than any single one would be capable to achieve by himself."

Bridge architect Gerd Lohmer who was awarded the Great Prize for Architecture of the Federal Land of North Rhine-Westphalia in 1963 for his "unusual influence as a designer on large bridge building of today", demands that the co-operation between engineer and architect start with the first site inspection and end only after the last detail has been finalised. According to Lohmer, it is very important that large modern bridges which appear like plastic art passable on foot or by car "be designed to such a scale and placed in its environment in such a manner that they do not irritate or destroy but incorporate themselves naturally." It is, therefore, the architect's task "to guide the engineer to the crucial points from where the bridge will later be seen and judged most, and it is only then that engineer and architect should start designing jointly. In the end they must have produced a highly finished structure. If everything looks very simple and natural, then you can say it is a good bridge."

But to proceed like this is still rather more the exception than the rule. At a time when every waste basket is a designer product – complains Lohmer – "there is not even a single stipulation that an architect has to be involved in the building of a bridge". But, then, even brilliant designs often only remain paperwork. Criticism is voiced from all directions. For instance, one can hardly fail to catch the disappointment in Herbert Schambeck's words: "A designer must be able to take it not only as an encouragement to do his very best when reading the sentence in the invitation to tender, "Particular importance is attached to good architectural design", but that the client intends to use this phrase as an aid to arrive at a decision and to answer for it vis-a-vis the Federal Court of Audit, when it comes to opting for a design which, in his view, is the best solution although being somewhat more expensive than the cheapest offer."

In spite of having been amputated on both sides, the bridge across the Fehmarnsund is a most impressive achievement. This can even get an engineer and building contractor as level-headed as Hans Wittfoht up into arms: "And what happened to the competition draft which had been so brilliant in its design? Cheaper dams now cut into the extensive water surface – what is left is a torso with few constant shore span openings . . . proportions, rythm and harmony have been interrupted, and gone is the tension which was supposed to exist between the many small and the large main opening, the actual navigation gateway!" Five out of nine openings remain on one side, and only two out of five on the other. The participating bridge architect thinks this an unsatisfactory result. Somewhat bitter, Gerd Lohmer asks: "Was it really worthwile to save the money? Who cares later how much the bridge has cost?"

The Bendorf Rhine bridge, on the other hand, is described by Lohmer as "the result of an ideal co-operation between all parties involved and a sympathetic building authority". "In front of the mountains and next to the old St. Sebastian's Chapel superstructures above the pavement would have appeared improper". An ideal example is the construction of the pedestrian's bridge across the Schierstein Rhine harbour entrance which is the donation of a cement factory to the city of Wiesbaden. Gerd Lohmer being the commissioned architect, he could benefit from this extraordinary situation and design the form, whilst the engineers made it as light a structure as possible, and even the client was prepared to accept considerable extra expenses over the cost of a simple girder bridge. This arched prestressed concrete bridge which was built in 1967 with a span of 92 metres and a vertex thickness of a mere 75 centimetres is one of the most remarkable light-weight concrete structures. Says the architect: "The bridge stands amidst the landscape like a piece of plastic art. The laterally cantilevered platforms which are unsupported, are suspended freely in the space above the water. At first, the engineers wanted to put a support under each platform, because that would have been cheaper. But in that case the bridge would have lost its elegant appearance". – Another prestressed light-weight concrete structure was built in 1968 near Osnabrück where a road bridge was erected across the motorway from the Ruhrgebiet area to the North Sea coast. The two cantilever arms built after the cantilever method have a span of 85 metres. The building height of the girder is 5.8 metres at the abutment, but only 1.2 metres at the vertex. Here, too, it is the flowing lineation which makes the building look so attractive.

The great number of bridges which have come into existence over the past three decades could not have been built, if aspects of economy had not been taken into account. Additional expenses for the execution of an aesthetically pleasing design are only rarely approved – a subject which could be discussed extensively. Nevertheless, the location of a structure should have some impact also. In a remote region, it is not justified to convert every glance of a passerby at a bridge into several thousand Deutschmarks of extra cost. On principle, the possibility to submit a special design for a tender has stimulated bridge building in the Federal Republic of Germany greatly and given it an unexpectedly high standard. Drafts submitted by government departments for important bridge constructions have been put into practice only in exceptional cases.

The "Düsseldorf bridge family"

This name has come to stay for the three bridges across the Rhine river designed and built in the capital of the Federal Land of North Rhine-Westphalia between 1954 and 1976 after the same constructive system and identical formal principles of design. Ever since, they have been a landmark in Düsseldorf's city landscape. All three of the buildings have been conceived as one urban planning entity by engineer Fritz Leonhardt and architect Friedrich Tamms.

The bridge trio are all cable stayed bridges with low bracing girders and slim pylons tapered towards the top. As a contrast to the dark grey paint of the steel structure, there are 60 cm high white cornicing stripes running from one bank to the other at all three bridges. They underline the light, indeed, the suspended effect of the bridges' shape. The pylons are not of the portal type but are free-standing. Also, the suspension cables are not run up to the pylon head in fascicles, but run parallel like in a harp and are attached to the pylons at an equal distance. This means that there is no complicated overlapping as is necessarily the case with the fascicle type with two suspension levels arranged laterally.

Although they are fundamentally the same, each one of the Düsseldorf Rhine bridges has preserved its individuality. To start with, one notices a difference in the number of pylons. The first one of the bridge ensemble, Theodor Heuss bridge, is suspended from four pylons, reaching a height of 40 metres above the carriageway. The Knie bridge's pylons - it was opened to traffic in 1969 - stretch up to 115 metres above the river promontory. The new Oberkassel bridge, on the other hand, received only one pylon placed in the centre of the cross section. Its top is 100 metres above the pavement. Whilst the supporting systems of the Theodor Heuss bridge are designed symmetrically, those of the Knie bridge are asymmetrical, owing to its locality. The suspension cables which are running parallel again, are led to join the pylons at different angles from the bank and the river side. The rope cables of the new Oberkassel bridge, on the other hand, are symmetrical.

Wherever you are in the city, you can see bridge pylons. Not only are they an aid to orientation, they also underline the location of the city on the river. Thus, bridge building evolved into town planning. Comments Rudolf Hillebrecht: "These filigree-like bridges create space and, at the same time, structure the wider space of the "citiscape" without interfering into or, worse, destroying it, and they let the city on both sides of the river emerge as an entity, as a modelled city structure: This is three-dimensional town planning."

Friedrich Tamms explains the constructive and design-related details as follows: "The Knie bridge, with its 115 metre high pylons, constitutes an effective conclusion, in town planning terms, before the Rhine landscape which opens up widely from here towards the West in the direction of Neuss. The space above the river is filled. The support system of the bridge is such that the optical bodilessness of the structure is also overcome. Pylons as well as cables provide the bridge with a third amply visible dimension. The eight suspension cables lift up the horizontal of the carriageway to the vertical of the large supports and combined they form an imaginary wall above the water. The bridge parapets where no differentiation is made between end posts and spaced fill bars, run like a cord over the various structural elements and link up with the chains of the carriageway lighting following the gradients of the bridge, as well as with the white cornices ... The pylons of the three new bridges are perforated at regular space intervals on the upstream as well as on the downstream side. In the interior space, glassprotected fluorescent tubes have been installed shedding their light on the river. All seven of the pylons end with red lights on top for air traffic safety purposes. At night, the illuminated seven columns are a guide to waterway traffic. During the day, they are also a widely visible connecting element between the Düsseldorf city centre and Oberkassel on the other Rhine bank."

Every little detail was taken into account when building the three Düsseldorf bridges. For instance, the river piers of the Theodor Heuss bridge are made of roughly sprayed granite in contrast to the steel bridge deck. The shape of the piers is based on hydrodynamic laws, i.e., the upstream pier cutwater is wide and stoutly rounded, whereas the lower part smoothly meets the fusing waves. The lateral walls are slightly curved in longitudinal direction, with the current joining in this movement. – And one more important point: For reasons of stability, the pylons which are constructed as T-shaped hollow bodies, require exterior stiffenings which, in the case of the Knie bridge, are not horizontal as is usual, but have been arranged to follow the gradient of the suspension cables. Thus, all details comply with the flow of forces.

The new bridge at Oberkassel which was built between 1970 and 1976 at an expense of 120 million Deutschmarks, had iniatially been erected next to the old bridge structure and, following the proposal of Erwin Beyer, was then pushed across into its final axis position. Never before in civil engineering history had a complete bridge weighing 12 700 tons been moved.

There is never a standstill in the evolution of bridge building. The second bridge across the Main river built by Hoechst AG near Frankfurt also testifies to this. Apart from two directional carriageways and a railway track, it also was to carry an extensive pipeline system, and all this with a 150 metre-wide opening for navigation and the construction height being limited to 2.6 metres. Thus, the world's first cable stayed bridge made of prestressed concrete and a multiple cable system came into being in the early Seventies. Even the pylons towering above the pavement at 52 metres' height, were made of prestressed concrete. Only 20 months were available from the initial planning stage to completion of construction. At first, the designers were faced with the problem of an oblique crossing angle between river and bridge. Architect and engineers solved this question by arranging the slim disks of the pier in direction of the stream and placing the pylons in a staggered position against each other in accordance with the oblique angle of the bridge in the plan view. The secondary piers were given a round shape, and they are therefore not directional.

At first, the Rhine bridge at Düsseldorf – Oberkassel which weighs 12 700 tons, was built adjacent to the old bridge and was then moved into its definite axis position.

The Knie bridge at Düsseldorf.

The first cable stayed bridge to be made of prestressed concrete was built across the Main near Frankfurt – Höchst in the early Seventies.

The pylon of the second Main bridge built for Hoechst AG near Frankfurt.

Since 1957, traffic on the B 9 Federal trunk road moves on an elevated highway near Unkelstein on the Rhine.

Near Ohlstadt, the Munich–Lindau Federal motorway has an elevated section of 1315 metres. The risk of floods and unfavourable conditions of the foundation instigated the present solution.

Elevated highways

The building of elevated highways is closely connected with bridge building. Elevated highways are not merely to be found in urban areas. Walter Durth, who is a university professor for road design and management, points out that an elevated highway built after the repetition method can be more economical than a high dam if the fill material – as is the case with the marshland around Hamburg – has to be procured from far away, and if the foundation has to be improved by exchanging the soil. It is all the more advisable to elevate a road in pressure areas, the higher the gradient is above the terrain, for the slopes of high dams require a lot of space. But even in the open countryside, an elevated highway may be more practical than a dam for crossing narrow valleys. The microclimate does play an important part here, too. Raised dams can cause cold air fronts which may put nurseries and orchards at risk. In addition, these fronts increase the danger of fog formation.

The advent of prestressed concrete produced considerable advantages also for the building of elevated highways. Apart from being economic material, it also gives buildings a look of lightness. The aesthetic effect depends to a great extent on the preparatory work prior to designing. In Düsseldorf, Friedrich Tamms has done some pioneering work in this field. He had a great number of models built, and, in some cases, even cross-sections on a 1:1 scale.

A new type of elevated highway, with only one row of columns in the middle, was realised in 1956/57 near Unkelstein on the Rhine. It forms part of the B 9 Federal trunk road which ran as a narrow, winding and repeatedly flooded road between the railway embankment and the river. To raise a dam at this location proved impossible for lack of space and, furthermore, this method would have constituted a severe interference in the river landscape. The 358 metre-long elevated road rests on eight piers the heads of which were enlarged in order to ensure stable support on roller bearings of the superstructure which was designed as a continuous girder. The acclaim which this elevated highway with only one row of columns had, made Ulrich Finsterwalder develop the "mushroom" road, the superstructure of which is permanently joined to the support. The mushroom-like junction of the pier and the carriageway is distinctly recognizable from below. The principle of this mushroom road was also applied when constructing the extension of the bridgehead of the Rhine bridge at Ludwigshafen, the Stadtfeld dam at Hanover and in many other places.

The tunnel beneath the Elbe river

Whilst bridges belong to the structures man built from the very beginning, the building of tunnels began to play a more important part in overcoming obstructions to the flow of traffic only by the mid-19th century. The development of blasting techniques and of mining engineering made it possible to open up transport routes through mountain massifs and below rivers. In the centre of urban areas, tunnels are of increasing importance, not only for transport by rail, but also in road building. Contrary to elevated highways, underground transport systems cannot interfere in the citiscape, they hardly have an impact on the available building space, and they avoid any kind of inconvenience caused to residents by traffic noise.

As early as 1907 and until 1911, the old Elbe tunnel was built in Hamburg after the shield driving method under compressed air. This tunnel is still being frequented today by several thousand pedestrians and vehicles. Both the tubes with a clear width of 4.66 metres each are 448 metres long. Their floor is 23 metres beneath the medium water level of the Elbe river. Access and exit on both sides is via elevator shafts.

Road tunnel under the Nord-Ostsee canal (linking the North and Baltic seas) near Rendsburg.

The new Elbe tunnel which was built at a cost of half a billion Deutschmarks, is used by up to 100000 vehicles every day.

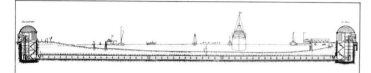

Profile of the old Elbe tunnel in Hamburg built at the beginning of this century which till the present day is being used by pedestrians and cars.

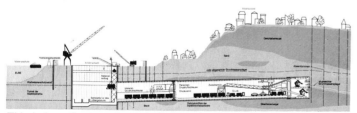

This is how the tunnel was built into the dry and sandy Elbe bank by way of the shield driving method.

In the new Elbe tunnel in Hamburg, the six motorway lanes are distributed over three tunnel tubes with two lanes each which have been manufactured on land after the shield driving method (middle), as open constructions (bottom), or as a reinforced concrete construction (top), and then are floated into position and sunk.

Querschnitt der Einschwimmstrecke, Baulos I
Stahlbeton-Konstruktion,
Seitenwände und Sohle Stahlisolierung, Decke bituminöse Abdichtung

8,40 m

41,70 m

Querschnitt der Schildvortriebstrecke, Baulos II
Röhren aus gußeisernen Tübbings

10,83 m

Querschnitt des Baulos III, offene Bauweise
Stahlbetonrahmen mit bituminöser Abdichtung

10,89 m

40,07 m

One of the most remarkable transport buildings of the Seventies is the new Elbe tunnel which is known to be the second largest underwater road tunnel of the world. The closed tunnel section which crosses under the Elbe and, on the North bank, a steep slope of dry and sandy layers, measures 2653 metres in length. The whole tunnel which was completed after a construction period of 7 years and opened to traffic in 1975 comprises six lanes. It forms part of the new motorway to the West of Hamburg carrying the traffic from Stockholm to Lisbon as part of the Europa Road No 3. Every day, up to 100000 vehicles pass through the tunnel which cost approximately 500 million Deutschmarks to build.

In 1938/39, a suspension bridge had been planned for at the very spot where today the motorway tunnel crosses under the Elbe river. This motorway bridge was supposed to have a 750 metre-wide middle opening with a clear height above the water of 85.5 metres. Furthermore, it was to have 180 metres-high pylons faced with square hewn natural stone, the sheer size and massiveness of which would have crushed the town picture. A compressed-air caisson which had been built at the time to examine the bearing capacity of the subsoil, was blown up after the war. The old plans were never revived. However, for a long time after the Second World War one did discuss the question whether the connection with the areas surrounding the city to the West should be improved by building a tunnel or a bridge. The decision eventually was in favour of the tunnel project because it exerted the least influence on the landscape, because the gradient of the route is flatter by about a third and because a bridge, however high, might endanger the future of the port of Hamburg. The six motorway lanes were arranged in three tunnel tubes with two lanes each, so that, in the event of maintenance or control works, one tube can be closed. There still remain two lanes each for traffic in both directions. The lowest point of the carriageway is 27 metres below the medium waterlevel of the Elbe river. The slopes are 2.6 and 3.5 p.c. respectively.

For the construction of the underwater section, one selected the sinking method which was developed in the Netherlands and applied already in the Federal Republic of Germany with great success to the tunnel under the canal near Rendsburg linking the North and the Baltic Seas. Since shipping traffic on the canal was to be impeded only as little as possible, a tunnel section of 140 metres length for the middle part of the 640 metre-long road tunnel at Rendsburg was prefabricated, floated into position and lowered into a transverse grove previously excavated in the canal.

The underwater section of the new Elbe tunnel was constructed in a similar manner, although, of course, the dimensions of the Hamburg project were of a different order. For the fabrication of the tunnel segments, the world's largest drydock was created with a surface of 170000 square metres, by blocking off and pumping dry the port section Maakenwerder Hafen. Within three years, eight tunnel elements of 132 metres length, 41.7 metres width and 8.4 metres height each were built here. The tunnel cross-section consists of a reinforced concrete frame with five cells. Between the three tubes, there are the large-scale supply and exhaust air ducts. The bottom deck is 1.1 metres thick, the cover deck 1.0 metre. When manufacturing the elements weighing 46000 tons, certain measurements had to be kept to the very last millimetre so as not to run into difficulties with sealing. Seven tugboats brought the first tunnel element into position exactly above the grove dredged in the river bed and the foundations. Lowering the element required precision work. Seven times the procedure was repeated which was followed subsequently by filling in sand under the hollow concrete boxes until a solid support was built for the entire bottom surface of the tunnel. Then, the sinking grove was filled up so that the top of the structure lies 3 metres below the Elbe bottom. Special profiles between the individual tunnel elements ensure proper sealing.

The 1114 metre-long section of the Elbe tunnel situated in the sandy slope of the bank was built after the shield driving method. Never before had this construction method been applied to a diameter this large (11.83). The three tubes are 4 metres apart and they have been armoured with 47520 cast-iron segments (cast-iron rings consisting of individual segments used for the development of watertight shafts). For the carriageways, reinforced concrete slabs were installed in the tubes. The lining is made of prefabricated reinforced concrete wall segments which are tiled with ceramic tiles, just like the walls of the underwater section of the tunnel. A suspended ceiling covered with sound absorbing material seperates the traffic section from the exhaust air duct. In order to make it easier for drivers to adapt to differing light conditions, the ramps have been roofed in over a stretch of 120 metres before the access and after the exit with a sheet aluminum grid structure. In addition, there is a graded adaptation lighting on a tunnel stretch of 200 metres. Three large ventilator buildings were erected for the ventilation and deaeration of the Elbe tunnel – which is controlled by a process computer. In total, 29 axial-flow fans have been installed of which 13 suck off the exhaust air from the tunnel.

Traffic as well as maintenance works in the Elbe tunnel are being monitored from an operation control desk which is manned day and night. To this end, the Hamburg authority delegates 44 employees who are joined by another 14 policemen. Apart from built-in fire-extinguishing equipment, two fire brigade vehicles and a tow truck have been stationed at the tunnel exits. To monitor and control the stream of the vehicles, there are a television system with 49 cameras, two traffic process computers, lane signals, conducting and closing gates as well as light barriers to control the vehicle height which is limited to 4.3 metres. In the tunnel, there are wall recesses at 100 metre intervals equipped with emergency help telephones. In the event of traffic disruptions, the operation control desk can inform drivers via a loudspeaker system. In addition, an aerial system has been installed in the tunnel so that motorist may be able to listen to the traffic news.

The motorway system in the Federal Republic of Germany and West-Berlin. Sections indicated by a broken line are being planned or under construction.

CHAPTER II Waterways and Ports

The Federal Republic of Germany has an efficient network of inland waterways which are subject to the sovereign rights of the Federal Water and Shipping Administration. Federation and "Länder" combined spend about 1900 million Deutschmarks on the 4300 kilometre-long navigation routes (in 1977, 450 million Deutschmarks of Federal funds were spent on maintenance and operation, whereas the main portion of 1100 million Deutschmarks went into investments). The big rivers, in particular, the Rhine with its tributaries Neckar, Main and Moselle, form the core of the waterway system, with a total length of approximately 3200 kilometres. The canals which have a total length of about 1100 kilometres interconnect the individual river systems across watersheds into one coherent network, thus, linking larger economic areas and intensifying the communication of the seaports with their hinterland.

Waterways contribute a remarkable share to economic growth. Disregarding pipelines for the transport of liquid goods, inland vessels are the most economical means of transport for bulk goods and, since decades, they account for about one fourth of the goods traffic in the Federal Republic of Germany. In 1978, a total of 242 million tons were transported on the inland waterway system. Of these, 80 million tons were shipped within the Federal Republic, 149 million tons as part of the cross-frontier goods traffic, and 13 million tons in transit traffic. There is no other means of transport with an expenditure in energy and personnel as low as in commercial inland navigation, and in particular in pusher barge navigation. The waterways have been expanded, to a great extent, to be navigable by the 1350 t Europa-barge which is 80 metres long and 9.5 metres wide and which has a discharge draught of 2.5 metres, as well as by twin pusher barge formations of 185 metres long, consisting of one push barge and two (engineless) push lighters. At an equal discharge draught of 2.5 metres, such a pusher barge unit is able to transport 3300 tons.

In modern civil engineering hydraulics, the concept of canalization is a taboo in converting rivers into navigable waterways. When expanding the Moselle river in 1958–64, the engineers exerted great cautiousness so as not to interfere with the character of the winegrowing landscape. The picture shows the Moselle barrage and lock at Enkirch with power station.

The conversion of the Neckar river into an international waterway

Since 1958, Stuttgart has been connected to the waterway network, and disposes of an inner harbour. Ten years later, the conversion of the Neckar into an international waterway was concluded with the opening of the port of Plochingen. The conversion of this river to Europa-barge standards had taken 48 years. The 27 barrages with weir installations, locks and power stations have a total lifting height of 161.5 metres. The shipping route from the point where the Neckar debouches into the Rhine near Mannheim all the way up to Plochingen has been shortened by means of lateral canals and crosscuts by 10 kilometres to 201.5 kilometres.

When planning the Neckar waterway, all parties involved were at pains to have regard for the landscape. In Heidelberg, heavy controversies had been raised because of the location of the barrage beneath the castle, in spite of the surface level having been limited to a mere 2.6 metres. Paul Bonatz, whose co-operation in the construction of the Neckar barrages had been requested in 1926, reports in his memoirs, "The university's aesthetes wanted spire turrets and arches, whilst the movement for the protection of the countryside demanded things totally different". The building permission for the barrage had been subject to the condition to top the pillars with spire turrets for trial, "but this", writes Bonatz, "we then duly forgot." The many alterations of the plans give evidence that the architect made the greatest efforts to arrive at a good design. Originally, the weir piers were supposed to be arranged in steps at half level above tailwater in order to provide a support for the gangway. This gangway would then have been high above the tailwater. Instead, the gangway was run above the topwater, so that the high pillars protruded from the tailwater without terracing. Bonatz sees this alteration as follows: "What is low is underlined, made even lower, and what is high is underlined, becoming higher still." Heidelberg has long forgotten the disputes of 1926. For where the river is populated today by goods and passenger vessels and sporting boats, there generally used to be but a rivulet in summer.

What Paul Bonatz was mainly after, when designing the barrages on the lower course of the Neckar river in the Twenties, was to make the function obvious through the form. The pictures (*above and below*) show from upstream the weir, the generating station and the twin locks at Neckargemünd.

Power station and weir near Marbach on the Neckar.

As, for instance, is the case of the Poppenweiler Neckar barrage, the high superstructures remain a strange addition to the river landscape in spite of a meticulous natural stone facing.

Particularly in the case of the design of the Ladenburg barrage and lock with its three sets of twin lock towers (at the upper, middle and lower gates) and the three weir openings, Bonatz attached great importance to making the function obvious through the form. Says he: "All individual parts were stressed in what made them individual: the heaviness of the weir pier row, the lightness of the mounted cavities for the machinery, the lighting strips, in short, every technical requirement for weir, locks and power station."The barrages on the lower course of the Neckar are characterised by the high and slim weir piers. Bonatz also made sure that the buildings blended into the colour scheme of their environment: "When building in an area with red sandstone, Jurassic limestone was added to the monolithic concrete giving it a greyish-rose coloured glimmer. In flat country, as near Ladenburg, we were not concerned to use concrete. But when running into shell limestone near Hornberg (castle), we used visible shell limestone masonry instead of the ordinary brickwork." In order to keep the lock towers as low as possible, the waterway administration developed, in co-operation with steel construction firms, sinkable lift gates for the upper gates, and folding lift gates for the lower gates. Stone mattings were used to fortify the embankments, and these were soon overgrown with greens. By building up the embankments "in a living way" with trees and bushes, the upper edge of the artificial bank stabilization was hidden already after a few years.

Although engineers and architects were at pains to achieve a good formal design when working on the expansion of the Neckar, the high superstructures of weirs as well as powerhouses and locks, remained foreign bodies in the river landscape. However carefully chosen the natural stone facing was, the awkward effect could not be completely eliminated.

The "Moselle construction method"

When, in 1958–64, the Moselle was expanded, a completely new method was applied. In 1956, the Federal Republic of Germany, France and the Grand-Duchy of Luxemburg had concluded an interstate treaty in which was laid down the decision to develop the Moselle into a large shipping route with a navigable depth of 2.9 metres so as to make it navigable for 1500 t-ships and twin pusher barge formations. It was imperative to avoid building obstrusively formed structures dominating the landscape of the narrow Moselle valley. Says Karl-Josef Großheimann: "All parties involved in the canalization of the Moselle spared no means to live up to the demands for a solution respectful of the landscape.It was not so much the alteration and redesigning of the Moselle valley, but rather finding a succesful way of complementing and improving the natural circumstances, that the engineers, architects and landscapists were equally faced with as a task and an aim."

For the first time in the history of civil engineering hydraulics it was possible "to erect structures which are nearly free of any problems in their appearance", as Professors Walter Henn and Udo Maerker of the Braunschweig Polytechnic, who were both involved in the project, put it. One hardly notices the considerable interference with the landscape caused by the construction of 12 barrages between the French border and the Moselle-Rhine junction, because the hydraulic installations have been kept extraordinarily low. They are almost immersed in the storage water level of the river. This was only possible owing to new technical solutions which have become known among experts as the "Moselle construction method".

Normally, river generating stations are equipped with Kaplan turbines with a vertical shaft. On the Moselle barrages, however, a new construction developed by the Rheinisch-Westfälische Elektrizitätswerk AG (RWE) was used for the first time in which the turbines are arranged slightly horizontally inclined in the flow direction. In order to keep the generator measurements to a minimum, the turbine's speed is increased by a coaxial intermediate drive. Generator as well as turbine are located in a steel casing immersed in the water stream and are accessible from the engine room. The water stream runs through the generating station without any special deviations so that one can do without the structural elements, such as spiral intake and toggle suction pipe, which are characteristic features of the vertical shaft Kaplan turbine. Due to the new type of construction, a new structural unit is created, differing substantially from traditional power stations in its internal layout as much as in its external design. The power generating installations on the Moselle are not only significantly lower, but also shorter by one third due to the smaller axle spacing, in spite of the crane installations being arranged inside.

According to the "Moselle construction method", the height of the power station block depends on the necessity to arrange the supply and exhaust air ducts in such a manner that they will be above water level, even in the event of the river flooding. The ventilation slits of the Trier generating station are seen as a band beneath the roof of the powerhouse from the downstream as well as from the upstream side. In the case of the Palzem power station, situated on the upper course of the Moselle, the upper edge is only 1 metre above the maximum storage level. The powerhouse is 4 metres below water level when the flooding river reaches its highest level. Ventilation, in this case, is by an underground duct leading to the embankment.

The only facade of the Moselle power stations is formed by the tailwater wall which is usually made of fair-faced concrete and faced with natural stone only in exceptional cases. At Trier, the concrete surface dissolves into a grid pattern. The roofs of the powerhouses are flat and slated or lined with a copper foil. Daylight can enter the engine room through acrylic glass domes. The only operation installation rising above the powerhouse roof, is the rack cleaning machine the design of which was greatly influenced by the architects. As far as the weirs on the Moselle are concerned, there, again, high superstructures were avoided by installing hydraulically controlled sector gates which, in the event of flooding, are lowered into a concrete chamber and immersed in water. The narrow weir piers the upper edge of which is only 1 metre above the maximum storage water level, are not too much in evidence with medium or low water levels. The barrages on the Neckar and Main rivers and other waterways, on the other hand, are built with highly protruding pillars for the hoist machinery which are required for the actuation of vertical lift gate and cylindrical barrage weirs and have to be arranged in a flood-free position.

The hydraulic engineering installations on the Moselle are kept to such a low level that they almost are immersed in the storage level of the river. Contrary to the other Moselle barrages, the navigation locks have been moved downstream by several hundreds of metres from the 9 metre-high Detzem barrage.

Since the development of the Moselle, gravel and sand banks no longer appear at times of low waters. The extended water spread also exerts a beneficial influence on viticulture. The picture shows the 7 metre-high barrage near Neef and St. Aldegund's.

The operation of such weir types requires a gangway which underlines once more the high superstructure of the weirs. An inspection tunnel was built into the weir foundation of the Moselle barrages, linking, at the same time, the lock and the powerhouse.

The Moselle locks have a uniform length of 172 metres and a width of 12 metres, allowing for two 1500 t-ships or a pusher barge formation using the chamber simultaneously for the ascent and descent. The head gate is of the vertical lifting type equipped with counterweights, with small drive houses on both sides. Together with the operation building, they are the only high structures in the weir and lock installation, the superstructures having been built as small and unobtrusively as possible. The drive for the hydraulically operated mitre gate at the lower lock gates are situated in the operation building basement. In addition, each barrage has a 18 metre-long and 3.5 metre-wide boat lock for small ship navigation, for canoes and row boats, as well as fish and eel ladders.

As a rule, one tried to forego alignments and cuts in the development of the Moselle river. The surface levels were limited to 6 to 9 metres in order to maintain the waterfront, although some insignificant changes were unavoidable, in order to create the necessary ground areas for the locks with their long upper and lower parts as well as for the inlet and outlet channels of the power stations, and to enlarge the navigation route to the required width.

The task of blending the installation unobtrusively into river course and landscape was entrusted to a team of several expert consultants, amongst whom also was Alwin Seifert. Long stretches of the Moselle were given a green belt as a harmonious transition from level reach to the shore and the slopes of the valley. The ugly silted gravel and sand banks which formerly became visible with low water levels, have now disappeared thanks to the storage water. Also, the extended water spread has a beneficial effect on the viticulture practised on the Moselle slopes. The solar heat absorbed by the water during the day is released at night into the air so that the average nightly temperature has risen, consequently improving the microclimate. The reflection of the sunrays from the water surface onto the vineyards also proves an advantage for viticulture.

The German Council for Landscape Preservation commented particularly positively on the development of the Moselle and pointed out: "The Moselle river was not given the character of a canal-like waterway, because dams were avoided, the bank surfaces were heightened in the storage range, and the channels were deepened in the upper third of each level reach.

The location of the barrages was chosen carefully and correctly, bearing in mind landscape aspects. The barrage installations and power stations are of an attractive design, as much from an architectural as from a preservationists and landscapists point of view." Besides the relocation of some new industrial zones on the Moselle, the body expresses particular regret over the fact that along many sections of the embankment, roads have been developed for motor car traffic which made it necessary in several locations to erect high breast walls.

The world's largest mechanical lift

The 115 kilometre-long lateral canal of the Elbe, opened in 1976 after a building period of 8 years provides the Hamburg seaport with a first-class connection with the inland waterway system. Often, the water level of the upper Elbe river does not permit the vessels to be completely discharged. The canal reduces the distance by water from Hamburg to the Mittelland canal to the west and, thereby, to the industrial region of Braunschweig/Salzgitter/Wolfsburg, by 217 kilometres and to Magdeburg by 33 kilometres. Europa-barges and twin pusher barge formations can navigate the new waterway at a speed of about 11 k/h. Routing radii of less than 2500 metres were avoided with regard to pusher barge navigation. The canal was given a trapezoidal channel with a 1:3 inclination ratio of the slopes. No vertical embankments with sheet-pile walls were built. In the Aller valley, a 14 metre-high dam had to be raised for the waterway. In total, 63 million cubic metres of earth had to be moved. The difference in height between the Elbe river and the Mittelland canal is overcome by means of two barrages only.

The most impressive building on the Elbe lateral canal is the mechanical lift near Lüneburg. At the land wave between "Geest" (dry and sandy) and marsh land near Scharnebeck, it bridges a level difference of 38 metres. This corresponds to the height of a 15-storey building. Presently, this installation is the world's largest mechanical twin lift with vertical transport. In the lift, the vessels are transported between tail and top water in a water-filled trough, like in an elevator. Since the vessels, upon entering, will displace the quantity of water from the trough corresponding to its weight, the trough weight will always remain constant. This is compensated by counterweights which consist of 224 high-density concrete discs the volume weight of which is increased to 3.56 t/m3 by adding magnetic ore as an aggregate. Each of these counterweights weighs 26.5 tons and is suspended from a steel rope with a diameter of 54 millimetres.

The trough which measures 100 metres in length and which has a clear width of 12 metres and a water depth of 3.5 metres, has been constructed, as regards its walls, according to the orthotropic plate principle. It is moved along four counterweight towers which each consist of two chambers bearing weights, and of a core with a staircase well, respectively, an elevator shaft. The water-filled trough and the counterweights weigh approximately 12000 tons. This total weight is transmitted in the tower heads from the pulley on to a support structure and, from there, led into the towers. Reinforced concrete gangways linking the tower heads immediately opposite of one another, have the statical function of pull and compression member. There are four drives with 160 kw electric motors to lift, respectively, lower the trough within 3 minutes. All in all, the passage of one single vessel only takes as much as one quarter of an hour. As the Lüneburg mechanical lift was conceived as a twin installation for two independently working troughs, vessels can simultaneously pass the barrage on their ascent as well as descent. Both lifts are operated by one person from a central control board.

The Lüneburg mechanical lift on the lateral canal of the Elbe opened in 1976, overcomes a 38 metre level difference. Presently, the installation is the largest mechanical twin lift in the world with vertical transport.

This vessel in the Lüneburg mechanical lift is reduced to the size of a toy.

The load of the water-filled trough which weighs about 12000 tons, is compensated by counterweights moving in towers. It only takes 3 minutes for the powerful electric motors to lift or lower the trough.

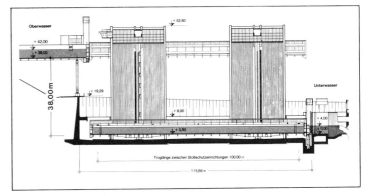

When the plant is running fully automatically, all he has to do is to push the ascent or descent operation button, once he has made sure that the vessels have been fastened in the trough. A closed-circuit television system facilitates control of traffic for him in the event of bad visibility.

The fore harbour of the upper reach is moved up to the troughs of the mechanical lift by two 42.5 metre-long canal bridges. The reach gate is of the lifting type. Air bubbling devices and sealing heating systems keep the gate area free of ice in winter.

At the lower gates, movable shield shutters are required, since the lower reach is connected freely with the Elbe river, and, therefore, the water level fluctuates by 4 metres. The operation-related water loss of the lift, by comparison with a lock, is only negligible. In order to compensate also for the loss of water in the middle canal reach caused by evaporation and infiltration, a pump system with a capacity of three times 2.24 m3/sec. was installed.

Initially, a steel truss structure had been planned for the lifting towers and counterweights. However, from the tests carried out on a land model, Gerd Lohmer, who had been called upon by the steel firms to act as architectural adviser, could see that this was not going to be a satisfactory solution: "The mass of the closed steel troughs would have moved among a criss-cross of steel girders. What was light would have carried what was actually heavy – a problem to which, in statical terms, one could certainly have found a solution, though lacking credibility when it comes to listening to one's gut feeling." The architect therefore proposed a concrete construction for the towers. Comments Lohmer: "The concrete masses had to be structural, however, so as not to appear as brutal massive concrete blocks, on one hand, and, on the other hand, also make apparent the function of the installation. In order not to make the towers look like hollow cases, the exterior of the structure was given a filigree-like grid of concrete combs. In doing so, the buildings do not only appear as a terse entity, but it is also possible to watch the lifting procedure though the grid which provides a certain sense of proportions." The bright colours of the steel structure constitute a successful contrast with the grey concrete colour. The troughs and the canal bridges were painted in blue. The bright red of the lifting tower for the reach gates is to signal, as it were, "stop". The trough parapets are of the same colour. This red band then continues all along the sides of the canal bridges.

The Uelzen lock

Approximately half-way on the Elbe lateral canal, near Uelzen, the presently highest lock in the Federal Republic of Germany, overcomes an elevation difference of 23 metres. The 190 metre-long and 12 metre-wide lock chamber can take in a pusher barge formation with two lighters or two Europa-barges. The installation was built as a lock with means for the economisation of water, because at every ascent locking, about 54000 cubic metres of water would have to be borrowed from the upper reach. Approximately 60 p.c. of the water volume required for one chamber filling for the lifting procedure are taken from three side ponds arranged in lateral terraces next to the lock. For descent locking, these ponds are filled again. The lifting and sinking velocities of the lock chamber amount to 2 metres/minute each way. An interchange locking takes about 45 minutes. The lock chamber has been equipped with floating bollards which are always on level with the vessel. The vertical lifting gate on the lower gates is moved upwards on both sides behind the end wall made of reinforced concrete by means of counterweights. Following the suggestions of the Hamburg architect Harro Freese, the corners of the tower-like superstructures at the lower gates have been rounded off, making the building look eye-pleasing. High above the lock platform there is the central control station, providing an excellent overview. Only one person is required to operate and monitor the entire lock installation.

From Fossa Carolina to Rhine-Main-Danube waterway

Already Charlemagne attempted to surmount the watershed between Rhine and Danube, the two vast European stream basins. The "Lorsch Annals" of 793 mention the project to build a "navigable trench" between the Suavian Rezat and the Altmühl rivers which were only 1500 metres apart. But what had been excavated during the day by 6000 workers in spite of heavy rains, "caved in again at night due to landslides". The political situation (an uprising in Saxony) may also have played a part in the suspension of the "Fossa Carolina" project. Some remains of "Charles' trench" can still be seen today in the vicinity of the village of Graben: There are earth dams of up to 6.5 metres in height and several hundreds of metres in length between which runs a 9 metre-deep water-filled gorge. At the vertex, these earth walls are 60 metres apart.

In the ensueing centuries, no attempts were made to put the plans into practice after all. It was only during the advent of mercantilism that interest in a waterway linking Rhine and Danube regained momentum, and it was Napoleon who took up the idea. During his time, however, little progress was made beyond the state of vague plans. This changed drastically under King Louis I of Bavaria. After a ten-year construction period, the 173 kilometre-long "Ludwigskanal" (Louis' canal) with 100 locks between the Danube and the Main was opened in 1846. The project which employed at one time up to 9000 people, gobbled up 17 million florins. But financially it turned out a big fiasco. With 196000 tons, the maximum transport capacity of the canal was reached in 1850. In 1912, no more than 64000 tons were shipped on the "Ludwigskanal", for, soon after the completion of the artificial waterway, the railways had developed into a successful competitor with the canal which only allowed for the passage of vessels with a maximum load capacity of 120 tons. In addition, the barges had to be towed – a time-consuming procedure – and locked at frequent intervals. After 1945, the "Ludwigskanal" was closed to traffic.

Contrary to the "Ludwigskanal", the new waterway, technically speaking, belongs to the top group of inland waterways.

Uelzen lock during construction.

This lock of the "Ludwigskanal" opened in 1846 has been kept in existence until the present day.

Contemporary presentation of the "Ludwigskanal" with the Altmühl bridge near Schelleneck.

Quay in Nuremberg harbour opened in 1972, after the 70 kilometre long Main – Danube canal section from Bamberg to Nuremberg had been put into operation.

The Kriegenbrunn water economy lock north of Nuremberg surmounts a level difference of 18.3 metres.

Strullendorf canal lock between Bamberg and Nuremberg.

The layout of the state harbour of Nuremberg points to the future. Harbour entrance and basin are 100 metres wide each.

A canal bridge conducts the Rhine–Main–Danube waterway across the Zenn valley near Fürth. The bridge measures 105 metres in length.

In order not to interfere with the historical image of the town of Würzburg, no lock house was built near the Main bridge dating from medieval times, and the drive and control rooms were accommodated in two bridge piers.

The Regensburg Danube power station was not only built with a reduced height of construction, but it was, furthermore, given a glass lantern-type roof so as not to block the view from the motorway on the towers of the dome.

For once, it makes the idea – toyed with already at the time of the Roman Empire – come true of creating a 3500 kilometre-long navigation link between the North and the Black Seas right across Europe. By 1886, the Main river had been developed into an efficient waterway from its mouth to Frankfurt, and by 1921 to Aschaffenburg. The prerequisites for a development of the Main by means of barrages beyond Aschaffenburg were met with the foundation of the Rhein-Main-Donau AG which was commissioned with the construction of the waterway and endowed with the rights to exploit, until the year 2050, the hydro-powers generated in those sections of the Main and Danube rivers running through the "Land" of Bavaria. These rights were subject, however, to the condition that the construction of the navigation route be financed from earnings from the hydro-power stations. Until 1962, 27 barrages with power stations were built on the Main between Bamberg and Aschaffenburg. The Main-Danube canal on which work commenced in 1960, follows the Regnitz valley from Bamberg in the direction of Forchheim, ascending subsequently towards Fürth and Nuremberg along the Western edge of the valley. The 70 kilometre-long Bamberg-Nuremberg section with its 7 locks is in operation since 1972. The 98 kilometre stretch between Nuremberg and the Danube near Kelheim is planned to be completed by the mid-Eighties. This link between the Rhine and Danube regions surmounts the Franconian Jura with a series of 9 locks, the normal water level of the summit level reach being 406 metres above mean sea level. This makes it one of the most extensive projects, from a technical as well as financial point of view, the cost being quoted as 1900 million Deutschmarks.

The technically as well as economically most viable solution evolving from comprehensive studies was a route consisting of 64 kilometres of still water canal and a stretch of 34 kilometres where the Altmühl river is to be expanded. Between Nuremberg harbour and the summit level reach, one lock with 19.5 metres level difference and three locks with each 24.7 metres level difference are planned. In the southern section, three locks of 17 metres height each, and on the Altmühl two barrages of 8.4 metres height each will be built. The effective chamber length of the 12 metre-wide locks will be 190 metres, allowing for two motor vessels of 90 metres length and 1500 tons load capacity to be locked simultaneously, or, alternatively, one twin pusher barge formation. At the largest among these locks, which even outstrip the Uelzen lock on the Elbe lateral canal, an interchange locking procedure will take about one hour. The journey time between Nuremberg harbour and the Danube will amount to approximately 16 hours.

Measures relating to water resources policy are of eminent importance in the building of the canal. At intervals, water from the Altmühl and Danube will be diverted via the canal into the Main basin so as to improve the water supply in the Franconian region where precipitation is scarce, but which is heavily industrialised. The locks of the Southern ramp, therefore, will be equipped with pumping stations which can haul up to 35 m³/sec. of water into the summit level reach and large reservoirs. The Northern ramp locks will be built with two or three side ponds. The special filling and drain system with openings in the bottom of the lock chamber enables the vessels to lie still during the locking process, thus, making it unnecessary for the vessels to be moored in the locks.

The still water canal which mainly follows the cutting in the terrain, is built as a trapezoidal channel with a 1 : 3 slope inclination. The water level is 55 metres wide, and at the toe of the slope the water is 4.0 metres deep. Sections where the water is level with the ground or higher, will be given an asphaltic sealing and, at the same time, an asphaltic concrete protection against damages from the river traffic. In deep cuts and for longer canal bridges, the canal is built with a rectangular cross-section.

63 intersection structures, amongst which two canal bridges, will have to be built between Nuremberg and the Danube. One canal bridge was already built in 1970/71 near Fürth, crossing the Zenn valley. The bridge is 105 metres long. The overall width of the steel bridge is 44 metres, 36 of which are taken up by the navigable cross-section, and 4 metres each by lateral operation walkways. The trough height amounts to 5 metres, so that, at a water depth of 3.5 metres, there remains a free board of 1.5 metres. The steel structure weighing approximately 1700 tons, carries a water load of about 14800 tons. The canal crosses the stream course at an angle of 75°. The abutments and both column rows had to be arranged parallel to the flow direction of the Zenn for current-related technical reasons, resulting in the bridge being supported at an oblique angle of 75° against the longitudinal axis of the bridge.

The construction of the Rhine-Main-Danube waterway provides a good survey of the development since the Twenties not only from a technical standpoint, but also as regards the design of the structures and their amalgamation with the landscape. In particular in the area of Würzburg, the technical installations had to be blended into and adapted to the historical town image carefully and unobtrusively. This is why the idea of building a lock house next to the medieval bridge was foregone and the lock drive and control rooms were accommodated in two bridge piers – a unique solution, one might say, putting up even with operational disadvantages. The fact that the old bastion underneath the Marienberg citadel had to be moved backwards by 23 metres, is only noticed today by "insiders", and demonstrates how painstakingly stone after stone was moved. Furthermore, the lock was faced with the shell limestone typical for Würzburg. – Another example: According to the original plans for the Regensburg Danube barrage, the powerhouse would have blocked the view onto the dome towers from the motorway. Nevertheless, architect and engineers succeeded in reducing the construction height, and the powerhouse was also given a glass lantern-type roof at approximately ridge level. Following the wishes of the local municipal architect, the lock house in Regensburg was designed in an octagonal shape similar to the old water towers, although this resulted in triangle-shaped rooms. – When building the Rothenfels barrage in the years 1934–37 in the particularly beautiful stretch of the Main river between Aschaffenburg and Würzburg, the lock, situated in a river bend, was built slightly arched, so as to achieve a harmonious adaptation of building and landscape. For the same reasons, the Jochenstein Danube barrage weir and lock was given an arched axis.

An aerial view of Regensburg. In the immediate vicinity of weir and power station runs the route of the motorway (left foreground). The lock is near the left edge of the picture in the background on a level with the medieval bridge across the Danube.

The "riverscape", as seen here near Volkach, has benefitted greatly from the Main development.

The Western Harbour is West-Berlin's most important harbour.

In order to counter the progressive erosion of the Rhine bed, the Federal Republic of Germany and France have jointly built in the Seventies the Gambsheim and Iffezheim barrages and locks, after the development of the river between Basle and Strasbourg. The Iffezheim plant (see picture) with its highly functional but nonetheless attractively designed lock houses, has two lock chambers of 24 metres width and 270 metres effective length each. They are closed by way of a sliding gate at the lower gates and a sinkable lift gate at the upper gates.

From the very start, the Rhein-Main-Donau AG tried to maintain the character of the river landscape. If at all possible, no embankment dams were built. The hydraulic engineers redirected the stream course in such a way, that the retained water, for long stretches in a row, fills the entire space between the embankments. Additional plantings give the embankments a natural look. With respect the landscape designer Alwin Seifert acknowledges that some sections of the Main river which had been planted already before the Second World War, have turned into "river landscapes of perfect beauty".

Comprehensive landscaping and design plans are elaborated by landscape architects for all sections of the waterway between Nuremberg and the Danube. The first such plan was submitted in 1974 for the narrow and charming Altmühl valley. The danger of creating a monotonous countryside is met by a constant exchange of the layout elements. In particular the inclination and length of slopes, yet also the planting of embankment zones, are frequently varied. Loops in the Altmühl river remain largely intact as dead stream branches, and by retaining smaller tributaries, it is intended to create additional water spreads. At the same time, areas flawed by gravel

When the 125 kilometre-long waterway system in West-Berlin was expanded, it resulted also in the creation of recreational areas along the embankments as, for instance, seen here on the Landwehrkanal.

pits and refuse dumps will be rehabilitated. In the dry region of the Franconian Jura, the canal will be an asset to the landscape, and all the more so since the routing chosen is constantly curving, and the water spread is supposed to be enlarged in places. Especially worthwhile looking at is the section of the Danube between Regensburg and Kelheim which has been expanded since 1978 with two barrages and locks, and has improved considerably through new water spreads and extensive plantings.

Bottlenecks hinder navigation to West-Berlin

The critical situation in which West-Berlin finds itself also comes to the fore in inland navigation. Before the Second World War, Berlin used to be one of the most important traffic cross-roads in Central Europe. All transport routes converged on this city like rays. Today, Berlin is a terminal for waterway traffic from the Federal Republic of Germany, and this terminal can only be reached by certain prescribed routes. Between the Mittelland canal and the Elbe-Havel canal, there still is a 900 metre-long canal bridge missing near Magdeburg which should lead across the Elbe river. The same goes for the Hohenwarthe mechanical twin lift. Work on both structures, situated today on the territory of the German Democratic Republic, was taken up before the Second World War, but has remained unfinished till the present day. Hence navigation between the Federal Republic of Germany and Berlin is dependent on the fluctuating water levels of the Elbe and its marked low water periods. The Spandau lock in Berlin is another bottleneck to overcome, its one and only chamber being but 70 metres long, so that 1350 t-Europa-barges coming from the West cannot reach the industrial areas located on the upper Ha-

The Duisburg harbours are considered the inland harbour system with the world's largest cargo traffic volume. In 1978, it amounted to 57 million tons, exceeding even the goods traffic volume handled in the port of Hamburg.

This vertical lift bridge for a combination of road and railway traffic serves as a link with the Mannheim harbour. Owing to the necessarily oblique route, the lifting towers were given a round shape. The bridge weight – the bridge span is 39 metres – is set off by counterweights inside the towers.

vel river in West-Berlin. In the meantime, an agreement has been reached with the German Democratic Republic on the construction of a second, larger lock chamber for the Spandau barrage.

When expanding the 125 kilometre-long West-Berlin waterway network, this also resulted in the creation of recreational areas along the embankments. The municipal harbour installations have been concentrated nowadays in four operation centres the most important of which is the Western harbour (Westhafen). It was here, in particular, that new warehouses and modern freight handling installations for all kinds of piece and bulk goods were built.

The North Sea – Baltic Sea canal

The 99 kilometre-long North Sea – Baltic Sea canal, known in international navigation as the "Kiel Canal", has saved ocean-going vessels the voyage around Skagen between the North and Baltic Seas since 1895. This equals a shortening of the route by 460 kilometres. The canal links the Elbe river near Brunsbüttel with the Kiel Fjord, crossing the lower-lying marshland and leading through the Geest ridge (dry and sandy coastal strip) which is up to 25 metres higher, and through the undulating country of Holstein.

To counter the fluctuating water levels of Elbe river and Baltic Sea, the canal is closed at the top and bottom ends by two twin locks each dating back to 1895 and 1914. The new locks are 40 metres wide and have an effective length of 310 metres. The locking time is 45 minutes approximately. The journey through the canal which, like the Rhine and Moselle rivers, is also passable at night, takes between 6.5 and 8.5 hours. Ships of a maximum length of 235 metres and a maximum width of 32.5 metres are admitted to pass. The elevation above water level is restricted to 40 metres, and all bridges across the canal have a clear height of 42 metres. Larger vessels and those with dangerous cargo may only meet or overtake one another in passing areas, or so-called "passes". The traffic is directed by central control stations in Brunsbüttel and Kiel-Holtenau.

Because damage to the underwater slopes had increased to an alarming extent after the Second World War, owing to a growing traffic density and the increase in vessel size, extensive protection and stabilization measures to halt the decay of the canal bed are being administered since 1965. The bed width of the waterway will be enlarged from 44 to 90 metres, the water spread of the canal, thus, widening from 102 to 162 metres. The water depth of 11 metres will remain the same.

Duisburg: The world's largest inland harbour system

The Duisburg harbours – a traffic cross-roads of the first order – owe their eminent position, first and foremost, to their location on the Ruhr-Rhine junction. Together with 14 factory-owned harbours and cargo handling installations, the public harbours constitute an inland harbour system which, judged by its cargo volume, is considered the largest in the world. In 1978, the cargo volume handled exceeded, with 57 million tons, the volume of the port of Hamburg. It is particularly ores, mineral oil, scrap, mineral raw materials, foodstuffs and grains which are unloaded here, whereas coal from the Ruhr region, iron and steel, machinery, refinery products and all kinds of industrial products are predominant in the haulage to other destinations. The public installations of the Duisburg-Ruhrorter Häfen AG alone comprise 20 harbour basins with a 2.13 square kilometre water surface. There are 43 kilometres of quais and embankments for the purpose of cargo handling and berthing. Even the largest of the Rhine-Sea vessels can be processed here. The harbours, amongst which there is one container terminal, are linked up with the Federal railway network via three connecting stations and 148 kilometres of track.

The port – Hamburg's lifeline

With 55 million tons (1978), Hamburg is not only the Federal Republic of Germany's most eminent sea port, but also its largest foreign and transit trade centre. The port is the lifeline of this Hanseatic city rich in traditions. Though the port being more than 100 kilometres away from the open sea, fully loaded vessels of up to 110000 t can call at the port. The channel of the lower Elbe river has been deepened to 13.5 metres at medium tidal low water level.

About 18000 ocean-going vessels originating from 80 countries called at the port of Hamburg in 1978. More than 4000 million Deutschmarks have been invested in the port over the past three decades for, after all, Hamburg has to defend its reputation of being a "fast harbour". In the port section of Waltershof, Europe's largest container cargo centre was built, controlling 18 container bridges and 62 portal lift trucks commuting between the vessels and the stowage areas. At Waltershof, operation is controlled by computer, and even for roll-on/roll-off traffic, Hamburg offers efficient installations.

Fanning out along the Elbe are the basins for ocean-going vessels of the Hamburg port, between which there are long jetties with sheds. The port area covers 89 square kilometres. The total length of the quay walls is 61 kilometres, 39 kilometres of which are deep enough for ocean-going vessels. Whilst the basins for these vessels are open to the sea, the inland navigation basins are facing inland. This separation of the traffic streams is not an invention of modern times in Hamburg. As early as in the Middle Ages, inland and sea port were separate.

The industrial landscape – in this case a large sea port with its variety of installations – is subject "to the same principles of urban architecture as a general urban organism", says Dietrich Kuntsche, chief architect of the Hamburg port authority. To him, the difference lies in "the preponderance of the economic purpose, the unalterable function, the clearly predetermined operation. So far, the architect is forced to move within the narrowest of limits, defined already by the

Hamburg is the most important sea port and foreign trade centre in the Federal Republic of Germany. The traffic connection with the Hinterland has been systematically developed. The motorway (Europa Route 3) leads past the Waltershof container centre through the port to the new Elbe tunnel. To the right, in the middle of the picture, the Köhlbrand bridge.

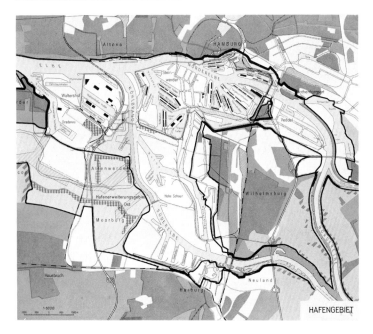

The Hamburg port area extends over 89 square kilometres.

practical programme. This is not a drawback – at least not so if the particular attraction of the task is seen to lie in filling the clearly staked out frame with a restrained, but nevertheless vivid inventiveness. Given these preconditions, it is possible to melt function and artistic urge into one uniform design; only this way it is possible for strictly purposeful installations to turn into buildings of architectural merit."

A city of harbour warehouses

Apart from the port basins with their crane installations, warehouses and quai sheds characterize the picture of a port. Basically, the sheds are nothing more than sorting tables roofed over. Here, the unloaded cargo is spread out, allocated to different destinations and re-grouped in cargo units for further despatch. Nothing must obstruct a speedy handling of the cargo. Hence the number of supporting pillars is kept to a minimum in the construction of sheds. There are about 80 sheds in the Hamburg port, measuring, on an average, 10000 square metres approximately. At the Waltershof container harbour, though, one will find sheds with a floor area of up to 25000 square metres.

At the end of the 19th century, the quai sheds in Hamburg were simple carpenter's constructions. The middle one of three hall naves rose above the other two, so that at a height of 8 to 10 metres a 2.5 metre high skylight could be installed. Both on the land and water side, the sheds were equipped with a ramp. The railway track was generally situated on the water side, horse-drawn carriages being parked on the land side. Apart from human muscular strength, only bag trucks were available for transporting goods on the quais and within the sheds. Over the past decades, the quai sheds have been built with prefabricated reinforced concrete pillars and wide span steel tube girders. The walls up to gate level are of brickwork with above a continuous light strip. The roof consists of corrugated asbestos cement sheets. It was endeavored to keep it to as light and simple a structure as possible. As the invention of forklift trucks has completely changed mobile industrial handling, ramps are no longer needed as they would only be an obstruction. Thus, a continuous plane surface has been created from the quay wall to the street on the land side.

Just how much specialised installations are subject to change, is demonstrated by the fact that the banana shed on the America Quay does no longer live up to requirements after only two decades. The banana bushes were hoisted from the ship's hold by means of lifts and placed into the air-conditioned sheds via hatches in the roof; then they were sorted and transported to the freight waggons or vans by way of conveyor belts. These costly haulage installations have become superfluous since bananas are dispatched in cartons placed on pallets. It is much easier to handle them with a fork-lift truck.

In the warehouses and sheds in the Hamburg free port, which covers an area of nearly 15 square kilometres and is surrounded by a 23 kilometre-long customs fence, import cargo is stacked up before customs clearance, until a buyer has been found. Particularly heavy containers or casks are stored in the one-storey warehouses, whilst more precious goods as spices, carpets, tea, coffee or tabacco are warehoused in the sheds. When it was decided in 1881 to establish a free port, three districts on the Elbe with almost 20000 inhabitants were vacated in order to build within only a few years a warehouse town there. On principle, all warehouses consist of a ground floor and five storeys, the so-called lofts, and have a street and a water front. On both sides, there are windows installed above the hatches. Office premises may not only be found on the ground floor, but sometimes also in the first loft. The buildings of the warehouse town were erected on close clusters of wooden driven piles of 12 metres length. Above these, strong concrete cross beams and the rising brickwork were placed. The inner structure of the 28 metre-deep stores was finished with wrought-iron supports, ceiling joists and longitudinal girders placed on top which are covered by a tongue-and-groove strip flooring. The fire lobby segmentation was commendable, each unit having a floor space of 400 square metres. The warehouse town, still in use today, offers a storage and office space of 415000 square metres.

Notes a contemporary source on the design of the warehouse town buildings during the two last decades of the 19th century: "When designing the exterior, great efforts were made to save the large, long rows of warehouses from a sober barrenness; to aim for a more favourable effect on the public without, however, attaching too much value to architectural ornament, except for the office forebuildings, which would not have corresponded to the purpose of the buildings. Taking into account the weather conditions, all warehouse buildings were built as brick carcasses." Even today, new warehouses are still being built of brickwork or faced brick, because these have proved the best building materials with respect to the extreme air pollution and, in addition, are cheap to maintain. Up till today, washed concrete facades remain an exception to the rule in the port of Hamburg.

The Overseas Centre and the St. Pauli Pier

The Overseas Centre of the port of Hamburg which was built 1963–1967, is considered the world's largest piece goods handling and distributing installation. The building covers almost the entire jetty. In the Overseas Centre, the collective shipments transported from inland by rail, road or inland waterways – approximately 20000 pieces of freight per day – are dismantled, sorted according to destination for further shipping and in some cases also stowed in containers. They are subsequently brought to the ocean-going vessels by van or in barges. The receiving shed is a 28000 square metre station roofed over, with 180 metre-long tracks on dual ramps 28 metres wide. The adjoining storage space, at 58000 square metres, has been designed for an annual handling volume of 500000 tons. The complex is subdivided into seven naves of 74 metres width, each of which is roofed over with two saddle back roofs, thus, leaving the interior sections of 37 metres width free of pillars. Like the receiving shed, the roofing skin consists of corrugated asbestos concrete sheets with recessed light strips made of corrugated wire glass. The exterior masonry of red frostproof brick has been extended far enough beyond the eave height of the saddleback roofs joined together as to give the impression of a cubical structure.

The roof of the 20 metre-wide ramp on the water side cantilevers beyond the quay arris by 25 metres, in order to provide protection for a dry loading of the barges under any weather conditions. (This principle reminds of the apron roofing at the Berlin – Tempelhof airport).

The water side roofing of the Overseas Centre rises above the adjacent shed complex, being distinctly seperated from the latter also by the profiled design, without jeopardizing the homogenousness of the complex.

Also one of the most remarkable buildings in the port of Hamburg is the Brooktor customs office built 1965–67, the platform complex of which is entirely roofed over evoking the impression of a station building. The tent-like roofing, seen before the back-drop of the old warehouse town, confers to this "main entrance" to the free port an appropriate character.

Harbour launches for the ferry traffic, the tourist boats for tours of the port, commuter vessels servicing the lower Elbe and the seaside resorts as well as the England ferry all land at the St. Pauli Pier. Because Hamburg is a tidal port with a range of tide of 2.8 metres occuring twice a day, a 700 metre-long and 18 metre-wide floating jetty serves as landing pier, where vessels can be moored. The pier which was renewed in 1954 consists of six reinforced concrete pontoons which have proved to have extremely stable floating properties. They do not require any rust protection and very little maintenance. On the pontoons also rest reinforced concrete superstructures housing restaurants, waiting rooms and shops as well as other facilities. The St. Pauli Pier is connected by way of a promenade with the Overseas Pier located several hundreds of metres upstream where cruise and other passenger ships moor. These facilities are also built on pontoons.

With 2136 bridges, Hamburg has by far the most bridges of any city in Europe. Outside the port area, Hamburg's waterways extend over more than 62 kilometres. More than 1000 bridges span water, some of them being balance or lift bridges to allow for the passage of larger vessels. At the beginning of the Seventies, the Kattwyk bridge was built across the Southern Elbe for the purpose of railway and road traffic. The 100 metre-long lifting section of this steel framework bridge can be lifted by nearly 46 metres, whilst the counterweights at the 70 metre-high lifting towers weighing 740 tons balance the lifting section's weight.

Water side of the warehouse town in the port of Hamburg which was built during the last two decades of the past century.

Land side of the Hamburg warehouse town. In the foreground the Brooktor customs office with the tent-like roofing of the platform complex.

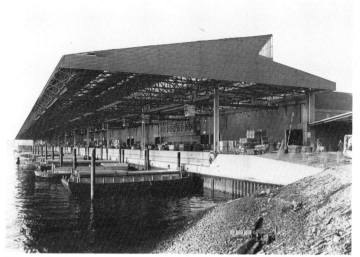

The roof of the water-side ramp of the Overseas Centre cantilevers 25 metres beyond the quay arris.

The Overseas Centre of the port of Hamburg is considered the world's largest piece goods handling and distributing installation.

The cantilever roof of the Overseas Centre ensures a dry loading of the barges, even if it rains.

The St. Pauli Pier, with its superstructures, rests on reinforced concrete pontoons of a total length of 700 metres, owing to the range of tide.

The 100 metre-long lifting section of the Kattwyk bridge across the Southern Elbe river can be lifted by almost 46 metres. Hamburg is the city in Europe with the largest number of bridges. The statistics of the Hanseatic town list 2136 bridges.

The Bremen ports

The port installations of the city of Bremen are known as the Bremen ports. They range in second place among the sea ports in the Federal Republic of Germany, with a cargo volume of 23 million tons (1977). With 60 p.c., their proportion of piece goods is particular high.

In Bremen, the changeover to container traffic was made at a very early stage, creating generous installations which for years secured a lead over all other sea ports. For when it became apparent towards the end of the Sixties, that the container handling installation of the City of Bremen port group would soon no longer be sufficiently big to cope smoothly with the rapidly expanding traffic of increasingly bigger special-purpose vessels, construction of a new container terminal began immediately near the Weser estuary which was opened already in 1972. This modern terminal which carries an investment up till now of 480 million Deutschmarks, commands a storage and traffic surface of more than 935 000 square metres as well as twelve container bridges. The quay length on the outer Weser river is 1600 metres, adding another 900 metres in the area of the Northern port which is an entrance lock dock. Almost 320 000 containers of a total volume of 4.2 million tons were handled in the Bremen ports in 1977. Practical plans have been drawn up for a generous extension of the terminal in the direction of the North Sea; it will cost several hundred million Deutschmarks to put these plans into practice. (In September 1979, the area was expanded already to 1 000 000 square metres upon the completion of a new construction section.)

In recent years, modern lash bases and roll-on-roll-off installations have also been added. In addition, the Bremen ports have special facilities for the export and import of all types of vehicles, silos and lifting devices for corn as well as generous installations for handling of annual shipments of 450 000 tons of bananas and 150 000 tons of other fruit. At the collective goods centre Weserbahnhof export goods are processed by the Bremer Lagerhaus-Gesellschaft (Bremen Warehousing Company) for shipping to all corners of the world.

The Wilhelmshaven oil port

Since 1958, Wilhelmshaven has an oil port on the Western Jade shore which is 46 kilometres from the open sea. The Jade channel has been dredged in various stages to a depth of 19 metres, enabling since 1974 fully loaded 250 000 t tankers to call at the oil port by benefitting from the range of tide. Approximately 22 million tons of crude oil are discharged in Wilhelmshaven every year.

A 1200 metre-long oil discharge pier extends parallel to the channel at 700 metre's distance from the main land to which the pier is linked by an approach pier. The pier installation, passable by fire brigade vehicles up to the pier discharge heads, rests on 32 to 44 metre-long steel tube piles. On these piles, prefabricated reinforced concrete segments were mounted. The tankers berth in front of the four discharge heads at elastic fender mooring post. The movable discharge booms can correct a level difference of up to 29 metres between smaller laden tankers at low tide and discharged supertankers at high tide. The Nord-West Oelleitung GmbH which has built the entire complex, has an oil depot ashore, with a capacity of 1.5 million cubic metres. Two pipelines with a diameter of up to 100 centimetres convey the crude oil to refineries located in the Emsland and Rhine – Ruhr regions.

Puttgarden ferry terminal

In the course of the "Vogelflugline" expansion works, the ferry terminal of Puttgarden on the Baltic Sea island Fehmarn was put into operation by the Federal Railways in 1963. Since the entrance between the two long moles is but 85 metres wide, the wave motion is decisively subdued in the 600 metre-long and at the baseline 700 metre-wide harbour basin. The ferry boats put into the two ferry beds in reverse and under their own steam. These beds are used alternatingly. The railway carriages are moved aboard via a hatch at the stern. On the Danish side of the Fehmarnbelt, the ferries moor with the bow turned to the shore. In doing so, it is avoided that the vehicles transferred have to turn about. The passport and customs control buildings are situated on the access and exit roads to and from the port of Puttgarden. There are car ramps on the side leading to the ferry boats. In the middle axis of the terminal, there is a 140 metre-long elevated gangway to the platform overpass of the station which is an integral part of the port.

At the container terminal of the Bremen ports situated on the Weser estuary, cargo handling – as everywhere else in the world – takes place under the open sky.

Harbour system of Bremen-Stadt.

The Puttgarden ferry terminal was put into operation by the Federal Railways on the Baltic Sea island of Fehmarn in 1963, as part of the Vogelfluglinie (The bird's flight line).

The modern container terminal at Bremerhaven commands nearly 1 million square metres of storage and traffic surface.

Since 1975, fully loaded 250000 t supertankers can call at the port of Wilhelmshaven where approximately 22 million tons of crude oil are discharged annually.

Lighthouses

The lighthouses on the North and Baltic Sea coasts display an endless variety. The oldest sea mark still to serve its purpose today in the Federal Republic of Germany, is the 39 metre-tall Neuwerk lighthouse. The massive quadratic masonry building which reminds of a fortification, was erected in 1310 in the days of the Hanseatic League. By comparison, the brickwork lighthouses on the islands of Norderney (built in 1870/71, 53.6 metres tall) and Borkum (1879, 60 metres tall) do live up to the traditional idea of such structures.

The 65 metre-tall Campen lighthouse built in 1889–92 which is a triangular strongly tapered steel grid structure, is a purely purposeful building in the middle of which an encased spiral staircase leads to the top. The Falshöft lighthouse (24 metres) was built from cast steel in 1910. The brickwork lighthouse of Mellumplatte built in 1939–42 carries today a helicopter landing platform, and similar to the Campen sea mark, the 16 metre-tall Fischerbalje lighthouse erected in 1960 consists merely of a steel skeleton. Three years later, the reinforced concrete structure of the Alte Weser lighthouse was built which enlarges into a conical shape towards the top. The reinforced concrete part carries a multistorey widely projecting steel structure. Other lighthouses were equally built from reinforced concrete in the late Sixties/early Seventies, some of them up to 64 metres tall (Wangerooge). In addition, steel lighthouses were erected in some places, the round shaft of which carry lantern-type roofs of all shapes so as to give each sea mark its individual character.

A new feature is the application of glass-fibre reinforced plastic. The Scheelenkuhlen beacon built in 1976 from this material projects almost 47 metres into the air. The lighthouse, however, whose top is lacking an optical closing stone, would hardly fail to be taken for a chimney. In one particular case, the Kiel water and navigation authority completely renounced the idea of a proper building for a beacon. When in Travemünde a hotel tower literally put the century-old lighthouse in the shade, the new beacon was installed in 1972/73 on top of the 113 metre-high hotel roof.

Neuwerk: Built in 1310, 39.0 metres, masonry.

Norderney: 1870/71, 53.6 metres, brick.

Campen: 1889–92, 65.3 metres, steel.

Borkum: 1879, 60.3 metres, brick.

Falshöft: 1910, 24.4 metres,
cast steel.

Mellumplate: 1939–42,
32.2 metres, brick.

Fischerbalje: 1960, 16 metres, steel.

Alte Weser: 1963, 38.1 metres,
reinforced concrete with steel head.

Altenbruch: 1967/68, 59.5 metres,
reinforced concrete.

Wangerooge: 1968, 64.1 metres,
concrete.

Inland waterways and ocean-side sea waterway boundaries in the Federal
Republic of Germany and West-Berlin. The dotted lines indicate sections
still under construction.

Track system of Frankfurt/Main main station, Europe's largest passenger train station.

Chapter III Rail Transport Installations

"In the entire history of building, the station was the first building owing its design, its dimension, its independent existence not to the traveller but to the technical object. This is when the architecture of transport first came into being", points out Wulf Schadendorf. In many cities of the nineteenth century, which was the century of the train, 'cathedrals of transport under the canopy of the railway heaven made from glass and steel' were created. As Theophile Gautier puts it: "These cathedrals of a new humanity are the meeting place of nations, the centre towards which everything gravitates, the nucleus of gigantic stars whose iron beams reach into the farthest corners of the globe".

The 'reception buildings' of the railways are splendid achievements of functional and stately architecture testifying to the social importance attached to the then new means of transport. Yet, surprisingly, a railway style proper never had a chance to develop. The buildings in the focus of the railway operations "were of a representative nature for they were to demonstrate their importance to each visitor. Often though, a stranger could only tell from the inscription on the outside of the building whether he stood in front of the station or the municipal opera house". This is how Richard Heinersdorff, a writer for professional magazines, explains the phenomenon.

As a rule, station buildings were built at the outskirts of the town which then extended in direction of the station. The frequency with which the streetname 'Station Road' (Bahnhofstrasse) occurs, still hints today to this urban development. The explosion-like growth of the cities was fostered by the railways. Whilst in former times it had been the nostalgia for far-away parts of the world which had attracted lookers-on to the station, these buildings began to acquire over the past decades a special social function: they became the meeting places of foreign workers in Cologne and Munich as much as in Frankfurt or Berlin. For these people who are often not integrated into society the station is a connecting link with home, this connection with the mother country being symbolized by the steel tracks.

The main station in Frankfurt/Main

Frankfurt's main station is the largest passenger train station in Europe. Every day, more than 1000 trains enter and leave this dead-end station. In addition there are approximately another 600 trains operating in the underground urban railway system. On weekdays, an average of 180000 travellers pass through this building benefitting from the extremely favourable location of the station vis-a-vis the city centre. The fact that this traffic volume is absorbed smoothly and without problems is evidence of an amazing far-sightedness and generosity on the part of the founders.

The reception building of the Frankfurt main station which was built from 1884–88 in neo-renaissance style is considered, with respect to its architecture and construction, as "certainly one of the most beautiful monuments of this epoch" (Mihàly Kubinscky). The basic concept of the entire installation which incidentally replaced three much older dead-end stations, was developed by the royal building supervisor Hottenrott. In 1880, a public bid for a competitive tender was issued among architects in Germany for the design of the reception building. 55 proposals were submitted. The first prize was awarded by the Prussian Building Academy to the then state building superintendant Georg Eggert from Strassburg who was consequently also commissioned the further development of the design – which covered everything up to the very last detail – and the execution of the work.

The centre of this representative building the layout of which is strictly symmetrical, is the 23 m high entrance hall with the ticket offices. The facade of the hall is crowned by a group of figures in hammered copper representing Atlas with the globe with the accompanying figures of steam and electricity seen as the 'driving forces of world transport'. Other figures on the corner pillars of the centre building symbolize the iron industry, agriculture, commerce and navigation. The entrance hall with its barrel-vaulted roof has two lower

This is how the reception building of the Frankfurt main station presents itself today. The building was erected from 1884–88 in neo-renaissance style.

Details of the rich allegorical ornaments of the entrance hall facade which is crowned by Atlas with the globe.

Frankfurt main station is being preserved today as a historic monument. All war damages have been carefully repaired.

This picture still dates back to the last century. In the 90 years since its construction, only very cautious changes have been made to the exterior building.

wings adjoining on both sides. On the sides, dome-vaulted towers form the corner-pieces of the monumental structure which originally was 210 metres long and built on a high granite base course from yellow sandstone from the Palatinate and Heilbronn regions.

Each stone of the facade had to be worked by a stone-mason, each ornament had to be carved individually. The steel structure of the platform halls with their huge curved trusses which span up to 56 metres, blends into the style of the reception building and with it forms a harmonious entity. The journalist Benno Reifenberg visualized 'iron palmtrees in the ramifications of pillars'. Looking at the exterior front, one can still guess how sumptuous and spectacular the decoration of the inside of the reception building must have been. Marble columns and splendidly moulded walls made up the interior decoration. Wide arched openings connected entrance hall, cross hall, waiting rooms and restaurants.

Even before the first world war, the constantly increasing traffic volume made it necessary to plan an extension. Whilst in 1888 the daily avarage of trains pulling in and out of the Frankfurt main station was 187, this avarage had reached well over 660 in 1914. From 1912 to 1924 another six station platform tracks were added to the existing 18 providing them with a roof with two additional platform halls. At the same time, the reception building was extended by 60 metres to 270 metres by adding on two side wings.

Although somewhat more moderate in their design, these annexes did harmonize with the older existing structure. With its 24 platforms, the Frankfurt main station is outstripped in Europe only by the Leipzig main station with 26 tracks and the main station of Munich (36 tracks including the Holzkirchen and Starnberg station). In 1969, a 25th platform track was added in Frankfurt, and since 1978 the installation includes another 4 underground railway tracks.

Since the mid-Twenties however, no substantial changes have taken place in the outer image. The damages caused by the war have been repaired and, in as far as the northern section of the reception building had to be pulled down for the building of the metropolitan railway, the station was restored in its historical facade, though with completely new layout and design inside. On the whole, the interior of the building has been subject, over the nine decades of its existence, to a great many alterations. The rooms for 'persons of high and highest rank' no longer exist. First class, second class and third class waiting rooms have undergone a metamorphosis and are now modern restaurants. There are even a post office, cinema and conference room. The duty rooms with the ticket offices, travel information and the luggage office have been modernized and live up to today's requirements. Sales premises and rows of shops have replaced a multitude of kiosks. – Owing to its importance to building history, Frankfurt main station is preserved today as a historical monument.

The entrance hall to the Frankfurt main station which measures 23 metres in height as it used to be formerly (above), and (below and right) after completion of the works for the metropolitan railway.

The curved trusses of the platform hall span up to 56 metres.

During the extension work to the Frankfurt main station from 1912 to 1924, two platform halls were added on each side.

The new reception hall of the Cologne main station which was built in the Fifties was given a glass facade the effect of which has been impaired though since the construction, in 1972, of the pedestrian platform in front of the cathedral (in the right foreground) known as 'Domplatte'.

The concrete shell-vaulted reception hall in Cologne opens up towards the station square.

The Cologne main station opened in 1894 has undergone repeated structural alterations.

The long building history of the Cologne main station, which is one of the most heavily trafficked in the entire Federal Republic, stretches up to the present day. In 1859, the 'Zentralbahnhof' (central station) was opened along with the first railway bridge across the Rhine immediately next to the cathedral. It comprised three station platforms with two through tracks and six dead-end tracks which were roofed over with a low double storey hall. In 1894, the main station was opened on the site of the former central station combining the facilities of a dead-end and through station. The reception building, measuring 165 metres in length and 50 metres in width, featuring elements of the renaissance style was overtopped by a 42 metres-high tower with the Prussian crown as a closure piece. From both entrance halls, large tunnels led underneath the track system to the back of the station building. The big platform hall consisted of a centre span of 255 x 64 metres and a top height of 24 metres as well as two aisles of considerably smaller size. The main span which, in terms of design, is one of the most valuable hall structures of the late nineteenth century, still exists today in its fundamental layout. Inside the hall, the central waiting room building had been erected in form of an island on platform level. It was an iron framework construction with infill masonry work niches decorated with colourful glazed facing bricks and terracotta blocks. Corner ornaments and towerlike superstructures gave the interior of the splendidly decorated building its structure.

Because the combination of dead-end and through station had not satisfied expectations, the station was completely reconverted and extended in the years 1909–1915. By pulling down the island building, the dead-end tracks could be linked up with the through tracks. Below the track system, new waiting facilities were created with a new porch building which still exists today unaltered. Again and again, constructive changes were made in subsequent times, until the main station which had been badly hit by bombs in the Second World War was reerected in the Fifties in various sections.

Sidehall of the Cologne main station.

The Stuttgart main station which was designed by Paul Bonatz and built from 1914 until 1928 has acquired its permanent place in the building history of the twentieth century. Subsequent railway station buildings have been influenced strongly by the Stuttgart example which was widely acclaimed even on an international scale. It is, thus, appropriate to speak of a pioneering building achievement. This is not only true of its functional arrangement but also in respect of its town planning qualities. The Stuttgart main station was planned as a utility building satisfying, at the same time, the wish for a representative structure.

It had been Paul Bonatz who, in 1911, had come out the winner of a design competition. However, his original design which provided for vaulted platform halls and a tower for the station forecourt, had little in common with the building that was eventually built later, conceived and designed by the architect in a process of maturation which lasted several years. The layout of the dead-end station has been developed in accordance with traffic planning requirements. The crowds of travellers arriving on the platforms gather in a monumental cross-hall. Adjacent to this, there are two asymmetrically and transversally arranged entrance halls differing in size according to their purpose. The larger one of these halls was originally intended for long distance traffic only, whereas the smaller one was supposed to receive the suburban traffic. Both access halls are recessed from the cross-hall, even in terms of height, by means of wide staircases. Comments architect Friedrich Tamms on the building: "Thus, a clear structure of the inner organism was achieved which finds its powerful structural expression in the large rooms . . . The arriving trains pull in under low halls so that the traveller coming from under the low area walks out into the large space, thus, creating a strong impression on him."

In respect of the classification of the Stuttgart main station in terms of urban planning, Tamms says: "Another new feature is the handling of the building masses which, against the traditional views of stately buildings, were arranged and balanced against one another in free play. Instead of being lined up symmetrically on an axis, they are accentuated wherever the location of the structural part within the urban organism so requires. The tower stands in the field of vision from the Koenigstraße which pushes foreward into the city centre; the large booking hall is where the searching eye of the departing traveller should find it; and the hall for the suburban traffic is right there where the office streets receive the stream of arriving traffic." Frank Werner points out: "And the wide station forecourt for the boundaries of which Bonatz was also to provide the design later, creates a certain distance to the set of old historical buildings, on one hand, and, on the other hand, a stage for the conceptions of quality of the new 'large town architecture', whilst the calculated absence of symmetry of the facade provides the observer with an optical 'movement' of the structural elements towards one another from every position."

The Stuttgart main station which was built from 1914–28 after the design by Paul Bonatz, is regarded as a pioneering building achievement not only because of its functional structure, but also because of its urban planning qualities.
The cross-hall of the Stuttgart dead-end station *(below)* has a monumental effect.

The rustic limestone ashlars contribute to the appearance of the building masses as one monolithic structure. This appearance of the building is "if anything, intensified by the long pillar arcade in colossal order, the huge, deeply cut triumphal arches and the sharp edged, thin eave cornices" (Werner).

"Blending purpose with a dignified expression"

The railway companies tend to want respectable buildings. It is hardly conceivable for avant-garde architects to feel attracted to such a large-scale administration. It is true that the railway architects do plan for the future and do not shy away from seeking new paths, but their work is judged and closely scrutinized in view of the cost by civil servants. A great deal does not escape unscathed. For instance, the railways have constantly improved things that have held good. Only very reluctantly have new forms been incorporated. In addition, there is such a lengthy time span between the beginning of the planning stage and the execution, owing to prolonged coordination and approval procedures, that the architect is not in a position to look into and react to new developments quickly.

As early as 1850, the Society of German Railway Administration Authorities published its stipulations for the layout planning of reception buildings. According to these, the requirements include "a spacious porch building which may be closed towards the street side, adjacent to the ticket hall and baggage handling counters, a post office and at least two waiting rooms with restaurants; furthermore, an office for the station master, a telegraph room and a small room for the conductor. The waiting rooms as well as the freight despatch must be directly connected with the coach hangar . . . It must be possible to board cabs and carriages under roof shelter."

In 1901, the Prussian minister for public works promulgated a set of rules under the title 'principles and layout patterns for the drawing up of designs for station buildings' in which it says, among other things: "The station building is to be arranged in such a manner that the traveller, after having entered the building, is able to see where the most important localities are and that a crossing of the various streams of traffic is avoided as much as possible when heading for the ticket offices, the baggage handling, the waiting rooms or the platforms. Since it is a habit to move to the right when making way for others, it is advised to arrange the ticket offices and the baggage handling to the right of the person entering."

At the beginning of the Thirties, the director of the German state railways, Hugo Roettcher, notes: "The construction of traffic facilities will always abide by its most important law which is to answer a purpose. The form in which this presents itself may change. The present time seeks to free itself from the styles created in building epochs of the past and designs the garb of the traffic installations, imprints itself on its form with a stronger and more conscious emphasis on the contents, and thus, the purpose and the masses, divisions and axis which follow from it.

This does not exclude that the purpose is given a dignified expression, in other words, that the reception building testifies to the importance of the transport company, that it demonstrates the important task which the station has to fulfill for commerce and progress, and that it ranks as a significant link in the spectrum of significant city buildings."

Imitations of earlier stylistic epochs are rejected. It is regarded as an advantage to take into consideration the use of local building materials. Preference is thereby given to sintered clinkers, since they can best resist the smoke issuing from steam engines. "A requirement for the traffic premises is light in near overabundance." In those days, towers are seen as an architectural counterbalance to the long horizontal lines of the wing buildings. Platform halls are regarded as 'the station's most beautiful distinguishing attribute'. And the following proposal may almost appear modern: "The inconstancy of the traffic requirements on the reception building and the necessity of frequent conversions can be expressed visibly in the structural de-

In 1855, the first reception building was erected in Landau in the Palatinate.

For nearly nine decades the second reception building served its purpose in this town in the Palatinate.

This reception building was built in Landau in the Palatinate in 1961/62.

With the shutdown of the passenger train services on the subsidiary line to Baden-Baden, the reception building erected from 1892–94 had become useless to the German Federal Railways.The town purchased the building to use and maintain it for new purposes.

In the mid-Seventies, the main station of Bonn was also meticulously renovated.

sign in such a manner that only the main premises are formed with supporting walls or pillars, and partitioning of the secondary premises with thin and easily removable walls."

Only few of the projects which went into planning after 1933 and which are characterized by the typical monumental style of the national socialists were ever executed. Alterations to buildings which had already been started earlier were more frequent. For instance, the facade of reception buildings were decorated with ornamental figures, in the true spirit of the epoch, and even waiting rooms as well as booking halls displayed works of art in the official style.

New reception buildings

Railway installations, and in particular the reception buildings of the stations had suffered badly under the consequences of the war. In the beginning reconstruction concentrated exclusively on the operating installations. At first, the remaining parts of buildings were reused in building construction. Slowly but gradually, however, it was possible to elaborate new solutions, and in so doing, the volume could be reduced by more than 50 per cent in some cases by making rational use of the available space. Often, one could still tell from the reception buildings erected in the Fifties that the architect had been at pains to catch up with the international developments. It was only in the mid-Fifties that a brisker building construction activity set in at the German Federal Railways. As regards their design and materials, these new buildings are rather diverse.

From 1945 till 1955, the new Heidelberg main station was built which was moved from the centre of the town to the Frankfurt-Basle main line. The traveller has access to the platforms from above via crossarms – the most convenient arrangement for the passenger after the dead-end stations. The facade of the reception building is almost exclusively made of glass. Other new station buildings also opened themselves up to the traveller. For example, booking halls are frequently sections of the station forecourt seperated only by a glass front.

Other new station buildings which distinguish themselves by their wavy and flowing shapes, were also built after the shell construction method. One of these buildings is the reception hall of the Bochum main station (1956/57) with its canopy full of movement, and the Wolfsburg station (1955–57). In the course of the reconstruction of the Cologne main station, the new reception hall, so characteristic for the entire installation today, was built from 1955–57. It is vaulted by a concrete shell opening towards the outside. The demarcation line with the station forecourt is formed by a glass facade, thereby releasing not only an early view on the neighbouring cathedral to the arriving traveller, but also extending optically the rather cramped space. The shell roof sloping towards the back and faced inside with

small mosaic ensures, in addition, a good lighting of both the upper floors of the office wing which is situated between the reception hall and the first platform.

In Braunschweig, a new reception building was erected in 1959/60 following the influence of the new Rome main station, though – judging from the traffic volume – it has turned out to be too big by a few sizes. In Pforzheim (1958) the new reception building already announces the tendency to restrict building to a mere functional form. Forced by the need to be guided by the absolutely necessary offer to the traveller and the economic possibilities of the enterprise, the Federal Railways, over time, broke away once and for all from buildings which, as dominant features in the cityscape, were living documents of the railway's importance and official ostentation. This is why in the end sober and functional small-scale buildings were erected which, like the reception building of Frankfurt-East (1959), are hardly recognizable any longer as station buildings.

The Federal Railways present themselves as 'department stores for transport performance'. Theodor Dierksmeier, the former head of the construction engineering division in the German railways headquarters, describes this development as follows: "As regards form and function, the 'hard line' will be predominant. The decisive characteristic for the buildings of the future is the cubus. This uncompromising industrial form will be seen through with all materials used."

Grid pattern facings for station facades were, however, only used sparingly by the Federal Railways. Among the exceptions is the reception building of the Munich main station which was completed in 1960. Twelve years later, wing buildings were erected, equally with aluminium curtain facades. This type of facade design was met, for a long time, with restraint, so that one can notice a "retreat from the grid pattern". Everyone spoke of the "barrenness of the grid" resulting in "urban planning boredom".

In recent times, the Federal Railways show a tendency, when building new large-sized passenger stations, to incorporate the reception building in the city organism as an integral part of multifunctional installations. Large stations are of course in themselves multifunctional, for they constitute a "supply machinery" in which the traveller does not only arrive or depart, buy his tickets, register his baggage or make use of postal services. He will find, in addition, several restaurants, a series of shops and service facilities, and even hotel facilities in some of the stations, as for example in Stuttgart and Munich. All these different functions, however, relate to travelling. The new idea is to reject this limitation. The stations which once were built in the open, later proved to be obstructions to urban planning.

Today, station facilities are meant to be integrated in buildings the function of which is totally different, so that the bolt formed by the strands of tracks is, as it were, bridged. The latest example for this development is to be seen in Hamburg-Altona.

In Braunschweig, a new through station was created in 1958–61 on the outskirts of the town to replace a dead-end station dating from the mid-nineteenth century.

The reception building of the Munich main station – it was completed in 1960 – is one of the few examples where the Federal Railways had a grid facade built.

Opening up towards the station forecourt is the glass facade of the new reception hall placed in front of the reception building in classicistic style of the Wuppertal-Elberfeld station.

The canopy of the reception building projects far into the forecourt of the Munich main station.

The platform hall of the Munich main station is always full of bustling activity.

The large canopy of the Ludwigshafen station (1967–70) counterweighs the pylon carrying the elevated road which leads across the track system.

It does not always have to be a flat roof. In the mountainous region of the Weserbergland, the Federal Railways had this reception building erected as part of the Bad Pyrmont station.

The reception building of Hanover main station with the Passerelle, or passage way, making the Bahnhofstraße accessible to foot traffic on two levels and undercrossing the station.

Ticket offices in Hanover main station.

Centralized transport and sorting facility for baggage and express freight in Hanover main station.

Hamburg-Altona: The station department store

By drawing together the service functions and the essential operation services in the new building of the Hamburg-Altona station, space was created for a department store (right) with a ground area of 2000 square metres.

In the course of the construction of the metropolitan railway city line, the Hamburg-Altona station received the third station building in its history. It replaces the reception hall designed by Georg Eggert which was built in the mid-Nineties of the last century and whose plastically conceived and richly ornamented brick facade had suffered irrepairable damage during the war. The distinctly compact new building, has concentrated, in spite of higher standard requirements, the passenger-related service functions and the essential operation service in such a manner as to make room, at the same time, on the station grounds for a department store with a ground area of 2000 square metres. The larger part of the reinforced concrete skeleton construction was erected on the floor of the metropolitan railway tunnel. Identical materials were selected by the architects for the reception building as well as for the adjoining department store. In order to animate the forecourt, a restaurant was placed in front of the department store.

Modernization as a means to create 'marketable stations'

Continuous white strip lighting elements with pictograms installed in the course of the reconversion of some stations - as can be seen here at Frankfurt main station - have proven their worth.

Theodor Dierksmeier (the former head of the building construction division at the headquarters of the Federal Railways) raised the question in 1973 'whether we will continue - as building history has shown - to create buildings as monuments, or whether it wouldn't be more appropriate to look at a building in terms of a commodity which, after having served its purpose, may disappear again without too much of an effort or expense and be replaced by a new and more up to date commodity'. In spite of the prevalent necessity for flexibility, the building policies of the Federal Railways have not resulted in a 'disposable architecture'. It is rather that the buildings dating to the early days of the railways attract more and more attention, particularly so, since their maintenance seems often more sensible and, in terms of advertising, more effective.

In undertaking the alterations to the reception buildings in large cities which had become necessary in the course of the construction of the metropolitan railways, the Federal Railways were at pains to achieve a 'marketable' design of the station buildings. Easy accessibility, purposeful operating installations and an inviting overall appearance are the features with which the Federal Railways intend to hold their own in the competition with other means of transport. The internal functional structure of historical railway buildings and halls has to be adapted to the demands of today's customers. Comments Guenter Bergbrede, in charge of the building construction division in the Federal Railways' headquarters: "This modernization process requires a lot of empathy in order to be able to combine the nineteenth century railway architecture with the facilities needed in the twentieth century. The times of the 'waiting rooms with meal services' are of the past. Today, the customer expects to find in the station restaurants and retail outlets with a broadly based assortment equivalent to the shopping areas of large towns". At the same time, the access and parking facilities have to be improved, since more than 50 per cent of all long distance travellers use a passenger car for transport to and from the station.

Nowadays, large city stations are connection points for many different means of transport and the location for a variety of service installations.

Often, the traffic takes place on several levels which cannot be taken in at one glance, therefore, making it necessary to install orientation aids. In many stations, continuous white stripline lighting with pictograms, location and direction information have proved to be very helpful. In addition, traffic information and operating installations are colour-marked. Timetable showcases as well as indicator boards, for instance, specifying the coach sequence of the trains and the destinations are painted in red. Because through stations with subways and overpasses are in the majority, it is intended to install a greater number of escalators or lifts, just like in undergrounds, airports and in department stores where, for a long time, they have been commonplace features. Thought is also given to escalator-proof baggage caddies or oblique conveyor belts as there is normally little room on the platforms for oblique ramps. Efforts are to be made to lift the height of the platforms in order to make boarding and getting off the train easier and faster. The head and the end of long trains usually extending far beyond the sheltered portion of the platform, waiting rooms glazed on all four sides with 15 to 20 seats each are to be built on long distance platforms.

In the future, tickets will be sold in large stations from ticket offices located immediately in the traffic stream. Open counters will replace the former ticket booth. As in air transport, the Federal Railways also intend to attend to the traveller 'with one hand', possibly including handling of baggage. Great importance is attached to the passenger station contributing to a uniform image of the German Federal Railways so as to consolidate reputation and position of the enterprise. Apart from logo, inhouse script and a company colour scheme, the sales offices are to be fitted out in a uniform way.

Postal stations

Particularly at the beginning and at crossing points of important railroad lines, the German Federal Post have at their disposal, in connection with parcel post handling and other facilities, their own postal stations with an extensive track system. Whereas first installations of this kind were built directly next to the passenger stations, the trend was changed in Cologne as early as 1895 by physically seperating postal and main stations.

In Frankfurt main station, the offices of the four largest post offices of this town are drawn together in new buildings (1972–82) into one postal centre which will be among the most important ones in the Federal Republic. Over a normal working day, 200000 individual parcels and packets, 10000 small parcel bags, over 3 million letter post items and 16000 bundels of mail advertising have to be handled by 4400 postal clerks. The first construction stage comprises, further to a twenty storey administration building, a multiple storey operation building and the 18 metres-high glass hall of the postal station which is 96 metres wide and 220 metres long. The ten tracks for loading and off-loading post and freight wagons are spanned by a three-dimensional steel framework.

Adjoining to the hall of the postal station, there is the 240 metres-long and 85 metres-wide operation building the roof of which is designed as a parking deck holding 700 cars accessible via a double lane turning ramp. Disregarding the extensive operational installations, the construction costs for the first stage of the postal centre alone amount to 272 million DM.

Another remarkable building is the parcel post office of Hamburg 2 which was put into operation in 1973 after a construction period of eight years on the grounds of the former Kaltenkirchen station in Altona. Part of the extensive complex the facade of which consists of red washed concrete curtain elements, is the postal station with its own track system and signal box as well as a 145 x 110 metres large hall with twelve tracks.

Whilst the roof structure of the track halls in Hamburg and Frankfurt rests on supports, the folded arch of the Munich postal station built in 1966/67 spans 148 metres, the rise being 27.3 metres. The complicated bearing structure of the 124 metres-long hall assembled from prefabricated concrete units ranges among the masterpieces of civil engineering. The clear form of the construction of which the end walls are glazed is captivating.

The shunting yard Maschen with 112 forwarding tracks

In the Seventies, the German Federal Railways built their largest shunting yard in Maschen to the south of Hamburg. The installation which carries an investment of more than 800 million DM, extends, at a width of 700 metres, over about 7 kilometres. Approximately 300 km of track, 1014 switches, 47 bridges and 36 buildings had to be erected in order to be able to concentrate in Maschen the tasks of five outdated and uneconomical shunting yards. No less than 112 forwarding tracks link up with 34 receiving tracks. Every hour, up to 350 freight wagons roll over each of the five metres-high humps. 11000 wagons can be handled daily. The process computer-controlled operation runs, to a very great extent, fully automatical. The new shunting yard does not only facilitate a more rational operation, but is meant particularly to accelerate commercial transport. From Hamburg, another fifty large towns are 'within one night's reach'. Entire landscapes had to be redesigned for the construction of the Maschen shunting yard. Layers of peat several metres thick had to be stripped before a new foundation could be silled by pumping in dredged materials. The Federal Railways planted 200000 trees and bushes as well as hedgerows which do not only mark the boundaries, but also serve as a protection against smoke.

Already since the Thirties, the railways intended to build a new shunting yard to the north of Munich. Although the project was cut down to half its size in favour of a park, and in spite of revetments being planned, the local residents are still bitterly opposed because of the expected noise nuisance.

Freight handling hall in Hagen/Westphalia.

The arched folded plate roof of the Munich postal station built in 1966/67 spans 148 metres support-free.

At Maschen to the south of Hamburg, the German Federal Railways have built their largest shunting yard. The installation comprises 112 forewarding tracks, the costs amounting to over 800 million DM.

There are ten tracks leading into the new postal station of Frankfurt/Main.

85

The railway architecture of the past decades has been marked to a substantial degree by the buildings housing power signalling installations. To the left the central signalling installation in Munich, in the middle the central signalling installation in Frankfurt/Main built in 1956/57, and to the right the signalling installation in Cologne-Ehrenfeld.

In Uhlerborn on the Main, the Federal Railways have built life size models of bridges, tunnels and other man-made structures for the purpose of testing and assessing constructive elements for projected new track.

Power signalling installations

Within the German Federal Railways, the construction of modern signalling installations has come to be of such great importance that these buildings are almost as much a characteristic for the railway architecture of the past decades as the new station buildings. Signaling installations are seen as 'front runners' in the railway's efforts to rationalize its operations. At large traffic junctions, the mechanically operating installations have been replaced by large new buildings with a push button system. This technical system allows for a considerably larger number of signals and shunts to be operated from one signalling desk. Since the Second World War, more than 600 new buildings have been erected for power signalling installations.

Since the personnel is able to follow the operational sequences closely on the mosaic-like track screen, this type of signal building, theoretically speaking, does not need any windows. However, without the possibility to cast an eye on the track system, the work of the officials would be too abstract and too remote from the movements which take place under their control. This is why the operation rooms have all-round glazing. Until the beginning of the Seventies, the window panes were mostly inclined towards the inside or the outside in order to avoid reflection. Often, there was a horizontal sunshield above the glazing where no anti-sun-glass had been used.

Contrary to the operation room, the extensive other technical installations, such as the relay rooms, the standby generating set and the air-conditioning, had to be largely shielded off towards the outside. It is a difficult but nonetheless challenging task for the architect to accomodate the different functions in an attractive building on a nearly always limited construction site. The function related differences between the individual premises frequently result in an interesting contrast in the design of the structure. Although this building task has been solved in rather different ways, one can hardly fail to notice a change in style. The Federal Railways' first large central signalling installation was put into operation in Franfurt/Main in 1956/57. The building which dominates the track system of the Frankfurt main station, falls into the 'weak period' of signal box architecture. It winds up in 1964 with the central signalling installation at the Munich main station. From the end of the seven-storey building facing the dead-end station cantilevers the octagonal operation room. This cantilever aspect is emphasized still further by the extreme inclination of the glazing and the horizontal sun screen. The outer walls have been lined with large format aluminium plates.

How much architectural ideas have changed can be seen from the central signalling installation of the Stuttgart main station in operation since 1978 with the severe cubic structure without any pulpit. Behind the dark curtain-like aluminium panels of the four top floors it is impossible to recognize from outside the operation room situated in the top floor. The signalling building blends into the facade structure of other new buildings and, thus, is a distinct contrast to the main station. The signal building number 8 which was built in Stuttgart at the same time appears, with its pulpit-like extension, 'like a design by a playful architect fed up with the highly technical and functional buildings', although this design ensues from factual requirements.

The situation of the German Federal Railways

More than 140 years ago, the railways have given man a mobility of a degree hitherto unknown, and have boosted the development of the beginning industrialization process. The country was thrown open by the rapid expansion of the railroad system. In the days after the Second World War, the railways were the most important means of transport. But then it became subject to the pressures of a mounting competition. From 1950 till 1977, the share of the German Federal Railways in the transport of passengers fell back from 40 to 7 per cent. In the same period, 60 per cent of the long-haul traffic volume were still transported by rail. In 1977 however, this proportion had sunk to a mere 29 per cent. Today, the Federal Railways transport every day more than 4 million passengers and about 1 million tons of freight. The annual losses run into several thousand million DM. A considerable portion of the payments made by the state to the railways (1978: 13 500 million DM) is meant as a compensation for politically required services, in particular in the social sphere. In addition, the state subsidizes the local passenger transport on rail where only a fourth of the total expenses are covered from ticket sales.

Shorter journeys through new lines

The 28 500 km long rail system of the Federal Railways still dates back to the last century. The quality offered has been improved though by electrification, continuous welded rails and modern rolling stock. The journey times have decreased, and the passenger is offered more comfort. Since 1979, the most important cities in the Federal Republic of Germany are linked by an on-the-hour intercity train service.

In order to relieve the obsolete network, new sections are being built which allow for a speed of 200 k/h and over. The 105 km long new route between Mannheim and Stuttgart under construction since 1976, is supposed to be available by the mid-Eighties. The travelling time of TEE and intercity trains will then be reduced from 80 to 38 minutes. The construction costs amount to 2500 to 3000 million DM. 23 per cent of the line are taken up by 20 tunnels of which the longest, on the Pfingstberg, measures 4.5 km in length. 114 bridges, amongst which 9 are viaducts, and elevations will have to be built. The route is built mainly in the cut or on fills. Only 8 per cent of the line section are at ground level. The design speed was fixed at 250 k/h, the curve radius, as a rule, measuring 7000 metres.

Extensive landscape plans were developed for this new line. In order to reduce noise to a level acceptable to the local residents, earth embankments or acoustic wall boards are being erected along some sections. Thanks to a new type of bridge construction on steel as well as prestressed concrete, the sound level for a bridge is brought down to the one for a free stretch of track. As is the case with almost every large scale building project, citizen action groups have formed along this new route, too, bent on bringing to bear their ideas on the planning or on stopping the entire project altogether. Since there is at least one group which intends to make full use of legal recourse, it is hardly possible to assess the delays that may ensue.

In 1978 began the large scale construction work for the approximately 330 km-long new route from Hanover to Wuerzburg, the costs of which are assessed to be around 8000 million DM. In addition, the development of existing lines by extensions totalling 1083 km is to be pushed ahead until 1985.

The elevated track of the magnetic railways which, contrary to motorways and railway lines, do not form a barrier in the landscape, are to be assembled from prefabricated reinforced concrete or steel units. The required space as well as the implications for the environment are regarded as being small. Due to the friction-free drive, there is, theoretically speaking at least, no limit to the magnetic railway's gradability. In spite of the high speed, the strong transverse inclination allows for narrow curve radii. These properties, combined with the elevated structure, enable the route to be better adapted to the terrain. The stations for the system can be incorporated in the traditional passenger stations and other buildings.

Magnetic rail suspension system: Flying at zero altitude

In the future, a high capacity rapid transit system, the tracks of which will run above the old-fashioned railroad system, will close the speed and distance gap between the railways and the airplane which is uneconomical for short distances. The magnetic rail supension system is to transport long distance travellers at a speed of 400 k/h and over, achieving a speed of approximately 300 k/h on short distances. The Federal Ministry of Research and Technology has been subsidizing the new technology with substantial means since the early Seventies. The concept is aimed at high transport performances at reasonable prices and cost along with moderate energy consumption and a high degree of safety and comfort.

In the summer of 1979, the Transrapid 05 magnetic rail suspension system was first introduced to the broad public on the occasion of the international transport fair in Hamburg, after an extensive series of tests and trial runs. The track being limited to 900 metres, the 68-seater rail car type vehicle could only reach a maximum speed of 90 k/h. The drive via a Langstator linear engine is situated, in the case of this system, in the rail which consists of one single elevated girder. Rapid reaction electric magnets in the vehicle make sure that it hovers above the rails at a distance of about 1 cm. Track holding is likewise controlled via magnets, so that the vehicle follows the route contact-free.

With the show installation in Hamburg an important milestone in the development of the magnetic rail suspension system was reached. The next step will be the construction of the 31 km long Transrapid test installation in the Emsland designed for speeds of 300 to 400 k/h, and which is to help acquiring experiences applicable to the everyday operation. The first section of a magnetic railways open to the public could be started in the mid-Eighties. It is unlikely that sections of a European rapid transit network can become reality before the end of this century.

Magnetic railway at the international traffic fair 1979 in Hamburg. This is how the future stations of a high performance rapid transit system could look like.

This circular course built in Erlangen to test the new technology has a diametre of 280 metres and a track inclination of 45° towards the inside. It allows for the magnetic rail suspension system to be tested at continuous running speeds of around 200 k/h.

The track of the Transrapid magnetic railways consists of an elevated girder. The construction time is reduced by the use of prefabricated concrete or steel units.

During the international traffic fair 1979 in Hamburg, the Transrapid 05 magnetic railways was for the first time introduced to the broad public.

Detail picture of the test track in Munich-Allach.

In 1974, this 2400 metres long test section was built in Munich-Allach for the Transrapid 04.

Motorization has led to substantial interference with the city substance. Because it is impossible to make the idea of an 'automobile heaven in the city' become reality – as it rather endangers urbanity –, local public transport is subsidized by the state with considerable funds. This aerial view shows the intersection of two Federal trunk roads in Karlsruhe.

CHAPTER IV Urban Transport and Relevant Constructions

An avalanche of cars jeopardizes urbanity

Thanks to the motor car, man has come to enjoy a mobility to an extent hitherto unknown. Yet the increase in the quality of life as a result of motorisation is starting, to a certain degree, to turn into the opposite. This is a phenomenon particularly in evidence in the larger cities which are no longer able to cope with the advancing avalanche of cars. Locked in the traffic jams, which are a common-place feature of the daily rush hour, the motorist is a prisoner of technological progress, and in his time-consuming search for parking he turns into his vehicle's slave. It is the future of the city, according to Alexander Mitscherlich "the cradle of civic liberties", which is in danger. Hence the solution of the traffic problems is one of the "central tasks all large cities are faced with, for without these a purposeful urban development is inconceivable" (Hans-Ulrich Klose, First Mayor of the Free and Hanseatic Town of Hamburg).

Cities are not only mere agglomerations of buildings and streets, but rather "existential premises for the entire social, economic and cultural life". This is particularly true for large cities the life spheres of which extend beyond the city boundaries and embrace a whole region. The pronounced trend to live in the country, the flight from the "inhospitability of our cities" (Mitscherlich) has accelerated this development at an almost fatal rate. The more people turn their backs on the traffic noise and the confinement of the inner cities with their polluted air, the faster the depopulation of the centres progresses. At the same time, however, the demands of the region on its nucleus, the city, with its high-standard shopping facilities and cultural institutions, increase. Owing to the excessive accumulation of individual traffic the inner cities are threatening to collapse, and the landscape's "suburbanisation" progresses.

The urban traffic problems require urgent solutions so that the residents may feel sheltered again in the social environment of the town. If this does not happen, the city centres are perverted into ghost towns after offices and shops close, the entire urban region loses its centre, and the population is threatened by spiritual and psychological isolation. Urbanity is in danger. Yet urbanity is, in the view of Edgar Salin, "education, well-being of body, soul and spirit; but it is . . . dependent on the fruitful contribution of man, the political being, to his and only his political sphere".

Even the German automobile association ADAC notes: "The city cannot be "carproof". But it cannot do without the car either". On the occasion of the opening of the 1979 International Traffic Fair in Hamburg the then President of the Federal Republic of Germany, Mr. Walter Scheel, spoke of the "carproof city" as an "obsolete concept", even if this news had not yet spread to the farthest corners. "The human town is much nicer. In it, one lives a lot better and more neighbourly, and, ultimately, it is also better justifiable from an economic point of view". In retrospect, Scheel observes, "we have tailored our patterns of settlement so much after the car that a good number of our citizens wouldn't live where they live if it weren't for the car. Thus, the car has turned from a convenient accessory in our life into a necessary one. This, however, means nothing more and nothing less than that we have become dependent on the car . . . We will now have to give thought as to how we will design our traffic system in the future. And, in view of the present situation, this means that we will have to call a halt to a possibly limitless expansion of car traffic . . . We must learn to make reasonable and conscious use of the car, lest one day traffic suffer an infarct . . . Every working day, morning or evening, millions of citizens are subject to the depressing experiences of the rush hour: jams, stench, stressed nerves, frequent accidents, the search for parking, the time wasted. Surely, most people no longer enjoy this kind of driving."

In Scheel's view, one of the indispensable prerequisites for the people to be prepared to leave their cars at home, is the availability of, at least equivalent, public transport facilities. He evoked the Bavarian capital, Munich, as an example: "Before the Olympic Games in 1972, metropolitan railways or an underground did not exist in Munich. By far the majority of all professional and shopping trips were made in private cars. Today, after the construction and installation of efficient short-distance transport systems, more than 70 p.c. of the working and shopping traffic is carried by those amentities. The consequences are a tremendous relief for the roads, a much better quality of air, a lot less noise in the city centre and a visible rekindling of inner city life causing even long-standing "connoisseurs" of Munich to be impressed time and again." Scheel was of the opinion that the Munich example should induce many a mayor and his councillors to consider the possibilities of an attractive mass transport system instead of brooding over plans for new routes to be built.

New traffic routes are created below surface by means of highly modern construction techniques.

It is not only in the large cities that traffic jams are a common feature in daily life. This picture was taken as early as 1958 on the Cologne Deutz bridge.

Construction of a section of the Munich underground. The tube has been lined with reinforced concrete cored segments.

Rapid transit systems to counter the collapse of traffic

In order to preserve the towns which have grown historically, it is necessary not only in metropolitan cities, but also in medium-sized towns to shift mass passenger transport from the surface to the underground. Metropolitan railways and undergrounds are the economically most viable means of transport where the traffic pressure is at its highest. A metropolitan railway requires no more than a 5 metre-wide route for the transport of 32400 passengers per hour, whilst the individual traffic would need to the same end a 55 metre-wide motor car carriageway with 16 lanes, not to speak of the parking facilities. Wolfgang Vaerst, First President of the German Federal Railways, has pointed out that the traffic requirements could not be sufficiently met, even if the development of the road system for individual traffic was pushed to the very limits of its financial and environmental capacities.

Pressure areas demand a "custom-made" transport system in which railway lines, bus lines and passenger cars complement each other. The backbone of public short-distance transport must be the rapid transit systems which accommodate the main traffic streams, with buses (and trams) taking up the functions of collecting and distributing spacially. This logical division of labour was made an official policy for the first time - if one sets aside Berlin - in Hamburg.

To counter the traffic collapse in pressure areas, a committee of experts set up in 1964 as a consequence of a law passed by the German Federal diet, the Bundestag, in 1961, established that the transport-related tasks of the municipalities can only be solved jointly by the Federation, the "Länder" and the Communes, and that priority must be awarded to the development of public short-distance rail transport systems. The financial basis was created in 1966 by increasing taxation of mineral oil. Beside the building of underground lines in the larger cities, suburban lines of the Federal railways in pressure areas have since been developed into metropolitan railways. Here, the cities of Berlin and Hamburg whose populations have long been counted in millions, and where the metropolitan railways have proved their worth now for decades, have set commendable examples. The priority given to short-distance "passenger" transport on rail also manifests itself in a restrictive road-building policy alongside the rapid transit lines which are intended to become the axes of development within pressure areas by way of town and country planning policy measures.

One of the aspects in favour of a construction of metropolitan railways in extreme pressure areas in the Federal Republic of Germany is that frequently the existing facilities of the Federal railways, which reach into the centres of pressure areas, can be put to good use. Thus, the linking up of the country with the city is facilitated considerably in a great number of cases, and traffic conditions can be improved more rapidly at relatively little expense and short construction periods.

As a measure to eliminate competition between the individual public means of transport, transport and fare pools have been founded in Hamburg (1965), Munich, Frankfurt, Stuttgart and in the Rhine-Ruhr region which offer a uniform schedule and fare structure. A passenger can change from one means of transport to another with one and the same ticket. The Rhine-Ruhr transport and fare pool was established in 1978 between the German Federal Railways and 19 communal transport authorities in the region between Dortmund and Mönchengladbach, embracing the largest pressure area on Federal territory.

Approximately 5000 million Deutschmarks have been raised mainly by Federation and "Länder" to put metropolitan railways into operation, after Berlin and Hamburg, in another four pressure centres. A further minimum amount of 7000 to 8000 million Deutschmarks is to be invested in the development of metropolitan railway systems. In 1979, the Federal Railways' metropolitan railway line network comprised 1232 kilometres of which 832 kilometres are used purely for metropolitan railway services at relatively short and scheduled intervals. The remaining 400 kilometres serve as regional railway lines and transport similar to metropolitan railway traffic. The modern tripartite metropolitan railway trains of the ET 420 series can be adapted to passenger volume according to requirements, running as a short train with 3, as a full train with 6, or as a long train with 9 coaches which accommodate a total of 1450 passengers. In only 40 seconds, these trains reach their maximum speed of 120 k/h.

Today, and even in the future, underground stations are an exception, because this rapid transit systems is not meant as a means of urban transport, but rather as a connection between large city and hinterland. The metropolitan railways make use largely of existing lines which, however, have to be expanded with additional tracks in some places so as to let the trains run as per fixed schedule, and unimpeded by long-distance traffic. In the case of the Munich metropolitan railways - the presently largest coherent system with 410 kilometres of track - only 5 of approximately 132 stations are subterranean. In Hamburg, only 7 stations of the metropolitan railways' city line are underground stations. Stuttgart has 4 (in future 5) and Frankfurt 3 (in future 6) subterranean stations, whilst there will be only one sub-level metropolitan railway stop in the Rhine-Ruhr-Wupper region. When expanding the station facilities for metropolitan railway traffic, the platforms were raised so as to be at level with the coach floor (95 centimetres above the rail top) or to leave no more than a small step of 19 centimetres. The metropolitan railway platforms are, as a rule, connected to the street network directly or by pedestrian underpasses. In most cases the platforms were roofed over individually or were given glazed waiting-rooms. All stations were equipped with automatic ticket machines and information facilities.

The Munich metropolitan railways

With the opening of the Munich metropolitan railways in spring of 1972, the radial lines of the Federal railways have turned into diagonal lines crossing the city centre. The response to the metropolitan railways was beyond all expectations. A maximum of 220000 passengers had been forecast in the prognoses. But in 1973, the daily number had already reached 430000, and three years later, as many as 507000 passengers travelled on it every day.

Lack of space forced the metropolitan railways platforms to be raised above the tracks of the long-distance railways in Frankfurt/Main–West station.

The Galluswarte metropolitan railway station in Frankfurt/Main is six metres above street level.

In 1976, 93 000 transfer passengers between the metropolitan railways and the first 19 kilometre-long unterground line were counted on working days at the joint station below the Marienplatz. The second underground line, with three further connecting points with the metropolitan railways, will be put into operation in 1980. By the mid-Eighties, a third underground line with four metropolitan railway connecting points will follow. By creating such a closely knit rapid transit system, its attraction is enhanced greatly, and this is all the more so because the metropolitan railways facilities will be developed also.

The 4.2 metre-long tunnel section of the Munich metropolitan railways between the main and Eastern stations runs underneath lively shopping thoroughfares in the heart of the city. Apart from the construction of the Isar river tunnel, it was driving a tunnel underneath three historical buildings (Karlstor, Old Town Hall and Isartor) which presented technical problems particularly difficult to overcome.

At the subterranian metropolitan railway stations of the main station, Karlsplatz and Marienplatz, separate platforms for boarding and disembarking were built, owing to the heavy traffic volume. For boarding, there is a middle platform of a maximum width of 10 metres, whereas passenger get off the trains via 5 metre-wide outer platforms. Due to the dense development of the Marienplatz and the limited width of the street, the Marienplatz metropolitan railway station had to be laid out in two storeys. On each level, two outer platforms were built. Hence, the halting period of the trains can be limited here also to 30 seconds. The remaining tunnel stations were built with middle platforms only. Between the platforms and the street surface, every station has a pedestrian floor with several stair systems so as to provide direct access to each side of the street. At the Marienplatz connecting point, sets of stairs allow for a direct change into the underground which run below the metropolitan railways. In total, more than 60 escalators have been installed in the metropolitan railways area, with height differences up to 15.6 m as at Isartor.

Particular attention was given by the Federal railways to the development of the tunnel station interior. In selecting carefully matched materials, special importance was attached to them being easy to clean and resistant to wanton damage. The stairways and walls of the pedestrian floors with the shops were lined alternatingly with granite and puddingstone (conglomerate). For the mural decoration at platform level, ceramic tiles were used along with steel deck plates and asbestos cement plates. The supports on the middle platforms and the strings of the escalators have been lined with ceramic tiles in the individual marking colour of each station. The drop ceilings with built-in lighting consists of aluminium sections, and of light-weight metal panels with sound absorbing mats on the platform levels. The floor covering is of cast stone tiles, the steps of the stairs are covered with granite. In the proximity ot the stairs leading to the platforms, automatic ticket machines and information maps have been either put up individually or in wall recesses.

Upper right: Platform area of Marienplatz underground station in Munich. The generous lay-out bears in mind the importance of this station as connecting point between underground and metropolitan railways.

Upper left: The Odeonsplatz underground station is representative of typical Munich underground stations.

Middle: An example for a surface underground and metropolitan railways stations in Munich.

Lower right: The map shows the Munich transport and fare pool (MVV) traffic area. It also includes the more remote vicinity of Munich with its popular recreational areas.

Lower left: As can be seen at Erding, many stations display indicator boards for people looking for recreational facilities.

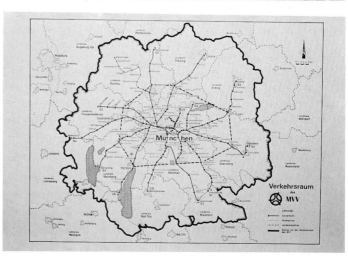

Connecting point Frankfurt main station

Since the metropolitan railways was put into operation in the Rhine-Main region (1978) – about 2.5 million people live here on an area comprising 2000 square kilometres – Frankfurt main station, with its new subterranean facilities, has come to be a modern traffic junction in keeping with a large city, and it is here that long-distance trains, metropolitan railways, tramway and buses – in short, all means of public passenger transport – are linked up with one another. About 20 metres deep below the platform hall there are the two metropolitan railway platforms with four tracks. Below the station forecourt, the metropolitan railways route intersects with the underground station at 13 metres depth. Above it, there is the extensive main station passage, a spacious subterranean distributing level for pedestrian traffic to the surface long-distance platforms as well as to metropolitan railways, underground and tram stops in the station forecourt. Two Federal roads run above the station forecourt, the most important North-South connection, apart from the motorway, in the Frankfurt urban area.

Although sufficient space would have been available, the project of routing the automobile traffic via a road tunnel situated immediately above the underground did not materialise. Thus, the chance of converting the station forecourt into a pedestrian precinct was lost. Nevertheless, a fairly large free space was created in front of the main station reception hall with lowered seating arrangements, with a bus terminal adjoining on one side, and short-term parking facilities for individual traffic and an extended taxi stand on the other. Plane-trees, plant containers and flower beds are to give the square an attractive outlook.

On the 12 000 square metre subterranean distributing level a small shopping centre consisting of 33 shops was created which are not subject to the law on shop hours, so that shopping is possible here also in the evening, as is the case in the reception building of the main station.

76 escalators, 10 passenger and 15 goods lifts carry the vertical traffic within the connecting point. Both the 120 metre-long middle platforms with two tracks each which constitute the underground station are accessible via a stairway and escalator system at both ends. Another set of stairs in the middle of the station leads, via an intermediate level, to the metropolitan railways. The latter's station, again, is connected directly with the main station passage by way of large escalator installations and, via another intermediate level, with the platform hall of the longdistance station. By building intermediate decks in the space between the metropolitan railway station and the long-distance tracks, three additional storeys became available which can be used as garage parking for 370 motor cars.

As regards the architecural interior design, the entire transport installation equals, in its layout and in its purpose, "neither a pure interior, nor a pedestrian precinct, although it has the characteristics of both". The light ground limestone which lines the walls of the tunnel structure, adds a friendly atmosphere to the "underworld" and, at the same time, harmonizes with the sandstone of the 19th-century reception building. On principle, the Federal Railways wanted to forego all fashionable effects for fear that they could be outdated soon. Since there is sufficient colour contrast from the shops and their displays, the greatest restraint was brought to bear when choosing the colours for the main station passage. As in the underground station, the round columns have been faced with ceramic tiles of a copper metallic colour. For the flooring, reddish cast stone slabs were chosen, and bright red stripes add extra colour to the covering. Contrary to the concrete angle-type steps of the inner stairs, the outer stairs which are equipped with an electric heating system, were built with reddish-grey granite. The drop ceiling with integrated lighting strips consists of aluminium panels. An aluminium grid ceiling, however, had to be installed in the passage as well as in the shops owing to the sprinkler system.

The pillars of the 210 metre-long metropolitan railway station are faced with yellow and orange ceramic tiles, whereas the outer walls are lined with 40 centimetre-wide white baking varnish steel plates. An orange indicator stripe with the station name and, as design elements, a continuous series of circles break the mural surface at medium level. In addition, a certain variety is derived from large surfaces for the line network plan and for advertising. The concrete slabs of the floor are coloured in green. The outer walls of the underground platforms are decorated with poster-size photographs with motifs of Frankfurt, framed by an aluminium-coloured indicator stripe displaying the station name. Directions and information are given and displayed according to the directives in force for the entire area covered by the Frankfurt transport association.

This stairway-escalator installation leads from the Frankfurt main station entrance hall to the extensive subterranean passage towards the city centre.

With the opening of the rapid transit railway services (1978), the Frankfurt main station, with its extensive subterranean installations, has turned into a modern junction for all kinds of public transport means.

In Frankfurt, the stream of pedestrians is led through a long-stretched subterranean distributing level, the so-called main station passage, where there are also many shops. The surface of the forecourt is reserved for motor cars and tramways.

The chance of accommodating automobile traffic in a road tunnel and to lay out the entire station forecourt as a pedestrian precinct, was lost in Frankfurt/Main.

Twenty metres deep below the platform hall of the Frankfurt main station, there are two metropolitan railway platforms with four tracks.

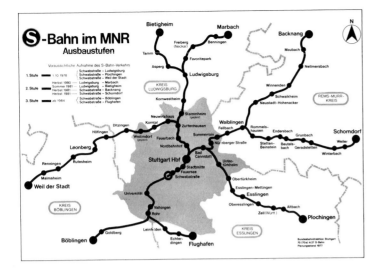

The network of the Stuttgart metropolitan railways is extended in consecutive stages into the mid-Neckar region.

"University" stop of the Stuttgart city railway (underground).

Even in the early afternoon, there is lively activity at the Schwabstraße metropolitan railway station in Stuttgart.

Pedestrian level at Schloßplatz underground station in Stuttgart.

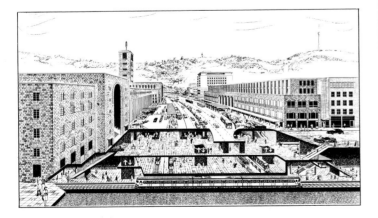

Several lines of the Stuttgart city railway/tramway intersect in the joint subterranean building at the main station with the metropolitan railways.

Rapid transit railways in the Stuttgart basin

In autumn of 1978, the age of the metropolitan railways began for the Stuttgart region and its population of about 2.3 million people. The solution of short-distance traffic problems does not come easy in a large city situated in a narrow basin. Since the basin only opens up towards the North-East, the strands of track from all directions are led from this side to the main station which is on the edge of the city centre. When putting into practice the 30 year-old proposal to extend the suburban lines underground through the city, gradients of the order of the stipulated maximum of 40/1000 had to be accepted due to the special topographical circumstances in the tunnel sections outside the stations.

At the main station, a subterranean 3-storey building was erected jointly with the Stuttgart tramways, where five city railways/tramways intersect with the metropolitan railways. The metropolitan railway station with its two tracks was advanced beyond the facade of the main railway station towards the city centre as far as the connection with the cross-platform of the long-distance station would allow. This means that passengers now only have to cover a distance of 130 metres to reach the pedestrian precinct of the main shopping street, the Königstrasse. The upper storey of this subterranean traffic installation features an attractive pedestrian zone with a great variety of shops. Along with the metropolitan railways, an underground parking was built near the main station, as was done in Frankfurt also. Furthermore, another stop in the centre of the city, "Stadtmitte", is being planned as a future connecting point with the city railway/tramway.

Since passengers generally consider it a drawback to have to climb down underground, the Federal railways, again, took the greatest care in designing and equipping the subterranean metropolitan railway stations so as not to create a basement atmosphere. The four subterranean stops, which were put in operation in 1978, were lined after one uniform system. In each station, the baking varnish steel plates covering the tunnel walls were given a different colour. The wall surface is livened up by a continuous white band displaying the station name. The marking colour of the station is repeated in the head mosaic of the round columns in the platform axis as well as in the coloured concrete slabs of the platform floor covering and the steps. The white panel drop ceiling has recessed lighting strips along the platform edge. On each platform, there is a control desk glazed in on all sides for the supervisory staff. For reasons of comfort, nearly all entrances to the subterranean stations have been equipped with escalators. At the main station and one other stop where level differences of 20 metres have to be overcome additional lifts are available.

As is the case in other large cities, the Stuttgart metropolitan railways have to be complemented by another efficient means of rail transport, and in particular in those areas where no plans exist to link them up with the metropolitan railway system and where the traffic volume is too heavy for bus services to cope. As an alternative to the traditional tramway, Stuttgart opted for a city railway which, as regards its routing, rolling stock and operational characteristics, ranges between an underground and a tramway.

The transformation from tramway into city railways has been scheduled for the Eighties, the aim being a separation from individual traffic as far-reaching as possible. Only where urban planning and other cogent reasons make a separation into two levels necessary, such a layout will be chosen for the dense urban areas. Otherwise, the city railways will be provided with its own railway right-of-way. This concept foregoes the creation of system ruins, for each section developed for city railways purposes, be it a tunnel or a railway right-of-way of its own, may be integrated into and put into operation with the other existing network. In doing so, every construction stage reached at any point in time might also be a viable long-term solution. The city railways, similarly to the metropolitan railways, helps to achieve considerable reductions in travelling time, but, above all, it is possible to operate more regularly and punctually by comparison with the tramway. The regional services are complemented by a dense bus network which will increasingly have the function of a feeder/shuttle to the stations of the rail-operated systems.

The short-distance traffic programme for the middle Neckar, i.e., the Stuttgart region, for the first time establishes co-ordinated plans of the traffic routes for public short-distances passenger transport as well as individual road traffic. In view of a competitive situation with the metropolitan railways, it is intended not to expand the capacities for individual transport any further. The communes in this region are called upon to tailor construction planning and investment programmes in accordance with and to the circumstances and possibilities given for public short-distance transport.

Hamburg: A rejuvenating cure with the help of a metropolitan railways in the city centre

The experience that neither the individual nor the commercial traffic of a large city can be absorbed by the road system, led to the city of Hamburg to begin with the construction of a rapid transit system as early as the turn of the century. Rapid transit keeps the city centre alive and contributes to a higher quality of life in the hinterland of Hamburg. The rapid transit railway network has been expanded from 139 kilometres in 1967 to presently 238 kilometres. The Hamburg transport association services a track network of about 1860 kilometres' length with rapid transit trains, buses and ships, and in recent years the so-called park-and-ride system has been persistently developed. There are 7200 passenger car parking spaces available at 48 rapid transit railway stations, a number scheduled to be increased to 20000 to 25000.

With the completion of the entire tunnel section of the city centre metropolitan railways in 1979, Hamburg received a second link between the main station and Altona which runs through the heart of the city. It was impossible to open up the very centre of town to the connecting line main station - Dammtor-Altona which had been routed peripherally more than 110 years ago. The maximum capacity of this section, which, since the beginning of this century has separate tracks for long-distance and metropolitan trains, was reached with six trains within ten minutes.

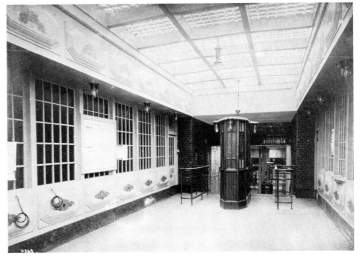

Historical photographs of the "Elevated and underground" in Hamburg, the construction of which commenced already in 1906. On the left,

Rödingsmarkt station in 1912, on the right, Feldstraße station at approximately the same time.

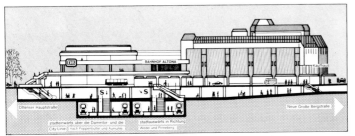

Metropolitan railway platforms, ticket hall and bus terminal are arranged one above the other at the Altona station in Hamburg, so that changing trains requires only a short distance's walk.

At the Jungfernstieg connection point in Hamburg, three underground lines and the metropolitan railways city line intersect on three subterranean platform levels.

The variety of design of the underground and metropolitan railway stations
in Hamburg.

The putting into operation of the metropolitan city line could almost be considered a "rejuvenating cure" for the Hamburg metropolitan railway network – the oldest on Federal territory. Since 1907, electric railcars are being operated in Hamburg. Contrary to all other metropolitan railway systems in the Federal Republic of Germany, they are powered via a live lateral tail with direct current. Hence the tunnel profile could be reduced by about one fifth when the metropolitan city line was built.

Building the metropolitan city line which required a four-track tunnel station instead of the ground-level metropolitan railway platforms, instigated the idea of reconstructing the entire station complex. The vertical arrangement of metropolitan railway platforms, booking hall and bus terminal allows for a short and convenient change of trains. This is the precondition for an integrated traffic system to be accepted. A central island in the completely redesigned station forecourt now houses the bus terminal.

Even more important as a "turntable" of transport is the connecting point Jungfernstieg built six years ago underneath the Binnenalster with an investment of approximately 150 million Deutschmarks. This is the junction on three subterranean station levels of three underground lines and the metropolitan railway city line. The centrally located station provides the possibility to change not only within the metropolitan railway network, but also to the boat services on the Alster and bus lines. Here, at this connecting point, public short-distance passenger transport takes place on five levels. Lifts are available to passengers in addition to the 37 escalators.

As regards the interior decoration of the metropolitan city line installations, one deliberately chose warm colours meant to create a "pleasant comfortableness" in places without natural light. The only exception is the Reeperbahn station the intensive blues and reds of which take up the dazzling appearance of this district with its colourful activity and the glaring neon signs of the entertainment establishments. The potential utilization of this station for civil defence purposes resulted in a lot of effort being invested: The drop ceilings reach beyond the tracks and as far as the external walls, which are tiled from the ballast bed up to the ceiling. The Altona metropolitan railway station, however, was subject to economies. No sound protection ceiling was installed above the tracks. The external walls have been tiled only in the platform section between the upper platform edge and the bottom of the ceiling. The walls of the stairs system leading to the distributing level, on the other hand, were particularly accentuated.

The first spade for the construction of the Hamburg "Elevated and Underground Train" – today's underground – was dug as early as 1906. In the meantime, the network has grown to 80 stops and a track length of 89 kilometres, 31 kilometres of which run below surface. Besides the underground lines, the Hamburger Hochbahn AG (Hamburg Elevated) operates an extensive bus network and the Alster shipping lines. The last remaining tram line was closed down in 1978. Already in 1955, the Hanseatic town had decided to replace the tramway, in rapid succession, by more efficient rapid transit railway lines or more flexible bus lines. 20 kilometres of new underground have been built since. On a working day, the Hamburger Hochbahn AG transports a scant 1.4 million passengers.

Over time, the underground buildings had to be re-adapted to the development of the traffic necessitating an increased service frequency and the use of longer trains. Substantial conversions had to be made to accommodate longer platforms. Simultaneously, faster access ways were created and escalators built. Most stations dating back to the early days were modernised where they did not have to make way completely for new buildings. Recently, the Hamburger Hochbahn AG endeavours to preserve those buildings from early underground days and to give them back as far as possible their original look. For instance, the St. Pauli station which shows a strong influence of Art Nouveau in its design, is presently being renovated and restored.

Berlin: From elevated to underground

The first electrically operated rapid transit train to be operated in Germany was opened in Berlin in 1902. Already at the end of the 19th century the street of the city centre could no longer cope with the traffic density and had to be relieved. The first line the lineation of which was determined less by the traffic requirements than rather by the principle of meeting the least resistance on the part of the authorities, did not touch what was then the city centre but in one stop. Originally, this East-West section had been planned all the way as an elevated railway. Since, however, the rich Charlottenburg district refused to tolerate the noise and a transformation of its street picture, the rapid transit railway was continued as an underground tramway. Later on, some sections were built in cuts and on dams.

In working-class districts, the comperatively inexpensive elevated was considered acceptable, whereas the rapid transit railway was designed as an underground in middle-class districts and in the tight city centre. It was sufficient to run the route in cuts in spaciously built-up areas, inasfar as this method did not constitute an optical or acoustic interference. Other sections on the outskirts of the city were built most economically by raising dams.

"The requirements of saving space in the building of the substructure, and of saving time through speedy construction as well as the utmost care in preserving the invested capital" ruled out a masonry substructure when the first elevated railway line was built. A contemporary report notes: "Necessity brings forth the iron viaduct". But the rigid structure of the first iron viaducts which blurred the city image considerably, soon induced the private "Gesellschaft für elektrische Hoch- und Untergrundbahnen in Berlin" (Company for electrical elevated and underground railways of Berlin) to call upon the services of architects. These did not confine themselves to simply decorate previously erected iron girders with rod-steel trappings. For example, the Bülowstraße viaduct was a product of close co-operation between engineers and architects, an organic entity of constructive shaping and a will for aesthetic design.This achievement which overcomes the rigidity of the rod-steel structure, is increasingly respected in recent times. The oblique positioning of the supports and the rounding-off of the corners of the iron structure create an impression of this traffic building being very light, indeed, of being suspended. The design took care of everything up to the very last detail.

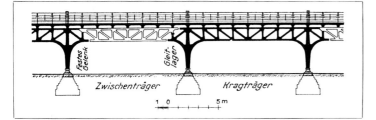

Iron viaduct of the first elevated railway section built in Berlin from 1896 to 1902.

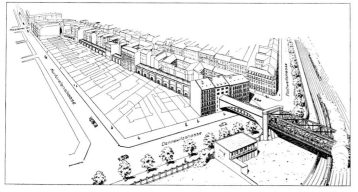

In the mid-Twenties, one even went as far as breaking through buildings in the construction of the elevated railways.

At the turn of the century, the Bülowstraße elevated railway viaduct was created in close co-operation between engineers and architects.

The Wittenbergplatz underground station was built in 1911–13 after a design by Alfred Grenander. This is a historic photograph of the station hall.

Bruno Möhring designed the elevated railway station built on the Bülowstraße in 1900/01.

As part of the efforts to adapt to the elegant environment of the Western districts of Berlin, the iron supports of another section were richly decorated with wrought iron trappings. At street junctions, stone piers towering high above the carriageway were erected which break the continuity of the elevated railway's horizontals.

The Berlin elevated and underground railway soon became very popular as a means of public transport. On one hand, the elevated position and routing of the rapid transit system was considered a flaw in the city picture and a health hazard for the residents living right next to it. On the other hand, it was regarded as a positive thing by the passengers that "they had to endure the less comfortable underground journey for a short while only", because they would regain "a stimulating contact with the external world" again where the underground turned into an elevated railway.

In some cases, the builders of the elevated railways even decided in favour of breaking through buildings. In order to limit vibration and avoid contact noise bridges, the supports of the rapid transit railway were provided with foundations separate from those of the buildings. A street overpass was built as an iron concrete structure closed on all sides in order to shield off the neighbouring houses from the noise of the trains. Yet, in spite of all these precautions, the ultimate decision was in favour of the underground. When building underneath an hotel in 1906-08, the tunnel was kept clear from the structural parts of the house, the foundations of which were laid far below the tunnel bottom. In addition, sound proofing materials were used so that the operation of the underground was hardly noticed in the house.

The great economic crisis at the end of the Twenties put a temporary end to underground construction works. Until 1930, the route network had expanded to 80 kilometres with approximately 100 stations.

It was only in 1953 that the construction of the underground was taken up again in the former capital of the "Reich", on the basis of a plan dating back to 1929 which made provisions for a 200 kilometre underground network for Greater Berlin. After the division of Berlin, the Berliner Verkehrsbetriebe (West) (Transport Operating Company of West-Berlin) were left with a mere 52 kilometres of underground track. Meantime the system in West-Berlin has been expanded to 96 kilometres. Underground and buses form the pillars of public short-distance transport. The tramway which had been started up in 1865, was closed in the Western zone of the city in 1967.

The underground stations of Berlin over time

From the stations of the Berlin underground it is possible to gather the mutations which architectural conceptions have undergone since the beginning of this century. The factual design of the generously glazed iron halls of the first elevated railway stations, which are today impressive cultural monuments, struck people around the change of the century as being too sober. A general competition was therefore opened amongst Germany's architects and engineers so as to receive proposals "worthy" of the Reich's capital's character. Thus, a pompous architecture of trappings evolved.

Several local architects were commissioned with the planning preparation for individual buildings of importance, but they did not always prove equal to the task. The Hallesches Tor elevated railway station turned out a "pompous piece of stone architecture with pylons crowned by vane-wheels, cartouches, baluster railings and a renaissance portal which wasn't a portal at all but contained a window, with the entrances next to it", to quote Klaus Konrad Weber. "The front of the station hall (Bülowstraße) . . . – totally superfluous as regards its function – has been stylised into a triumphal arc - like portico". Neither did one feel deterred from building bombastic gate piers. In order to create a dominating focus on Nollendorfplatz, a dome structure crowned by a round lantern roof towered above one part of the platform hall which simultaneously was to mark the completion of the first elevated railway section.

Although the design of the stations differed greatly, they were nonetheless similar in their conception which originated from the Siemens & Halske company. At the entrance below the viaduct the stairs started behind a little ticket box leading up to the platforms in two flights. The platforms were initially arranged on both sides of the double track. Middle platforms were only built at a later stage.

In the beginning, underground station platforms were also arranged laterally. Iron pillars were erected between the tracks. The only surface buildings were the cashier's box and gates richly decorated in Art Nouveau style at the stairs. In a publication from 1902 it says: "Little can be said about the underground railways from an architectural point of view. Underground stations of predetermined dimensions do not leave a great deal of scope for artistic initiative".

Yet, it was precisely this which was to change through the work of Alfred Grenander whose activities concentrated increasingly on the design of buildings for the underground in Berlin. He restrained himself in the modelling of his works, and was at pains to give stations a characteristic uniform look. According to Gustav Kemmann, he "generally contented himself to underline the effect of the forces in the structural parts by creative adaption and by co-ordinating and matching, where it was appropriate, the colour scheme of surfaces and structural parts". Some of the booking halls were given an elaborate mural and ceiling decoration of coloured terra-cotta. For the purpose of distinguishing the individual stations, Grenander introduced marking colours, a system which has proved its worth since in many a large city. When the underpass underneath the Spree river required a deeper lowering of the tunnel, the underground architect benefitted from the occasion to give the station more height and to plan a vault instead of the usual plane girder ceiling. In this case, the glazed facing slabs which otherwise were used exclusively for lining the walls, were continued to cover the entire vault surface.

Alfred Grenander attributed the architectural design to the technical necessities. Says Martin Richard Möbius in his monography, "it is one of his great merits to have brought his influence to bear, by setting examples visible to everyone far and wide, and at a time when a most dangerous confusion prevailed in this area, that the architect's supremacy was restored even in those tasks that were to some extent delegated to the engineer . . .

Alfred Grenander, again, was the architect of the Olympic Stadium underground station (1929/30). This picture was taken in 1978.

The Möckernbrücke station was built between 1934 and 1936.

At the Friedrichstraße station – now on East-Berlin territory – long-distance and metropolitan trains stop next to one another.

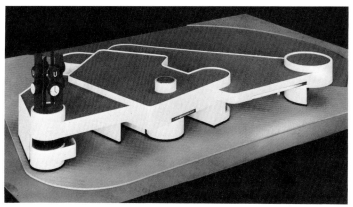

Model of the Fehrbelliner Platz underground station.

The Fehrbelliner Platz underground station built 1967–71 after a design by Gerhard Rainer Rümmler, is of a very plastic shape.

The portico of the Fehrbelliner Platz underground station with a wrought-iron gate dating back to 1913.

There is no fake, make-believe decoration and no artistic confusion in the buildings designed by Grenander. The building mass presents itself as a clear, single and completely harmonious shape, revealing immediately its purpose.

The stations of the Wilhelmsdorf line which was built in 1913 and elaborately decorated at considerable expense, deviate from this simple and factual underground station design. With the network expanding, buildings also rose where several underground lines or underground and metropolitan lines intersected.

The circular railways which had originally been meant to serve exclusively for goods transport but which also carried passengers after 1872, was built to create a connection around Berlin far beyond the then built-up area, of all railway lines ending in dead-end stations. In 1882, the town railway was opened which traversed the city centre and was linked to the circular railways. It was only in 1924 that the state-owned circular, city and suburban railways were electrified. By the end of the Thirties, the expansion of the metropolitan railway network of Berlin was completed, which also connected the most important long-distance railway stations with one another. The metropolitan railways which today do no longer play any significant part in the Western section of the city, is operated in West-Berlin also by the Deutsche Reichsbahn (GDR).

Striving for individuality

After the second world war, it took quite a while until the insecurity in the design of underground railway buildings was overcome. The diversified picture of the new buildings which have risen over the past decade and a half, show the fundamental influence of Gerhard Rainer Rümmler. Whilst the surface building of the Bayerischer Platz underground station presents itself in clear cubic shapes, the entrance hall of the Fehrbelliner Platz underground station equally built in 1967-71 is of a strong plastic shape, and is made to stand out, furthermore, owing to its facing of small red ceramic tiles to such an extent that one could speak of a signal effect.

In other respects, also, the tendency was to strive for "breaking free from monotony" in the designing of the stations. Since the marginal development of the Friedrich-Wilhelm-Platz dated back to the days of gas lanterns, this particular station was equipped with large glass bowl light fittings, supported by steel cantilevers fastened to a middle girder of the middle platform. At another place, the large ceramics were replaced by tunnel-high, colour-baked asbestos cement slabs. At the Schloßstraße underground station the architectural concept had its bearing even on the carcass: Walls, ceiling and columns were made of rough-shuttered exposed concrete which was concealed, though, in some places by blue plastic boards, red station signs and advertising bill boards.

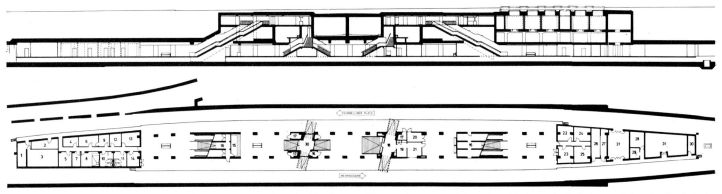

Longitudinal section and ground plan of the underground station Berliner Straße built between 1966-71.

These pictures testify to the efforts made to bring variety into the interior decoration of new underground stations which were built in Berlin in the Seventies.

So-called media supports made of red and yellow plastic are suspended from the ceiling in the platform area. They are supposed to carry light fittings and indicators.

In order to give each station an individual touch, the outward image of the buildings is constantly varied. Stylised depictions taken from the multitude of shapes of machinery and from the fundamental inventions of the Siemens company are a characteristic feature of the Siemensdamm station, whereas the Konstanzer Straße station is decorated with strip mosaic in the colours of the Konstanz city-arms and the Wilmersdorfer Straße station with the Bourbon lilies from the Wilmersdorf city-arms. In other stations, a relationship with neighbouring industry is established by making use, for the interior decoration, of aluminium and coloured polished steel. Bricks of the medieval monastic format are supposed to create a reference with the historical landscape at the Juliusturm station. The Richard-Wagner-Platz underground station has been decorated with mosaics displaying medieval scenes which stem from a former restaurant. The platform walls tiled yellow show pictures from Wagner's operas, framed by a continuous ornament of deep blue ceramic tiles.

The construction of the Hanover underground:
A means to improve life in the city

The city of Hanover does not only look towards building an underground as a way of solving traffic problems, but also as "an instrument to improve city quality, or rather life quality – in short the whole range of aspects which make up man's vital consciousness". Continues Klaus Scheelhaase, head of the underground construction authority: "The construction of the subterranean transport installations constituted such a strong interference in the urban structure, that it would have been a short-term solution to deal exclusively with traffic problems, in particular, as it is unlikely that another transformation of the urban structure will be possible during our generation for economic and political reasons. In view of the huge investments, one cannot limit oneself to merely move a means of transport below surface and to simply fill in the earth above the tunnel. It means having to redesign the entire city centre at the same time. It takes to restore the former functions of the centre, which it has maintained over centuries and which it only lost to the motor car, so as to give a nucleus to the region with which people can identify – be it the churches, the market square, the town hall in former times, or department stores in the present day. The aim was and is to create places of encounter, meeting places, which rekindle the functions of the market and of representation".

The good accessibility of the inner city by way of the underground in Hanover has created the basis for far-reaching restrictions imposed on individual transport. A 5 kilometre-long walkway network for pedestrians criss-crosses the centre. This network integrates the underground stations and the main railway station in such a manner that users of public transport can easily reach their destination in the city centre. The automobile traffic is led around the centre via a tangential ring road. There remains but a residual system of motor roads for delivery vehicles and to provide access to the car park buildings. Thus, the city authorities have taken the consequences from the realization that a satisfactory development of the city centre through and for the motor car is neither possible nor desirable.

In order to counter the threatening separation and displacement of the city centre's functions, the utilization of the scarce ground in this area was optimised. Extensions and new buildings, for instance, of department stores and authorities, were built in the immediate vicinity of the underground stations. In particular near the Kröpcke Station – where three underground lines will intersect in the near future – the satisfactory accessibility through public transport allows for a dense structural concentration. Above this particular station rises an eleven-storey office and commercial building.

With determination the traffic planners in Hanover persued the integration of Federal railways and metropolitan (underground and tram) railways in their urban planning programmes. The expansion of the city centre beyond the main station which had been put on paper already at the beginning of the Fifties implied that the dividing effect of the railway installations be overcome. When in the course of the underground construction the tunnel was driven under the main station, and the latter was converted, this occasion was used to the full. Instead of refilling the remaining building pit, a 700 metre-long pedestrian tunnel, the so-called "Passerelle", was built. It is part of a 2 kilometre-long continuous pedestrian connection accessible via four metropolitan railway stations and which links up the residential district of "Lister Meile" located near the inner city with the centre. All means of short-distance public transport are connected with the "passerelle" in such a way that passengers may conveniently change from one system to the other via the shortest distance, without being exposed to the weather. In this context, a new central bus terminal with direct access to the "Passerelle" was also created near the main station.

"The user of the public short-distance transport systems should find better conditions than those he meets with when driving into the city with his own motor car". This is the point of departure for Scheelhaase's reflections. Hence the special importance which was attached in Hanover to arriving at a good architectural design of the underground stations. Whereas in many other towns architects were commissioned only with the interior development and decoration of the subterranean stations, making them feel like "upgraded wall paper hangers", the joint deliberations of urban traffic planners, engineers and architects commenced in Hanover already after establishing the exact location of a future station. This no doubt enhanced the looks of the entire installation.

In Hanover, the exits from the subterranean installations have been orientated towards prominent buildings so that pedestrians and passengers may find their way more easily. In addition, these exits end in pedestrian precincts to avoid conflict with the automobile traffic. In the design of the underground stations, great care was given to establish already on the platform a relation with the town picture which the passenger expects to find upon meeting the daylight.

Above: The major part of the Markthalle station has been devised as a double-storey hall. In compliance with Marktkirche (market church) and Altes Rathaus (old town hall), the walls have been lined with red brick masonry.

Bottom: Street art in the underground: Two walls of 110 metres length and 3.3 metres height each have been decorated as "jet underground" after a design by the Parisian artist Jean Dawasne.

Left from top to bottom:

The Kröpcke station in Hanover is an intersection for three underground lines. Urban planning furthered a dense structural concentration in this area.

Every underground station in Hanover has its own unmistakable features. Here the Mühlenberg station the tiled walls of which are decorated with three millstones.

Pedestrian level at the Werderstraße station in Hanover.

Page at right: The barrel-shaped roof of the Lister Platz underground station entrance provides, at the same time, an optical closing stone for the Lister Meile pedestrian precinct.

More than in any other city, thought was given in Hanover to establishing a communication between the subterranean and surface buildings. The results can therefore be considered to have a model character.

For the Markthalle station which is in the immediate vicinity of the old town, a mural lining of red brick masonry and floor coverings of red ceramic tiles was selected in compliance with the old town hall and the market church. In order to achieve good visual communication between entrance and platform level for a better orientation of the passengers, the major part of the building has been conceived as a double-storey hall. In the description of the work content it says: "Leaving the station through the Köberlingerstraße exit, one sees in front the towers of the market church. One exit leads the passer-by directly into the newly built arcades of the extension of the town hall completed in 1882, another stairs system provides access to the market hall".

Contrary to the Markthalle station, there is no point of reference for the main station underground stop. This is why one decided in favour of a "self-portrait of our generation", taking up the idea of a street art programme. The concept "to display art not merely in museums, but in a further dimension also in streets and squares and, thus, making it accessible to a broad public" was persistently put into practice. In the underground station two concave walls each 110 metres long and 3.3 metres high have been decorated after the designs by the Parisian artist Jean Dewasne, an almost unequalled master of the large surface design. The effect is described as follows: "The individual mural motifs begin and end with the colours black and white and turn more and more colourful towards the centre, growing into one uniform, dynamic composition. According to the contemplator's position, a wall can appear shortened, following the concave form, or, as it were, as a film when trains pull in and out of the station. Seen from the opposite platform, individual motifs are drawn into picture groups by the columns and shear walls placed in front of them, thus creating cut-outs whose coherence with the neighbouring section remains nevertheless noticeable. By the trains pulling in and out on four tracks, the clear shapes and colours are temporarily and in some places completely concealed".

About 150000 passengers will be confronted with these mural paintings which are called "jet underground" every day, once the entire metropolitan railway network has been completed. The main station stop will then have a double level intersection for three underground lines. The stream of boarding and disembarking passengers will be kept separate from the transit traffic.

In the centre of gravity of the Lister Meile pedestrian precinct which was built after completion of the underground, there is a station the external mural surfaces of which have been lined with a yellow rod facing so as to form a vertical flute. Together with smooth and textured exposed concrete columns, it gives the two subterranean levels their specific character.

Due to the local conditions, the Lister Platz station installations had to be built in a double-storey formation, i.e., one above the other for each of the directions. This difference is high-lighted by different colour compositions on the platform storeys. Sandstone and ceramic reliefs saved from the demolition of old buildings in the underground station point out the fact that the Liststadt was created in the 19th century. Although this connection between the design of the subterranean building and the town picture on the surface does not immediately catch everybody's eye, it nevertheless has a subconscious effect, as Klaus Scheelhaase and his staff have been able to observe. The urban planning features of the Lister Meile pedestrian precinct is topped off by the barrel-shaped roof of the underground entrance. It simultaneously provides shelter from bad weather for passengers changing between city railways and bus system.

At the "Hauptwache" (the main army post) in the centre of Frankfurt, a transport building comprising five levels was built in the Sixties in the course of the underground construction works. On the lowest floor (D level), there is the station with two lateral platforms for the first underground section built in Frankfurt. It is crossed by the metropolitan railways and another underground line. For these rapid transit railways, a large underground station with a middle platform used by the metropolitan line and two lateral platforms for the underground was built at C level. In addition, this floor houses extensive operating premises, amongst which the central control desk for the entire underground network. Above both stations, there is a 15000 square metre subterranean pedestrian precinct, known as B level, which serves at the same time as a shopping centre and from which one also has access to the basement levels of to department stores.

The lay-out of B level and the surface space was determined mainly by traffic planning considerations. All proposals to free the space near the Hauptwache from the encumbrance of the automobile traffic had been rejected in the Sixties. At that time it was argued in Frankfurt that automobile traffic could not be shifted unterground because this would obstruct the approach to local residents' premises. Plans to run the East-West traffic through a long tunnel underneath the "Zeil" and the "Hauptwache" were equally turned down on the grounds that this would not allow for a junction with the South-North traffic stream, and would have given it, furthermore, the characteristics of a motorway, i.e., a rapid transit road, which was condidered out of place in the city centre. The traffic planners in the mid-Sixties, therefore, insisted on a six-lane street junction at the "Hauptwache". Yet this principle made the design of the city's hub very difficult. Pedestrians who wanted to cross the square had to be sent underground. But then one did not feel like referring pedestrians on their way from East to West to a "mousehole" staircase near the junction beyond the square. Hence the idea of the architects, Wolfgang Bader and Artur C. Walter, to lead the pedestrian below surface slowly but gradually. In order to have a smooth transition between the surface and subterranean levels, very wide, fanned-out stairs systems were built on both sides of the North-South motor road which cuts the square in two. One of these stairs systems even opens up onto an intermediate level into a little drop square. The large openings with the stairs interrupted by landings and ramps for prams have expressly been overdesigned with respect to the traffic load as it was the intention to simultaneously create a place to linger with shops on both flanks. To suit pedestrians who are in a hurry, escalators leading to B level were installed.

It was not merely the transitional zones, but also the entire B level which were regarded by the planning staff as being integral part of the street. This was to be expressed in the utilization of identical materials. For walls and floors, the architects suggested granite or silver quartzite which would have given a certain brilliance to the building. But it was precisely this that frightened the authorities away in view of a minor economic recession. The architects, for their part, rejected the washed concrete proposed by the civil servants, for "this material does not age gracefully". Tests showed that, given the aggravations caused by the underground construction works, a mural design with site-placed concrete was impossible. The mural surfaces and the floors were therefore finished with textured concrete slabs. The manufacturing of these cast stone tiles with an "artisticly designed ondulated surface" required expenses of such a degree that there were hardly any savings made by comparison with the natural stone facing proposed initially. But the political optics were safeguarded, although not for long. The transport building had hardly been inaugurated and the entry into the "age of the underground" welcomed in 1968, when the Frankfurt population started to abuse the "concrete desert", the "desolate and grey concrete landscape", and some even went as far as to speak of a "constructional cadavre". The fact that the "Hauptwache", built in 1729/30 as a guardhouse for the Frankfurt military, and which had been dismantled for the purpose of the underground construction works, had been reassembled in its original historical form and also housed a café as before, did nothing to relieve the disappointment over the new environment of this familiar building. Sqeezed in from three sides, the building now appears lost, an erratic mass. The open transitional area leading to B level immediately next to the "Hauptwache" building is known amongst the population as nothing more than "the hole". Even the city authorities have not been able to think up a more appropriate designation but they do know about a lot of complaints that the floors, walls and even ceilings of B level are very hard to clean. The textured flooring slabs have shown not to be able to resist to the extreme wear and tear of neither goods deliveries nor cleaning machines; they break constantly and have to be replaced continuously. And in other respects also, B level, meanwhile home of the tramps, was the cause of great aggravation.

Ten years after its completion, the municipality decided to redesign the B level which, apart from its role as a traffic junction, had also turned into a "meeting place, strolling alley, some kind of grandstand to watch urban life, a permanent dwelling place for marginal groups". Since the new design was to take into account this concomitance, the reporting experts declared a "merely cosmetic superficial change" as not sufficient. In their report, Toni Sachs-Pfeiffer and M. Th. Krings-Heckemeier stated that "the social behaviour of people on public premises is influenced in its pattern by the built-up environment as a whole". If one, therefore, wants architecture to live up to man's needs, it will have to take into consideration the variety of social aspects which are enhanced, respectively impeded by the built-up environment. The influence exerted by the signal effect of elements of design must be recognised". If eye contact with the surface is missing, as in the case at the Hauptwache, an "unreal" atmosphere results, a sensation of being separated from one's normal environment, which, psychologically speaking, opens up the possibility of "unrealistic" behaviour patterns. The experts speak of a disorientating interior design and visual obstructions in almost all areas of B level which, on top of it, is unclear in its lay-out, with often ambiguous sign-posting. Due to the low and dark ceiling, spatial perception is impeded. In addition, the space of B level appears almost overbearing with the grey colour of walls and floor. "I feel as if I were in a shaft", commented a passer-by. In interviews, the experts could discern "a need for beauty, variety and stimulus". "The value of experience which the built-up environment holds for the passer-by, can be enhanced substantially by way of a diversified design. People are looking for stimuli on the path they are treading daily". In the text of the tender with which design proposals for the new interior development were obtained from a limited number of architects, it says among other things: "The new design is to improve the quality of orientation as well as to exert a positive influence, in an urban sense of the word, on the behaviour of its users".

Much to everyone's surprise, it was the architect of the transport building, Artur C. Walter, of all people, who exceeded the predetermined scope farthest of all in his proposal for redesign by not limiting himself to "new wallpaper" only, but by even interfering substantially into the structural substance. In doing so, he drew the conclusions from a meantime transformed surface situation. The street junction project has been shelved, the "Hauptwache" has become a focal point for extensive pedestrian precincts. Walter therefore proposed to "put a lid" on the "hole" next to the 'Hauptwache' and to restore a complete plane at the surface. This would not only bring to bear much better the eminence of the historical building, but the de-

The intention to carefully "lead pedestrians into the underground", owing to serious planning premises, resulted in the creation of this controversial "hole" near the Frankfurt "Hauptwache".

The stipulation to maintain a six-lane street junction at the "Hauptwache" forced pedestrians "to go underground". For the architect, the ensueing solution was a self-willed one, a gradual transition into the "underground". The model picture clearly shows the situation.

The pedestrian level beneath the Frankfurt "Hauptwache", with its textured concrete slabs, looks so dreary and "unreal" that the municipality opted for a new design, ten years after its completion.

The Eschenheimer Tor underground station in Frankfurt/Main.

This station was built in the Sixties in the north-western area (Nordwest-stadt) of the city.

Pedestrian level at the Theaterplatz underground station in Frankfurt/Main.

The Frankfurt underground continues beyond the city centre, as here on Eschenheimer Landstraße, on surface in the middle of the road. The fencing of the tracks makes the people living here feel more separated from their neighbours on the opposite side of the road than by a river.

Nuremberg, too, has become an underground city. The Lorenzkirche underground station in the heart of the historic town reminds of a grotto. The stylised rosette of St. Lorenz points out the way to the sights of this town rich in traditions.

This design of the Alte Oper (Old Opera House) underground station in Frankfurt/Main provided for a double-storey platform hall, by reducing the pedestrian level to a minimum and – by slanting the square surface minimally – an opening towards the surface. Thus, daylight would have penetrated the station as far as the platforms. But the design was rejected.

molition of the intermediate level would result in a two storey-high space on B level where the variety of experience could be enhanced further by a gallery. This proposal met with technical reservations. In the end, however, it most likely foundered on the fact, that those responsible for communal policies did not want to go this far.

The new interior decoration of B level which was recently approved will feature lighter and pleasanter colours. The floors will be tiled with smooth cast stone slabs of different tints of brown and beige, and the walls will be faced with nile green small tiles, both of them materials which are also easy to clean. The setting plan for the flooring and the design of the new lighting are supposed to make orientation easier for the passer-by. The entire pedestrian precinct will be subdivided in walking and dwelling zones. On one hand, the linear arrangement of the light fittings emphasize the transitory character, whilst a focus is created in another place by the polygon-shaped strip lighting. Circular lighting around the columns and white bands in the wall lining underline the heavily frequented access area to the metropolitan railway. In addition there will be a secondary centre with a fountain. The extensive construction work which is scheduled to end in spring of 1981 have been assessed to cost about 10 million Deutschmarks.

An antipathy against catacombs

Many people feel uneasiness whenever they are supposed to go below ground. In order to relieve them of this kind of "threshold fear", everything possible has to be done in the construction of subterranean traffic installations to avoid giving the impression of catacombs. With cheerful colour designs alone this problem cannot be solved. Even the simplest of road underpasses are regarded dangerous buildings in the late hours of the evening. And the fear of being attacked or mugged is all the much greater, the less visual control one has over the subterranean installation. This is particularly true for rapid transit stations. Everything must be done, therefore, during the planning stage, that the stations are as open to the view as possible from the entrance. The ideal is the situation where the entire platform area can be overlooked from above at one glance.

It was these considerations which induced Artur C. Walter to "discard everything that was not absolutely necessary", when planning the new Frankfurt underground stations. This included, first of all, the B levels the range of which he reduced to a minimum of approximately 5 metres before and behind the gates. His new stations have two storeys and are conceived in such a way that from the entrance area one immediately overlooks the full extent of the platforms. It goes without saying that this is also to the benefit of orientation. In close co-operation with an engineering firm, Walter developed a structure with floor, walls and ceiling forming a static compound which does not require any supports. Vaulted trusses of 15 to 21 metres' length span the entire length of the underground station. From the platform to the lower edge of the girder the height is 5 to 7 metres. The impression that the ceiling could fall on one's head will hardly come to mind.

The Frankfurt underground stations "Westend" and "Oper" are being built after the described concept. The architect suggested to open up the station near the old opera house by an ascending vault and by lowering simultaneously the surface in the pedestrian zone by 2 metres. This would have meant that normal daylight would have reached the platforms, and it would have revealed interesting spatial relations. The Oper underground station could have become one of the finest in the Federal Republic of Germany. But the authorities in the Main capital had had enough with the "hole" near the "Hauptwache". Neither did the idea materialise to build all stations on the new line after the same construction principle, but to differentiate them clearly in their interior decoration.

It is still in the future to create, wherever an opportunity will present itself, a window from the underground to the surface letting in day light – for instance by way of an amphitheatre-type slanting in the terrain. Thus, transparency can be brought about for wherever people can see "a patch of sky" from the underground, they will no longer feel enclosed in the catacombs. An experimental design of subterranean transport installations has to be developed from within the carcass. Decorations cannot be but contraptions.

Traffic planners, engineers and architects must be moulded into a team

It is amazing to see how little attention is paid in the multitude of professional publications to the archtitectural design of subterranean transport installations. All the more space is devoted to subterranean construction methods which have made great progress over the past two decades. Without any doubt, construction engineering took precedence over architecture. This is particularly true of the new subterranean metropolitan railway lines the installations of which lack any specific character, giving the impression that they are not only unimaginative, but also interchangeable in their design. Looking at these metropolitan railway stations, it is immediately clear that planning is in the hands of the municipal authorities whose civil servants, as a rule, remain anonymous to the public. It may even happen, in long-term projects of this kind, that two or even three people succeed each other in this responsibility, and in a large administrative machinery the individual tends to feel rather an exchangeable little wheel in a large mechanism than being personally responsible for his work. Given these circumstances, readiness to break new paths and develop new concepts can hardly be at its best. But also in (communal) underground construction, architects have had to experience that co-operation with the engineers of the construction firm is frequently better than with the representatives of the authorities. Architects need engineers as their partners with whom they can come to an understanding over the issues in the interest of the joint work. On both sides, the will and the capability to maintain an intensive dialogue must be present.

The authorities, on the other hand, voice a certain regret over the fact that many an architect is too biased in favour of the creative-artistic aspects and are not sufficiently equipped to penetrate the technical-constructional facts of a situation. For instance, the obvious must be stated expressis verbis: "Architecture must not impair functionalism".

Skilled architects should be called upon already when routing new lines so that they may develop ideas and concepts at this very early planning stage. In reality, however, this is hard to put into practice, as a rather long lapse of time may occur before the actual planning of the section starts at which point in time only the architect is awarded the commission. Consulting contracts might be a way of eluding such a dilemma. The positive or negative remarks of the architect on the location of a new station could be a valuable assistance to the traffic planners if they are really concerned with and after an urban planning-related impact of the project.

Any rapid transit railway section should have its own design concept. Although one can never be sure how an underground system will continue to grow and develop in the future, the overall coherence of the network remains. The passenger will find it easier to orient himself if a station or a line does not look like a duplicate of any other, but rather is strikingly different. Unconscious perception requires less of an effort than reading the station names. This is why of late more and more work is done with models and also with periscope cameras in order to be able to represent the spatial perception from the subsequent user's perspective. Thus, valuable aids are given to those responsible on a municipal level in their decision, as they are experts themselves only in exceptional cases.

The Wuppertal overhead railway

A metropolitan railway of a special kind is the supension railway built in Wuppertal in 1901. Though it has long since been declared a technological monument, it has not lost any of its importance as a means of mass transport with its daily traffic volume of 50 000 passengers. As the construction of an underground had to be ruled out owing to the rocky supporting medium, and it seemed unsuitable to build a traditionally conceived overhead railway in the narrow winding valley of the Wupper river, the decision in Wuppertal had been in favour of a monorail overhead railway after the system developed by the Cologne engineer Eugen Langen. Thus, the population of Wuppertal was presented with not only a second traffic level at a very early stage, but also with a unique transport installation. On a stretch of 10 kilometres, this railway follows the Wupper at 12 metres' height. The structure consists of truss bridges, resting on 742 socketed stanchions. Modern double-hinged coaches seating 204 passengers run at three and a half minutes' intervals on the 13 kilometre-long section with its 18 stations.

Over the past two decades, the remodelling of large junctions required some alterations to the railway structure. When a new overhead station was erected in Wuppertal-Barmen in 1968, the old scaffold structure was replaced by a 172 metre-long steel supporting system spanned by means of steel ropes from four pylons. In another location a spider-like bearing structure was built consisting of an arch with tieback between raking frame legs with an overall span of 92 metres.

The Wuppertal overhead railway opened in 1901, which still carries a daily passenger volume of 50,000, has been classified as a technological monument.

This modern arched girder structure of the overhead railway looks like a giant spider. It has a span of 92 metres.

New short-distance transport systems: Cabin railways

Only one fourth of all journeys made in short-distance traffic in the Federal Republic of Germany are covered by public transport which, in most cases, have to share routes with automobile traffic. The construction of an own track bed for the tramway frequently meets with difficulties. In addition, this does not mean that there are no waiting periods at junctions for a clear road. Even the lanes reserved for scheduled buses can only reduce these difficulties, if they can be arranged at all, but cannot solve the actual problem.

A solution might be found in the cabin railway systems which have been developed in recent years with subsidies from the Federal Mi-

The overhead railway cabins the largest one of which seats 41 passengers, are suspended from an elevated narrow carriageway girder. The picture shows a small test installation in Düsseldorf.

The technical test installation for the cabin taxi short-distance transport system in Hagen/Westphalia. The elevated carriageway may be used by standing as well as suspended cabins seating 12 passengers each. In Hamburg, a show installation with a 1.7 kilometre circular course is presently being built.

nister for Research and Technology. They develop the space above the roads as a second traffic level, making their operation independent from the other traffic. Since small curve radii and extreme uphill grades are possible, the routing is highly flexible. The cabins which differ in size, can also be arranged in train formations.

The overhead railway (H-railway) whose technological development is about to be concluded, is seen as an economical solution to the inner-city passenger transport problems and can also serve as a feeder railway for metropolitan and underground. The overhead railway cabins which seat and stand up to 41 passengers, are suspended from an elevated narrow carriageway girder supported by columns. The construction of an overhead railway requires a substantially lower investment than a tunnel railway. The newly devised system boasts a high transport capacity due to the cabins following each other in short sequence and at high speed; it can be adapted flexibly to traffic requirements thanks to the cabins coming in different sizes, it reduces personnel cost to a considerable extent through mechanization and does pollute the environment neither through noise nor through exhaust gases. The system is driven by electric rotary motors or via a linear motor. In 1977, a 1.4 kilometres test line was put into operation in Erlangen.

For demonstration purposes the so-called "C-railway" is being built in the northern part of the Hamburg city centre, which was developed by the "Cabin taxi working group" (Arbeitsgemeinschaft Cabinentaxi). The elevated carriageway for standing and suspended cabins with 12 seats each consists of a steel drive girder which runs generally 8 metres above street level and is supported every 30 or 40 metres by steel or reinforced concrete piers. Two platforms arranged one above the other – one for the suspended and the other for the standing cabin trains – form the C-railway stations. These platforms with two processing units each are accessible via stairs and lifts. The demonstration installation which is planned to open in 1981 comprises a circular course of 1.7 kilometres length with three stops, one of which will be directly on a metropolitan railway station. In Hamburg, the operating speed of the cabins which are equipped with linear motors will be 36 k/h. If the C-railway stands the test it will be expanded into a whole network. It is possible to operate this system automatically, on demand as well as on schedule.

The special characteristic of the magnetic railway (M-railway) is its drive concept based on the Langstator linear motor and the permanently magnetic load technology. The vehicles do not have a drive motor, but are driven contact-free by an electric travelling field in the carriageway. This results in a considerable cabin weight reduction. Presently, an M-railway trial installation is being tested on the grounds of the Braunschweig polytechnic (Technische Universität Braunschweig). The Deutsche Messe- und Ausstellungs-AG (The German fair and exhibition company) is planning to build an internal passenger transport system after the M-railway technology on the Hanover fair grounds once the trial runs have been completed in Braunschweig. If cabin railways should turn out viable and widely applied means of transport, the architecture of transport will be faced with new tasks.

Urban motorways

In the early days of motorway construction, these rapid transit roads were not run as far as the immediate vicinity of the cities. The city centres were linked up with the motorway network by means of "tributary roads". But soon one started to plan orbital motorway routes around the outskirts of large cities which were connected with the motorway system as well as the main outward-bound roads. With motorisation progressing, the demand was voiced to lead automobile traffic via motorways not only to the city boundaries, but also via urban motorways into the heart of the city. In doing so, the existing urban road network could be relieved and live up again to its original function: The streets of the city will become the arteries of urban life again.

The construction of urban motorways is not devoid of problems, though, because it requires an interference in the structural substance and threatens to dissect organically grown town districts. Traffic planning increasingly finds itself in a head-on collision not only with the local residents, but also with broad groups of the population. The zest for technical perfection has changed the "citiscape" in some places to such an extent that it appears questionable whether it will come off with grace in posterity's eyes. Add to this the considerable aggravation caused to the local residents by noise and exhaust fumes.

It is not the speed, in the case of urban motorways, which is important for mastering immense traffic volumes. Routing and cross-section, therefore, differ from those of cross-country motorways. As a rule, the design speed of an urban motorway is between 80 and a maximum of 100 k/h. The lane width is generally reduced to 3.5 metres. The Berlin urban motorway makes do with a crown width of 27 metres for three lanes in each direction, whereas cross-country motorways with two lanes and a shoulder have a cross-section of 30 metres. Beside the horizontal lineation, the lay-out of the gradient requires very high skills from the designer. The planners must work with constant conscious consideration of their responsibility vis-a-vis the people living in the close vicinity of these rapid transit roads.

The Berlin urban motorway system

The urban motorway network of West-Berlin boasts 70 kilometres, 31 of which have been completed, and a further 17 being under construction. The remaining sections are in various stages of building preparation or planning. Compared to previous considerations, the network has been reduced by 30 kilometres. It now comprises one orbital motorway route, three connecting motorways and six motorway branch-offs into neighbouring urban regions. The connecting motorways' objective, other than providing access to the urban regions through which they cut, is to link up the inner urban orbital motorway with the outer orbital motorway situated in the German Democratic Republic for supra-regional and long-distance traffic.

It is attempted, with the development of the urban motorway systems, to eliminate accident-prone spots, alleviate environmental detriments and to advance especially areas which are structurally weak. The Senator in charge of housing in West Berlin regards the construction of motorways "in urban pressure areas as the most appropriate means to master individual traffic, including commercial traffic as well as that portion of public short-distance passenger transport (buses) which is affected by road". And he notes further: "Because it separates the traffic elements, the motorway is a safe traffic route, and owing to the continuity of the traffic streams, one that is to be judged positively in terms of environmental protection".

The opening to traffic of new sections of the Berlin urban motorway relieves streets running parallel to it by 40 to 60 per cent. Traffic in the city centre also decreases, because vehicle streams approaching from outside are absorbed by the motorway. The accident rate on urban motorways is by two thirds to four fifths less than the one for ordinary city streets. Whilst a city street can handle only about 800 motor vehicles per lane and per hour, an urban motorway has an hourly throughput per lane of 1200 to 1600 vehicles.

On motorways, exhaust gas concentration is – as could be established in West-Berlin – up to two thirds lower than on comparable urban roads. This can be attributed to the constant flow of the traffic on urban motorways, whereas the carbon monoxide ejection as a result of acceleration, braking and stationary periods with the engine running – for instance at junctions and light signals – may soar to well over three times the exhaust gas volume.

The continuity in the traffic flow on the motorway also has a positive bearing on noise development. Whilst on city streets the only way of protection is to equip neighbouring houses with noise-reflecting windows, there are a variety of sound proofing measures available on motorways. Planted revetments minimise the noise-related aggravations to local residents by 5 to 10 dB (A), but they do, however, require sufficient space. Protective walls, which usually are 3 to 5 metres high, may also help to reduce the noise level by 10 to 20 dB (A). Of course, it is often a problem, in terms of architectural and urban planning, to amalgamate these noise protection walls with the environment. The routing of the motorway through a tunnel warrants absolute sound proofing. But then such underground engineering works do not only generate enormous construction costs, but also high current expenses for lighting, ventilation as well as drainage.

Great expenses for an environment-conscious design

The Allee tunnel and the Eastern by-pass in Frankfurt/Main produce an example for the expenses that may be incurred in the construction of urban motorways. Frankfurt is the one large city in the Federal Republic of Germany which, with the highest degree of motorization and the highest number of commuters, has the smallest number of roads at its disposal.

Charlottenplatz in Stuttgart is no longer a square in the proper sense of the word, but rather a multi-level traffic junction.

View from a pedestrian overpass onto the orbital urban motorway in West-Berlin.

In Frankfurt, the urban motorway is to be routed through a tunnel under the Alleenring. Costs for the 2.5 kilometre-long section are estimated to amount to 350 million Deutschmarks.

Urban orbital, motorway and motorway triangle junction near the Berlin radio tower.

Because the built-up area borders directly on the road on both sides of the Alleenring, the planned urban motorway will be running through a 4, respectively 6-lane tunnel over a stretch of 2.5 kilometres. This environment-conscious lay-out will account for 170 million Deutschmarks of the total cost estimated at 350 million Deutschmarks.

The Frankfurt Eastern by-pass, a 6.5 kilometre section of urban motorway with 4 to 8 lanes and three junctions, closes another gap in the motorway network. Two valleys will be spanned with expensive bridges, the length of which has been determined in accordance with a meteorological expertise so as not to block cold air streams in lowlands. Over long stretches the motorway runs in cuts. The environment-conscious design which, besides generous plantings, comprises also retaining walls and noise protection installations, doubles building costs to 260 million Deutschmarks.

According to expert prognoses, the traffic in the inner city will diminish considerable due to both the urban motorway projects which, after their completion, will enable to completely by-pass and circle the city of Frankfurt. The pressure on the main traffic routes is expected to be reduced, on an average, by 50 per cent. More than 40000 citizens will benefit from this relief measure. On the other hand, however, there are approximately 1000 citizens who will be adversely affected by the construction of the new urban motorway sections, and some of them are determined to fight the project. Nothing seems to be able to deter them from filing their appeals, not even the fact that formerly peaceful residential streets are now misused as dodges, polluting the air with exhaust gases in the highest concentration possible.

In some cities overhead roadways have come into existence with the purpose of relieving intersections and bridging track systems or entire industrial zones. Often, these extended buildings look like bridges devoid of abutments. For stilted carriageways like these there are plenty of good as well as bad examples. It requires good design skills and dexterity to make an overhead roadway blend in harmoniously with the town picture. On principle, the negative effect is all the less, the slimmer the superstructure and the narrower the piers of the building.

One of the most beautiful overhead roadways spans the Jan-Wellem-Platz in Düsseldorf. The prestressed concrete building, designed by Friedrich Tamms and built in 1961/62, produces an impression of lightness and elegance due to its carved lineation. The overhead roadway which measures 540 metres in length and has three lanes, carries the North-South traffic, dividing it into two strands which are led back to even street level on two lanes each. The stilted carriageway was not designed as an angular hollow girder, but displays a double curved sinusoidal curve which dissolves into two simple sine-like bottom booms where the carriageways split. Although the shuttering required the highest of qualities, the construction of the overhead roadway cost only half as much as a tunnel whose cut ramp would have rather marred the town picture. The carriageway of the overhead roadway is supported by individual steel piers placed at 25 metre intervals and branching out at the top in a V-shape. Behind the bifurcation of the structure into two branches, trapezoid steel piers were erected. The steel cable of the railing is supposed to serve as an elastic impact absorber for vehicles veering off the road and guide them back onto the roadway.

As part of the "Western Vicinity of Hamburg" (Westliche Umgebung Hamburg) Federal motorway, the 3.8 kilometre Elbmarsch overhead roadway was built which runs through the port and industrial district in the western area of the Hanseatic city and on to the Elbe tunnel. Aspects of aesthetic design were superseded by the need to find the most economical solution possible to a technical task when this structure founded on large bore piles and made largely of prefabricated reinforced concrete units was erected.

One of the overhead roadways which were built under particularly difficult conditions, is the Rudolf Wissel bridge in Berlin built from 1958 till 1961. The 906 metre-long building traverses the access road to the Charlottenburg goods yard, an allotment garden colony, tracks for goods trains and the metropolitan railway, the Spree river, a lock and an embankment road; its twelve sections span between 68 and 85 metres. The 477 metre-long and 36.5 metre-wide shore span of the Cologne Zoo bridge spans, besides several major traffic routes, extensive factory grounds. Construction of this prestressed concrete bridge from 1962-65, with its spans of up to 99 metres, was only possible after the cantilever method.

The 1824 metre-long and 25 metre-wide Berliner bridge in Duisburg for which the cantilever method was also chosen as the most appropriate construction method, because it had to bridge water courses, traffic routes as well as factory installations, is made partly of steel

The overhead roadway above the Jan-Wellem-Platz in Düsseldorf was built in 1961/62. It could almost be described as elegant.

and partly of prestressed concrete. Its location in the mining subsidence area necessitated special measures for the protection of the bridge against ground shifts. Neoprene pot bearings conceived specifically for the given conditions safeguard a longitudinal flexibility of ± 60 centimetres and a transverse flexibility of ± 39 centimetres. In addition, the bearings which will support a surcharge of up to 1633 megapond, can be vertically readjusted by up to 80 centimetres. Between 1966 and 1969, a 542 metre-long and 24.5 metre-wide steel overhead roadway was built in Ludwigshafen which is led over the new main station and the tracks of the goods yard. The structure is subdivided into a 280 metre stayed cable bridge and an adjoining deck bridge. This method was chosen because the railway installations allowed for bridge piers to be erected only in very few places.

A prestressed concrete bridge which can be disassembled, was built in the course of the "Middle Ring" in Munich. The units are part of a component system.

On only five weekends, 60 mechanics built this 600 metre-long steel overhead roadway on the Aegidientorplatz in Hanover.

The design of overhead roadways and sound protection walls can cause quite a lot of problems because traffic structures of such importance are almost impossible to integrate into the urban picture. The drawing shows a design by Friedrich Tamms.

The 75 metre-high pylon trestle and its four posts which join centrically at the top are a landmark visible from afar. As a dominant feature of urban planning, it indicates the location of the new main station. At the top, the pylon block carries a rhomb-shaped cable chamber which is 15 metres long and 7 metres high, and from which the 38 tendons emanate holding the pavement deck.

In Hanover, 60 mechanics had merely five weekends to assemble a 600 metre-long steel overhead roadway weighing 1200 megapond at the Aegidientorplatz. Through the rapid assembly of this overpass after a component system method the traffic remained undisturbed on weekdays. After completion of the assembly, the construction works on the underground could start in this area without obstructing the traffic flow.

The requirement, based on the anti-emission law, to build overhead roadways with sound protection walls of at least 3.5 metres height, is in contradiction with previous design principles for such structures. In Düsseldorf, a U-shaped structure open towards the top was developed with internal side walls of 3.5 metres height. Remarks Friedrich Tamms: "The 45 centimetres ledges of former overhead roadways now become a 5 metre-high structure the lower edge of which is, in itself, 5 metres above street level. This 10 metre-high building is equal in height to a three and a half storey-building. Also, not least because of its length, it cannot be overlooked in the "citiscape" and, thus, constitutes the opposite of aesthetically dissolving buildings of earlier days". Tamms strove to divide the surfaces horizontally several times by way of light and colours, so as to optically reduce the mass of the building and its height to acceptable proportions: "The upper half ot the supporting exterior wall is to be slanted towards the outside in oder to divert the rain water and to reflect the light. A white colour band interrupts the grey concrete over its full length where the supporting wall has sufficient thickness. It forms a ledge from which the water can drip away. Underneath, the structure, in the deepest of blues, recedes towards the cross girders and, thus, loses its optical importance, pushing back the substructure into areas difficult to catch with the eye". In spite of these efforts, it will hardly be possible to integrate traffic structures as massive as these into the town picture. It is to be expected, therefore, that the construction of road tunnels will gain impetus.

Parking garages and underground car parks

The number of passenger cars and vans in the Federal Republic of Germany has risen to almost 22 million. Only for every fifth motor car there is a garage or parking space available outside the public traffic areas. In order to maintain the flow of traffic in the cities, middling at least, parking in the streets will have to be restricted even further. This is why the so-called "stationary" traffic is more and more shifted to multi-storey parking buildings. Optically, the best solution are underground car parks the like are built not only under squares and new buildings in the cities, but occasionally also in housing estates in order to maintain green areas.

Notwithstanding the construction of parking garages and underground car parks it is impossible to provide parking facilities in the city centre for the tens of thousands of commuters who work there. It is here that the traffic policy measures of the municipalities begin. In order to scare away long term parkers, progressively increasing parking fees have been introduced, e.g., in a number of municipal car parks in Frankfurt/Main. In addition, the number of the permanently leased bays is limited. In order to halt the exodus of citizens from the city centre, residents in the centre are given reserved spaces in streets and on squares against payment of a nominal fee. A collapsible iron post secured by a lock ensures that no abuses are possible.

There is as much variety to be found in the architectural design of parking garages as in their structure, but their quality, in terms of urban planning, differs substantially. Many a thing which was meant to create contrast looks ugly or even brutal, such as, e.g., a steel construction looking almost naked, placed next to a Gothic church. Quite often parking garages are regarded as foreign bodies in the city landscape, as dull, functional buildings in which cars are piled up on top of each other – a necessary evil resulting from motorization. On the other hand, entire urban districts may become desolate, if no parking facilities are made available. Parking facilities, therefore, are a must. But then they must also be well-shaped in their design, at least as far as their facades are concerned. Furthermore, it is the location which decides over having to equip parking decks with a railing only or with a parapet.

There is a variety of ways of how to design a facade, even in the case of "hand-me-down parking garages" as they can be erected within only a few months, e.g., after the Krupp-Montex construction method. The supporting structure is a steel skeleton into which precast concrete slabs are inserted. From a series of lined-up basic elements, column-free parking buildings of random length and, as a rule, 16 metres width are created. In spite of normal factory production, it is frequently difficult to see, due to the skillful work of the architects, that these buildings are parking garages.

The parking garage with 500 bays hardly differs from the rest of the street front.

121

At first glance, no one would possibly guess that the building on the right is a parking garage. It was built in Straubing after the prefabricated construction method and accommodates 310 motor cars.

Parking decks at the Wilhelma zoo in Stuttgart with 800 spaces.

Left from top to bottom:
This parking garage adjoins a department store in Hamburg. On the inside of the ramp there is a 7 metre-wide traffic lane. 220 spaces for passenger cars are arranged along the outside.

In the city centre of Hanover there is this parking garage of a department store. To contrast with the horizontal division of the building, the parapet slabs have a vertical texture.

This building in Hanover offers parking space at the top and versatile leisure facilities at the bottom.

Park and ride

Above the tracks of the Langenhorn-Markt underground station in Hamburg a parking garage was built in the Seventies which accommodates 480 cars on four decks. By means of an elevator, motorists have direct access to the platforms. The location selected for this park-and-ride installation (p + r) is very favourable, expecially since several main traffic routes merge at this station. Parking is free of charge if one transfers from the car to the underground. The trip to the Jungfernstieg in the centre takes only 24 minutes. Monthly season ticket holders are given a p+r badge, whereas other people have to draw a permit from an automatic distributor with their ticket.
In 1977, a p + r underground car park with 400 spaces was opened at the Gerstedt underground station in Hamburg. Of these spaces, 300 are allocated to underground passengers and the remaining ones are open to the customers of a new shopping centre. In that year, there were 6700 p + r parking spaces in Hamburg available at 43 rapid transit railway stations.
Owing to the extreme shortage of parking facilities, a 25 million Deutschmarks programme for the construction of further p + r installations was agreed upon which provides for about 600 new spaces. A survey revealed that the motives of saving time and convenience determine largely the choice of the rapid transit system as a means of transport and, consequently, also location and design of the p + r installations. The location of metropolitan railway stations, however, can be guided by p + r considerations only in exceptional cases, since the number of passengers parking their car near the station account for only 7 per cent. It is, therefore, of decisive importance to co-ordinate the location favourably with the metropolitan railway stations, as motorists transferring to the train are not too willing to accept to walk for more than 200 metres. Even if the surface is not restricted, this may lead to multi-storeyed parking installations. So far, no parking decks have been built yet at the Munich metropolitan railway stations, because there has been sufficient space – for the larger part in possession of the Federal Railways – in the immediate vicinity of the stations. In Munich, the use of p + r installations is free, also.

Via the elevator motorists have direct access in this park-and-ride installation to the platforms of the Langenhorn Markt underground station in Hamburg.

The central bus terminal at the Hanover main station (above and below) was awarded a prize for architecture.

Bus terminals and truck stations

The easier it becomes to transfer between the different means of transport, the greater chances are for public short-distance passenger transport to win motorists as passengers. Bus terminals should, therefore, be integrated as closely as possible into rapid transit and long-distance railway stations. The bus terminal at the Wandsbeker Markt in Hamburg, opened in 1962, is situated above an underground station and was considered, in its time, to be the most modern installation in Europe. Not only does it fulfill its purpose, it also has an attractive design. The large roof areas were skillfully "loosened up" by staggered slopes. Generally, the bus stop roofs provide the only possiblity, besides the lay-out, to vary the looks of large bus terminals. This opportunity, then, is often put to good use.

For instance, narrow barrel-shaped elements were arranged side by side for the central bus terminal at the Hanover main station. Traffic and parking facilities in the cities are also relieved by the 42 motor stations belonging to the Straßenverkehrsgenossenschaft (SVG) (Road traffic co-operative) which are frequented, in the course of a year, by 1.5 million long-distance lorry and trailer units half of which park for longer than six hours. Since four decades, these truck stations also provide loading capacity allocation positions which function as freight exchanges. Then, there are hotels for long-distance lorry drivers, repair workshops and petrol stations.

The location of the International Congress Centre of Berlin (ICC) near the radio tower is particularly advantageous.

Car lobby in the basement of the Berlin Congress Centre

In planning the International Congress Centre (ICC) in Berlin, an unparalleled complex opened in 1979, special importance was attached to its good integration into the traffic system. The location opposite the fair grounds at the radio tower is not only subject to extreme urban traffic volumes, but is also situated on the intersection of the traffic arteries which couple Berlin with the Federal territory. The basic design assumptions for the traffic installations of the ICC were for a supra-local convention with 5000 participants who arrive within a very short period of time in 2000 passenger cars, 1000 taxis and in buses. From this inevitably ensued a division of the access road into two levels.

The ground level access road to the congress centre is to be used preferably by buses of the Berlin public transport company (Berliner Verkehrsbetriebe). Other buses will find parking and stopping space at a bus terminal which is only 200 metres away. Private motor cars and taxis are guided to the first basement level of the ICC via special approaches and are spread over eight lanes. From this "car lobby" escalators carry passengers up to the entrance hall. Vehicles leave the subterranean installation on five lanes. The congress centre has its own parking garage which extends in front of the congress building and which provides space for 650 motor cars. A computer-controlled indicator system around the ICC makes it possible to give alternative directions so that the approach to the car lobby is automatically blocked when it becomes overcrowded, and alternative access routes are indicated. The construction of this communication complex equipped with the latest of artful gadgets made it necessary anyway to redesign the neighbouring streets and junctions.

The congress centre is linked up, across the wide Messedamm, with the fair halls at the radio tower by a triple-storey bridge structure. At a later stage, the ICC will also be included in the underground railway network, when passengers will have direct access from the station to the entrance hall.

A triple-storey bridge connects the congress centre with the exhibition halls near the Berlin radio tower.

Pedestrian overpass at the "Landungsbrücken" pier in Hamburg.

Pedestrian bridges and conveyor systems

Since the time when extensive pedestrian precincts where created in the cities which do not only interconnect shopping streets, but also green zones and recreational areas, pedestrian bridges are no longer rated of secondary importance. Every fourth bridge in West-Berlin is exclusively reserved for pedestrians. The relatively small loads allow for the application of the most diverse construction methods and materials. Out of 122 pedestrian overpasses in this city, 17 are made of wood, and 13 of brickwork. The other structures consists of steel (35), reinforced concrete (33) and prestressed concrete (12), whilst with the remaining 12 mixed construction methods have been applied.

Frequently, pedestrian overpasses are built in place of stair ramps which, by preference, are built in a spindle-shape where greater differences in height have to be overcome. In order to avoid the inconvenience of having to mount stairs, longer distances are accepted. By far the longest pedestrian bridge in West-Berlin is the Goerdelersteg in the district of Charlottenburg. It spans the Western harbour canal (Westhafenkanal) and the urban motorway and measures, all three ramps included, 350 metres.

What pleasure is derived by designers from bringing variety into these transport buildings may be gathered from the fact alone, that there is hardly one pedestrian overpass in Berlin which resembles another. Here, transport architecture is farther than ever from a uniform component system.

In 1969/70, a 137 metre-long tension band bridge was built across a street junction in Freiburg/Breisgau. This 4 metre-wide foot-bridge connects the city centre and the municipal park with districts beyond the circular road. The tension band supported by two piers is only 25 centimetres thick. This structure is a suspension bridge in the true sense of the word, as carrying rope and stiffening girder are one. On the Düsseldorf fair grounds, the exhibition pavilions and other buildings are connected with one another by a 1000 metre-long network of pedestrian bridges. The upper portion of the foot-bridges which are closed on all sides, consists of acrylic glass mounted in aluminium frames. The bottom part of the structure is faced with enamelled aluminium sheets. With their oval cross-section, these pedestrian overpasses form a contrast with the severe looking cubes of the exhibition halls which was well intended by the fair architect. The bridges are mounted, at 15 metre intervals, on slim tubular columns of 4.2 metres' height.

This 137 metre-long tension band bridge was built in Freiburg/Breisgau in 1969/70.

Elegance is the word for the Sträßchensweg pedestrian overpass designed by Gerd Lohmer. The three openings are about 40 metres in width each.

Right: The Werdersee bridge in Bremen has spindle-shaped stairs as well as a spiral ramp with foot and bicycle paths.

Below:
An extensive network of fully closed foot-bridges connects the exhibition halls with one another in Düsseldorf. The main bridge features conveyor bands.

Escalators lead to the footpath network on the second level. Two conveyor bands of 225 metres length each run along the main bridge. At a speed of 40 metres/minute, these conveyor bands can transport 11000 people per hour in either direction. Since it is possible to reverse the direction, the conveyor band capacity increases to 22000 fair visitors during peak hours. At the outer sides of the bridge, next to the conveyor bands, there remain pathways of 1.4 metres width for those who prefer to walk.

Pedestrian precincts reactivate urban life

The definition, conceived in the USA, that "a pedestrian is a motorist who has found parking space" highlights the consequences of motorization. Scarcely has the mobilized citizen left his vehicle, when he must run the gauntlet in crossing the road, squeeze through parked cars. The motor car has supplanted the original function of urban streets and squares which was that of a meeting place. Particularly the main traffic routes in the city centre do no longer form a link, but a division not unlike that of a river.
Only the crossings at the traffic lights make it possible to "bridge" this gap. This development contributed greatly to the city centres losing their attractiveness, and reduced the life quality of the population.

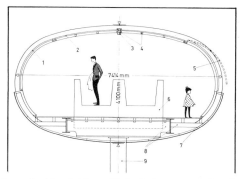

Cross-section of a pedestrian bridge with built-in conveyor bands.

To counter this problem, the idea was conceived in several large cities at the end of the Fifties and beginning of the Sixties to create "car-free" zones and turn them into pedestrian precincts. As a consequence of the positive results the picture of the city centre started to change, particularly in the Seventies, and increasingly larger "walking areas" came into being. In 1979, there existed already some 500 pedestrian precincts in more than 300 towns in the Federal Republic. Similar plans were already being examined in a further 150 towns. The neighbouring shops achieved the highest turnovers per square metre in the retail business, but they also paid the highest rents. A more distinct proof of how popular the pedestrian precincts are, can hardly be found. The days when shop and house owners objected against such projects are long gone. Since the beginning of the Seventies it has always been the local residents who repeatedly demanded, in some cases with massive backing, that pedestrian precincts be created, and even gave a financial contribution to this end. Drops in turnover in side streets lead to these being included into the pedestrian zone and hence to develop slowly but gradually a closed system.

Buildings too high on either side of the street do have an unfavourable effect, because they easily make it look like a gorge. On the other hand, pedestrian streets should not be too wide, either, i.e., they should not give the impression of almost being on a "square". This is why planners initially based themselves on the assumption that pedestrian streets must not be wider than 10 to 15 metres. A test carried out in Frankfurt by blocking off the 30 to 40 metre-wide "Zeil" to automobile traffic, revealed, however, that pedestrians make use of the entire width of the road. After the completion of the underground and metropolitan railway works, though, the wide road space will be filled in with structural and decorative changes. It is planned to create an area where one can linger. Projecting facades, corners and edges, in short, all these attributes which normally obstruct automobile traffic in a street enhance the lay-out of a pedestrian precinct. An uninterrupted series of buildings, as straight as the crow flies, do not offer points of interest for the passer-by's wandering eye. Staggered buildings, on the other hand, give the impression of looking at a series of lined-up spaces, an effect which can be further emphasized by a varied design of the facades. An expansion of the street space into squares may be used to the advantage of the pedestrian precinct design. Passages are very good as cross-sections between individual walking streets, and so are arcades which also provide cover when it rains.

Parking garages and underground car parks bordering immediately on the pedestrian precincts are an absolute requirement. The underground car park underneath the pedestrian precinct around the Dome in Cologne sets a good example. Entrance and exit are situated inconspicuously under the Roman-Germanic museum. It is equally important to ensure that pedestrian precincts are easily accessible by means of public transport. No traffic routes should run through this area, though, unless the vehicles make use of tunnels. At the most, one might tolerate the existence of tramways in walking areas, if the track dam stands out clearly in its surface modulation and if distances between stops do not admit high speed. Buses, on the other hand, are critical in that no pedestrian can say to which side they will pull over. Another problem is the delivery of goods. The most favourable way would be to have access for supplies to the back of the property or to have them delivered via a subterranean approach, so that there will be no vehicles in the pedestrian zones itself. Failing this, the goods traffic should be restricted to certain hours only – preferably in the morning – when it causes the least inconvenience to the flow of pedestrians.

Success depends on the structural design

To establish a pedestrian precinct it is not sufficient to put up signs saying "closed to motor vehicles" at the beginning and the end. "The success of a pedestrian precinct depends, last not least, on the structural design", states the Deutsche Industrie- und Handelstag (German head organisation for industry and commerce) in an investigation. The road research association has set down some guidelines which stipulate the following: "Pedestrian streets should preferably not be covered with bituminous surfacing, but rather be paved with setts or tiles. The surface must be even, and it should display as great a colour variety as possible". Materials and laying patterns must live up to a certain aesthetic demand. Interlocking paving and tiles made of grey concrete must not be used too often if one is bent on avoiding an impression of dreariness. In spite of all this, the pavement must be sufficiently strong for heavy vehicles (fire brigade) to pass.

Trees, bushes and flowers are more than just a colourful dot in the city landscape. The guidelines deal with that only briefly:"An attractive design, from the architect's and the gardener's point of view, of the pedestrian zone should be a self-evident condition". Here, one should call upon the help of experts.

In the pedestrian precincts, garden cafés, beer gardens, ice cream parlours with sunshades and Frankfurter stands in the streets are as much desirable as anything else which has the character of a market or a bazaar. This entails stands in the open air, book shelves in front of bookshops, flower stands and fruitsellers with their mobile carts, waffle bakeries, etc. Weekly markets which have become a point of attraction again should be included, if and where at all possible, into the pedestrian precincts.

Fountains are particularly popular among the young as a meeting place. In many towns sculptures are erected. Seating facilities where there is no obligation to eat or drink invite the passer-by to linger for a moment in order to observe the colourful activity in the street. Baggage lockers are only found occasionally yet, although they make it possible to go for a little walk without the inconvenience of bulky shopping bags. Special attention is generally given to the illumination of pedestrian precincts, this being an important element of design. In several cities, e.g., old gaslights were installed.

Because Munich achieved "better than any other city to give back life and beauty to the heart of the old part of town by a well thought-out creative design", the architects of the pedestrian precinct were awarded in 1974 a prize for modern urban planning by the American Institute of Architects. Between the Karlsplatz – better known as

The Domterrasse in Cologne ends in the square in front of the main station. Both are connected via generously laid-out perrons interrupted by landings. Underneath the Domterrasse is a street with bus-stops.

Already in Roman days, the Hohe Straße in Cologne was an important commercial street. It was here that one of the first pedestrian streets in the Federal Republic of Germany was created.

After completion of the metropolitan and underground railways works, the well-known "Fressgass" (grub road) was transformed into a pedestrian precinct.

The "Passerelle" in Hanover serves as a subterranean shopping street.

Pedestrian street in Darmstadt and roofed shopping street in a Darmstadt shopping centre.

A prize for modern town planning was awarded to the designers of the pedestrian precinct in Munich by the American Institute of Architects. This precinct stretches from the "Stachus" to the Marienplatz. Plant bowls and seating facilities are part of a pedestrian zone's "inventory".

"Stachus" – and the Marienplatz the characteristics of a throughroad were avoided and a space to linger in was created, where new impressions provide the stimulus to change the direction, to stand still and to participate in urban life. Smaller side streets have also been included in this pedestrian zone which has been "furnished" with fountains, beer and café gardens, fruit and other stalls, a multitude of plant bowls and show cases.

In a somewhat varied form, roofed-over shopping streets in modern city shopping centres seizes on the idea of the passages as they were built in some large cities in the 19th century. An exception is the subterranean shopping street called "Passerelle" in Hanover, in the design of which great importance was attached to giving it the features of a public street. The "Passarelle" has become a popular point of attraction due to its variety of shops, resting zones, fountains and squares as well as conveyor bands, escalators and ramps. The successful architectural design contributes greatly to this popularity. By means of many openings an entity was created, in terms of urban planning, between the sheltered subterranean pedestrian street and the street network on the surface. Here, the pedestrian who, for a long time, was given the feeling of being a "second-class road user" has regained his privileges.

Toning down the traffic in dense residential areas

Following the positive results achieved with pedestrian precincts in the commercial centres of the inner cities, the future task on which to focus is to tone down the traffic in residential streets. The following situation report is found in a study published jointly by the Federal Minister of Transport and the Allgemeiner Deutscher Automobil-Club (ADAC) (one of the German automobile clubs): "The street has become 'hostile'. This is not merely a consequence of the dangers it entails due to street traffic and environmental pollution, it also results from the fact that the motor car has acquired a paramount position in the street, whilst man has lost his ground there . . . The common-place residential street does not offer any impulse to the residents to go and meet there, to communicate, or to spend more time than necessary there walking."

In 1977, 865 out of 100000 children in West-Berlin were involved in a road accident. This considerably exceeds the average in the Federal territory (558 out of 100000 children). Half of these accidents happened on residential streets within the children's action and play radius.

But it is not only the children who are endangered, but rather all people. The growing automobile traffic causes noise, pollutes the air and makes it near-impossible to communicate or find recreation in front of one's own door. For decades, wide automobile lanes have been cut into the urban organism; formerly quiet and peaceful residential streets have turned into noisy throughroads; parked cars have been taking over an increasing amount of space in the streets. On the other hand, next to nothing was done for the sake of pedestrians – save perhaps the pedestrian precincts. Cyclists did not fare any better. The few bicycle paths that exist are frequently blocked by parked cars.

In Berlin, this sign indicates residential streets where traffic has been "toned down", i.e., restricted.

In the Nordstadt district of Bonn, motorists who hope to reach their destination faster by making a detour, are kept away by the above street lay-out.

Paved street sections in an extremely densely populated district with old buildings in Essen-Frohnhausen resulted in quieter traffic.

The strongest inducement to tone down the traffic in residential areas was derived from the Netherlands where so-called living courts (Woonerven) were developed, in which traffic is made to play an inferior part and the use of the space by the local residents takes precedence. If the street is to regain importance as a public place of communication in a residential area, the motorist will inevitably have to be restrained. Measures aimed at controling the traffic, such as speed limits, cul-de-sacs, one-way-streets and parking restrictions cannot be of more than a provisional nature during a transitional phase. Structural transformations, the design of which is still new ground to be broken by the experts in the most varied fields, must be first in line. Green areas, play grounds and recreation areas in all kinds of shapes have to be created. The citizens should be involved in the preliminary deliberations, for to act against the resistance of the population concerned, would mean to plan past the expectations. Toning down the traffic, however, must not restrict itself to individual streets or districts, but must be wide-spread.

Construction and design-related elements in this "appeasement of traffic" comprise the partial raising of the street pavement, the narrowing down of the carriageway for the purpose of expanding the sidewalk, the staggering of lanes along both sides of the road axis as an "optical brake", or even the total abandonment of the principle of separating carriageway and pedestrian reserves. This inevitably entails a limitation of the parking space in the street in favour of green areas. In some cases it will be necessary, therefore, to provide garages or parking bays for the cars of local residents in courtyards or parking buildings. These are measures which for the moment still remain unsolved as far as financing is concerned. In the Federal Republic of Germany, the task of toning down traffic in residential areas has not progressed, though, beyond some more or less hopeful model experiments.

The terminal of the Cologne/Bonn airport satisfies even the highest aesthetic demands. The motorway 'feeder road' continues along the centre line, and as with all modern passenger terminals in the Federal Republic of Germany, the approach road is subdivided in an arrival and a departure level.

CHAPTER V Air Transport Buildings

Apart from balloons and airships, i.e., "flying equipment lighter than air", it was only at the threshold to the present century when man's eternal dream was fulfilled of lifting himself up like a bird to conquer "the sea of air". The question who was the founding father of power flight remains disputed: The American of German origin Gustav Whitehead in 1901, or the brothers Orville and Wilbur Wright in 1903. Since these pioneering flights, not even 80 years have passed. Since long, the use of the airplane as the most modern and fastest means of transport has become commonplace. Jets have reduced distances to a minimum. Today, wide-body planes seating up to 500 passengers bridge oceans and interlink continents within a few hours only. The first civil supersonic airplanes achieve flying times no one would have dared to dream of fifty years ago. In 1977, a world-wide passenger volume of 620 million was counted. The airports in the Federal Republic of Germany alone were frequented by 42 million passengers, and already one can anticipate the transport of airfreight exceeding one day the transport capacity in passenger traffic.

During the young history of air transport, the airport installations had to be adapted again and again to the new ever larger and more powerful types of airplanes. The saying that nothing is more consistent than change has always held and still holds true as far as airports are concerned. Only in recent years, airplane manufacturers have also started to give more consideration to existing ground installations which represent investments of hundreds of billions Deutschmarks. For example, the wing spans of the triple-engine McDonnell Douglas DC-10 and Lockheed L-1011 Tristar wide-body jets are almost the same, the difference being not more than a few inches.

Man has mastered the art of flying by means of a highly developed technology. Today, the problems of air transport are mainly concerned with the organisation of the ground services so as to ensure that the time won even on short routes is not lost again due to long distances to and within the airport grounds as well as overcomplicated processing procedures. The processing of passengers, airfreight and airmail as well as the maintenance of airplanes require extensive building complexes which often become a blend of architecture and the technological requirements, the one conditioning the other. The variety in the solutions found is amazing.

The first building installation for aereonautic purposes was built in Germany as early as the Nineties of the last century, when Otto Lilienthal had his "flying mountain" erected in Berlin-Lichterfelde. A shed was built into the summit of this 15 metre-high artifical hill housing the flying machines. It was from this hill that this pioneer undertook his flying experiments.

Berlin-Johannisthal: Take-off for the world's first scheduled flight
Berlin-Johannisthal was the first airport created in Germany for commercial purposes. It was located on the edge of the city, in the 2 kilometre-long and 1.5 kilometre-wide area between Johannisthal and Adlershof. The aerodrome was opened on 26 September 1909 with a "grand flying competition of the first aviators". The day after, the first cross-country flight in Germany took place: Hubert Latham had taken off from the Tempelhof drill ground in an Antoinette single-decker built in France and had made a surprise landing at Johannisthal where he received an exuberant welcome – as well as a police penalty for "gross misdemeanour".

The largest building in Johannisthal was a board fence 4 metres high and approximately 7 kilometres long which forced the spectators to use the official entrances, for the enterprise had to be financed largely from admission fees. Some grandstands and a few wooden hangars had been erected around a more or less levelled landing strip with the turning masts and a booth for the jury. It is here that aircraft manufacturers like the Wright Flugmaschinen GmbH, the Albatros-Werke and the Rumpler Flugzeugbau established themselves. In Johannisthal, the first pilot licenses were awarded, two airship halls were built, and in 1912 the German aereonautic research institute (Deutsche Versuchsanstalt für Luftfahrt e.V.) took base here. The statistics for the year 1913 record 36817 take-offs and landings in Johannisthal, though the total duration of the flights only amounted to 4096 hours. Nevertheless, Reinhold Boehm, chief pilot of the Albatros-Werke, established a permanent flying record in Johannisthal on 11 July 1914 of 25 hours and 10 minutes, a record to be broken only 13 years later by Charles Lindbergh on his transatlantic flight. Long-distance flights covering up to 2079 kilimetres were made as a preparation to introducing a scheduled public air transport system. But this was only to happen after the First World War.

The world's first scheduled air traffic route was opened on 6 February 1919 in Johannisthal with the take off of a converted military plane which, besides 40 letters and 65 kg of newspapers, carried one single passenger to Weimar where the National Assembly was convened. The passenger sat astride a wooden board behind the pilot, in the open cabin. Further routes were established, among others, to Hamburg and Gelsenkirchen via Hanover. As early as 1922, there were connections to Amsterdam, London, Paris and Riga. The Johannisthal airfield could not keep up with the development in aereonautics. The buildings on the edge of the airfield did not allow for an expansion of the installation. In addition, the feeder service to Johannisthal, at 12 kilometre's distance from the city centre in an unfavourable traffic position, required considerable effort and expense.

Grandstands for the spectators – below: an air show in 1912 – were as important in Berlin-Johannisthal as the hangars.

The Berlin-Tempelhof airport at the end of 1928.

This is how the Berlin-Johannisthal air field looked like around 1912: Tarmac (1), main grandstands (2), restaurant (3), parking lot (4), LVG airplane factory (5), airship hangars (6), grandstand (7), Albatros airplane factory (8), turning points (9), grandstand (10), shed complex (11), NAG engine factory (12), Wright airplane factory (13), flying school (14), premises of the German aeronautics research institute (15), solid fencing (16), Rumpler airplane factory (17), shed complex (18).

Departure and check-in lounge at Tempelhof airport.

Central airport expansion plan from 1925.

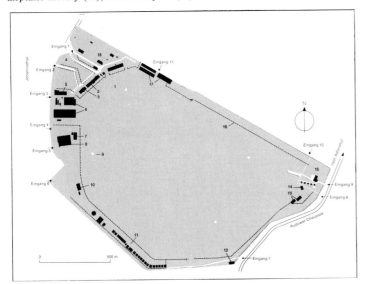

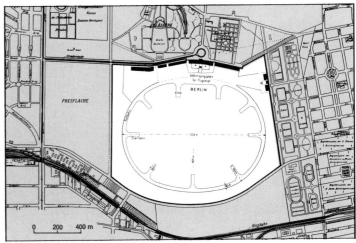

Berlin-Tempelhof: Europe's air junction

The former Tempelhof drill ground, where in September 1909 Orville Wright had demonstrated his flying act to a stunned public, lent itself well for the construction of a central airport. On an area of 1.5 square kilometres a temporary installation was created here for which the Minister of Transport granted a provisional concession on 8 October 1923. In the ensuing years this developed into an airport based on the then latest transport concepts and technologies which was to become "Europe's air junction". In those days, the five airplane hangars with bases of up to 2400 square metres and a clear height of 8 metres were regarded as technical masterworks. They were equipped with underground tank installations. The sliding gates on the apron side could open the hangars over a width of up to 40 metres.

Tempelhof became the home base of the Deutsche Lufthansa which had been founded at the beginning of 1926 by way of a merger of the Deutscher Aero-Lloyd and Junkers Luftverkehr companies with the German state taking a share in the holding. Already in its first year the Lufthansa route network included 53 airports amongst which Darmstadt, Baden-Baden, Augsburg, Essen-Mülheim, Karlsruhe, Mannheim and other towns which are no longer scheduled destinations today.

The passengers of the newly founded Lufthansa – in those days, its name was still spelt Luft Hansa – were checked in at provisional counters in one of the hangars since it was not until 1928 that construction of a departure building could commence. This long-stretched clinker building lay like a bolt between the approach road and the 100 000 square metre concrete apron where the planes stood ready for boarding. The check-in hall with its simple counters was then still rather modest. The visitor's platforms, on the other hand, which were arranged at ground level as well as on the roof, took up a large amount of space. On the occasion of sporting aviation events the Berliner Flughafengesellschaft (Berlin Airport Company) counted as many as 400 000 visitors.

The passage between the building and the tarmac was given a protective roof. Soon, air traffic became so intensive that the passages for departing and arriving passengers had to be separated. Beside an elegant restaurant and a hairdresser, the departure building even housed an "airport hotel" where travellers could rest or stay overnight until they took their connecting flights in the event of bad weather bringing air traffic to a standstill. A tower with a 110 cm swivel floodlight served as a beacon for the fully lit night flight route to Königsberg.

Wireless contact was then still in its infant stages. For years, aerial masts – wooden grid structures – were the landmark of Tempelhof. The "radio building" housed the "radio operator digs" and the weather service as well as the air traffic police which was in charge of flight operation and passport control. Whenever a black ball appeared on the radio building mast, the air traffic police had cancelled all take-offs and landings due to bad weather. Imminent landings were announced by the howling sound of sirens. From the smoke emanating from subterranean smoke ovens, the pilot could determine the direction of the wind. At night, an airplane silhouette mounted onto a tower and moving with the wind, was illuminated by strong floodlights. A small "control tower" built in 1928 was equipped with an optical indicator of the wind speed. Take-off permission was indicated to pilots of planes ready for take-off by means of a signal light system.

The new central airport: A futuristic monument

In the Thirties, Tempelhof and its traffic volume were ranking at the top in Europe. But with the rapid development of aviation, the old departure installations had turned into inconvenient bottlenecks. It was Ernst Sagebiel who was commissioned to develop a concept pointing towards the future for the Berlin central airport, a concept which was to be guided by the contemporary preference for monumentality as well as modern ideas of town-planning. The new complex was not only supposed to provide a long-term basis for a smooth operation of air traffic, but also to serve as an "air stadium" for grand air shows and, in addition, accommodate many authorities and institutions related to aviation. In 1936, work started after the bold plans on an enormous and unique air transport installation which was to set new standards. When the Second World War broke out, the buildings were nearly finished. Construction work progressed only very slowly and finally had to be suspended completely. But after redressing the war damages, the installation proved a viable one, even in the age of the jet.

Just to what extent the premise of building an "air stadium" determined the planning of the new central airport, can be gathered alone from the ground plan of the airport area trebled in size to 4.5 square kilometres. The tarmac was given an oval shape along the longitudinal axis of which the buildings were arranged in a strictly symmetrical order. At the oval vertex, the tarmac was confined over a length of 1230 metres by the rounded, long stretched ramp and hangar complex. The roof of this hall sequence was intended to become a grandstand for 65000 spectators. Furthermore, the plans provided for a stepped strip of green along the oval tarmac to accommodate 1 million people. This spectator zone was to border on the far side on a road for operating vehicles and on the near side on a 75 metre-wide taxiway which in the proximity of the hangars and halls opened up into a 300 metre-wide apron area.

In those days, paved runways were not yet required. On take-off or landing the pilot had to steer exactly against the wind so that a complete network of criss-crossing runways would have been necessary. For the then relatively low tire pressure values, a solid grass cover was quite sufficient, particularly since the airplanes were equipped with tail wheels at the rear instead of the nose wheel landing gear common today. Nevertheless, wheel loads were already great enough to require an expansion of the taxiway with 140-metre radius take-off head points. These head points and the wide tarmac allowed for a take-off against any wind direction. The anchorages in the middle of the tarmac appear rather curious to us today.

Here the planes could be anchored to ears sunk in the ground when the weather turned stormy. From there the planes prepared for the flight were supposed to be towed to the ramp to take passengers, freight and mail on board.

Owing to its ground plan, the new airport installations soon became popularly known as the "coathanger of Berlin". In the middle of the curved building which clings closely to the oval of the tarmac, a 380 metre-long ramp was built the one-strutter steel structure of which extends like a roof over the tarmac for 49 metres and provides a clear entrance height for the planes of 12 metres. Adjoining the ramp flanks are column-free hangars with an overall length of 850 metres. The motor-operated gates of the 49 metre-deep hangars have an access height of 12 metres.

On the land side, the 100 metre-long, 50 metre-wide and 19 metre-high departure lounge adjoins exactly in the centre line of the ramp. The entrance building in front of it, with a 90 metre-long and 80 metre-wide forecourt, almost looks like a bolt. This forecourt is flanked by triple-storey buildings with arcades which were intended to be used as main post office and offices. Other office buildings were supposed to encircle a large circle area. On both sides of the departure hall, subterranean airfreight and airmail handling areas with a double track railway connection in a tunnel as well as individual access and exit ramps for lorries had been provided for.

For the first time in the history of air transport architecture, the new Tempelhof central airport was to separate the traffic streams of passengers, visitors, baggage, airfreight and airmail on different levels. From the entrance hall with the counters of travel agencies and banks as well as stands selling provisions, the passenger proceeds via a wide staircase to the lowered departure lounge in the centre of which it was intended to establish all check-in services including ticket sales, customs and passport control as well as baggage check-in and claim. The plans provided for the passengers to be guided from the counter to the 380 metre-long passenger ramp, separated after domestic and international flights, from where twenty stairs formed a connection with the tarmac level. This concept was based on a separation of the ramp hall into an arrival and a departure section. Immediately after disembarking the passengers and off-loading luggage, freight and mail, the plane was supposed to be towed away and brought back to its given position shortly before the next flight.

It was also planned to load the checked-in baggage separated according to destination onto carriages in the departure lounge. These carriages were to be transported in lifts to the baggage level underneath which was on a level with the ramp hall. Electrically driven carts would have ensured a rapid baggage transport to and from the planes.

The lowest level was arranged 10 metres below the departure lounge, being intended for airmail and airfreight handling. It was here that not only a loading platform for the freight and mail wagons was planned, but space for a maximum of 300 trucks as well. There are wide ramps leading to the passenger ramp hall. The plans included a subterranean cargo yard, customs premises which can be locked, safes for articles of value and even cooling chambers for perishable goods. The visitors to the new central airport were not only to be given a view of the activity at the counters from the lateral galleries of the departure lounge, but were also to benefit from the view, through a wide window front, onto the ramp hall and the tarmac. On the sides, large elevators were planned to connect ramp gallery, main restaurant and roof terrace. Today, Tempelhof is no longer a commercial airport. It serves as an airfield for the Western allied forces and is also used for charter flights. In the event of poor weather conditions, it is an alternate aerodrome for Tegel airport.

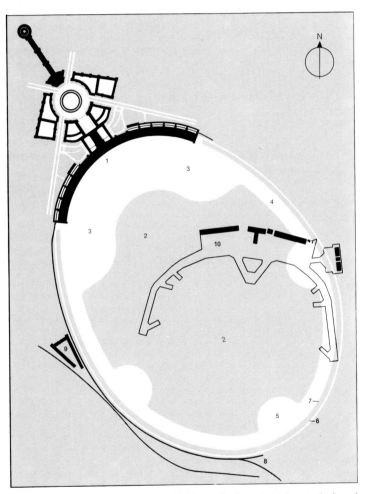

The ground plan of the new Berlin-Tempelhof central airport designed by Ernst Sagebiel bears the characteristics of an "air stadium": New airport buildings (1), tarmac oval with 2000 metre longitudinal and 1700 metre transverse axes (2), anchorages (3), 75 metre-wide paved taxiway (4), take-off heads with 140 metre radius (5), road for operating vehicles (6), stepped spectator area (7), railway connection leading through the basement of the main building (8), maintenance yard (9), old airport installations (10).

This aerial view of Tempelhof airport dates back to the year 1968. After the Second World War, all war damage was repaired.

Cross-section of the main building of the new Tempelhof central airport: Forecourt (1); arcades (2); main entrance (3); entrance hall (4); stairs leading to galleries (5); stairs leading to lowered departure lounge (6); luggage level (9) with ramp to mail and cargo level (10); railway tunnel (11); tunnel for utility piping (12); passenger ramp (13); ramp stairs (14); ramp gallery (15); plane positions (16); main restaurant (17); tower (18); canteens (19); roof terraces (20); festival hall (21).

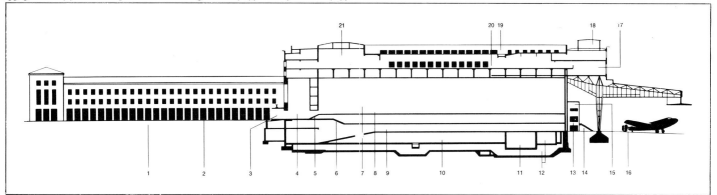

Departure lounge at Tempelhof airport (1962).

Airport capacities in 1978 (data by Arbeitsgemeinschaft Deutscher Verkehrsflughäfen) (Joint venture of the German commercial airport authorities):

Airport	Passengers	Air cargo (tons)	Airmail (tons)	Take offs/ landings
Berlin	4029360	11312	9321	54721
Bremen	667612	2710	1230	41630
Düsseldorf	6360320	38089	5035	113234
Frankfurt	15876717	605455	69000	216522
Hamburg	4159255	35318	8394	94945
Hanover	2097860	10634	2752	76584
Cologne/Bonn	2126964	79574	4939	88181
Munich	5624780	47857	7860	130172
Nuremberg	814628	6616	2912	52768
Saarbrücken	164365	406	–	21435
Stuttgart	2743171	22311	3841	90744
Total	44665032	860282	115284	980936

The airlift memorial – popularly known as "hunger's rake" – is to commemorate the 97 Americans, Englishmen and Germans who lost their lives during the "airlift" in 1948/49. The towering concrete arch symbolizes the three air corridors from and to West-Berlin.

Berlin-Tegel airport included, the Federal Republic of Germany boasts an exceedingly dense and efficient network of eleven commercial airports. The most important one of these is Rhein-Main airport in Frankfurt/Main. Due to its, in terms of traffic geography, favourable position for intercontinental traffic, it has developed into a main distributing junction the importance of which reaches far beyond the borders of the Federal Republic. As regards passenger traffic, Frankfurt ranks second in Europe behind London Heathrow, and is even heading the list in as far as air cargo and airmail is concerned. After the Second World War, Frankfurt airport has assumed the part which was formerly played by Berlin-Tempelhof as "Europe's air junction".

In terms of passenger volume, Düsseldorf-Lohausen airport takes second place. Owing to its location on the edge of the Ruhr region, with its numerous population, this airport handles more holiday travellers by charter traffic than any other airport in the Federal Republic of Germany. If only scheduled flights are taken into consideration, Munich-Riem airport ranks second behind Frankfurt.

Frankfurt Rhein-Main airport: Turntable between the continents

In Frankfurt/Main, aviation can look back on a long tradition. It was here that the first "International Airship Traffic Exhibition" was held in 1909, that the first official airmail service was established in 1912, and where, in the mid-Thirties, the 6.5 square kilometre Rhein-Main plane and airship field was built, replacing the Rebstock airfield which had become too small. Until the disaster of Lakehurst on 6 May 1937, the "Zeppelins" took off from Rhein-Main airport for their regular journeys to South and North America. Already in 1937, Frankfurt achieved second place in Germany with its capacity.

Shortly after the end of the war, American field troops built the first runway at Rhein-Main which initially was only 1800 metres long and 45 metres wide. As early as 18 May 1946, the first civil airplane landed again; it flew the colours of American Overseas Airlines which later was merged into Pan American World Airways. Three months later, Frankfurt was once again included into international flight schedules. During the blockade of Berlin, a plane took off from Rhein-Main airport every three minutes. Since these supply flights during the "airlift" had worn out the first runway very heavily, a second runway had to be built in 1949. In 1950, the number of passengers reached 195330. Only a decade later, there were nearly 2.2 million passengers. At the end of the Fifties, a passenger volume of 10 million was predicted for 1975. But this figure was already exceeded at Rhein-Main airport in 1971, the year in which the new terminal, popularly known as "jumbo station", was opened.

The building history of passenger terminals in Frankfurt covers two decades. As early as 1951, entries for a competition for a new reception building had been invited which was eventually won by the Frankfurt architects Alois Giefer and Hermann Mäckler. They joined forces with the airport planning expert Heinrich Kosina and opened a planning office on the airport premises. Initially it had been planned to commence work already in 1954. But in actual fact, the laying of the foundation stone did not take place until summer 1965. By that time, nothing had been left, though, of the first design. In the meantime, all efforts had been directed to amend and adapt the old facilities to the stormy development of air traffic by means of provisional extensions, by building cargo buildings and by creating a base for the newly refounded Lufthansa which concentrated its operation and maintenance activities increasingly at Frankfurt. Rhein-Main airport was a permanent building site. When the introduction of civil jet aircraft was imminent, it was decided to gather some experience first and to bide one's time. Years later, when eventually the decision to build the Boeing 747 had been taken, a substantial expansion of annual capacity to 24 million passengers was made – two years after the construction works had begun. There are reserves to raise this capacity to 30 million passengers a year. Just on time before the first landing of a jumbo jet, one pier head of the new terminal could be put into operation in 1970.

Fundamentally, a terminal is the junction between aircraft and ground-operated means of transport. This is why one also speaks of a land side and the air or apron side. In the planning process of the Frankfurt passenger terminal, special importance was attached to the extraordinary high proportion of passengers who switch at Rhein-Main airport from one plane to the other in order to reach their destination faster via Frankfurt. The share of transit passengers at Rhein-Main is 45 per cent. Two thirds of the passengers are on international flight. This traffic-related characteristic and the area being bounded on by two motorways induced the entire passenger traffic to be concentrated in one single terminal, instead of creating several self-contained smaller processing units – as is the case at other large airports. Transit passengers are thus saved time-consuming bus transfers and overlong walks. They will find all facilities concentrated under one roof, they can change from their jumbo jet to the train or get into their hotel room without having to leave the terminal complex. Building costs amounted to approximately 1000 million Deutschmarks, a sum equivalent to the price of not even a dozen jumbo jets.

The reception building with the counters for departing passengers and the baggage claim is nearly half a kilometre long. It consists of four adjoining halls with waiting zones being arranged in front on the tarmac side. From this complex of buildings passenger ramp piers are projecting far into the preparation area of the apron. The middle finger arranged in the centre line branches out after 200 metres at an angle of 45° and opens up after a further 200 metres into finger heads with five aircraft positions each.

36 aircraft can put in simultaneously at the three pier fingers of the Frankfurt passenger terminals.

Jumbo jets and other aircraft at one of the pier finger heads of pier B, the roof surfaces of which serve as a visitor's terrace.

Left: Extending over an area of 15 square kilometres, Rhein-Main airport with its two runways, is situated directly on the Frankfurt motorway junction. The runways which are 3900 and 3750 metres respectively, are presently being extended to 4000 metres each.

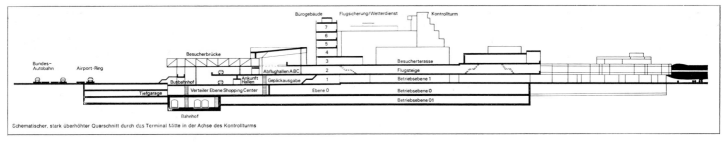

Cross-section of the Frankfurt passenger terminal

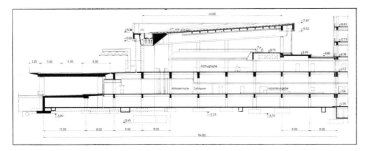

Cross-section of departure lounge and approach roads: In the basement there are the utility installations. The arrival lounges are at ground level, with the baggage claim conveyor belts, the meeting area and shops as well as service installations such as travel agencies and banks. Above this extend the departure lounges with a pillar-free roof span.

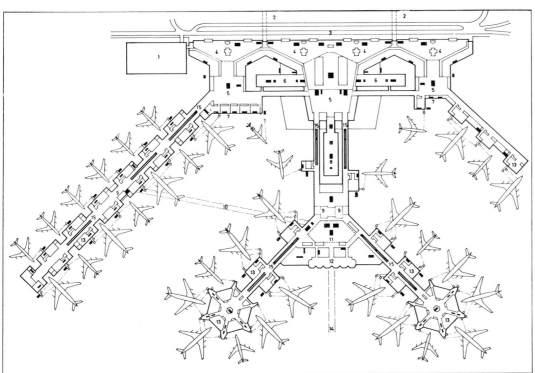

Ground plan of the passenger level (level 2):

1 Car park
2 Visitors overpass over approach roads
3 Approach road departures
4 Departure lounges
5 Waiting lounges, domestic flights
6 Apron bus stop, domestic flights
8 Air traffic control
9 Passport control
10 Tunnel for transit passengers
11 Waiting lounge, international flights, with access to bus stop, international flights
12 Waiting lounge, international flights, with view onto apron
13 Assembly lounges at ramps
14 Vehicle tunnel leading to external positions
15 Conveyor bands

The main supporting members of the departure lounges converging on one pylon span up to 55 metres.

Waiting lounge for domestic flights in pier B with flight information boards.

There are 1700 metres of conveyor belt in the terminal.

The pier marked as finger B, as seen from the land side, has the shape of the letter Y. This is where the aircraft of the international airlines are serviced.

At both ends of the complex housing the departure and arrivals lounges, two other pier fingers extend into the apron area at an angle of 45°. The Western finger designated A is approximately 400 metres long and reserved for Lufthansa aircraft. The Eastern pier finger C, allocated to charter flights, can later be expanded into the premises of an old cargo depot.

In total, there are positions for 36 jets on the three pier fingers, providing space for up to 30 wide-body aircraft. This means, that at any one moment more than 10000 seats can be offered immediately at the terminal. The large number of service positions is achieved by means of the space-saving nose-in arrangement whereby the aircraft is parked at a right angle to the pier. The length of the pier finger necessarily follows from the number of positions and the wing spans (nearly 60 metres in the case of a Boeing 747) of the aircraft which are to be serviced there. Telescoping passenger ramps which swivel horizontally as well as vertically establish a stepless connection between aircraft and terminal. Passengers are not subjected to adverse weather conditions when boarding or disembarking.

During peak traffic hours which occur four times a day and which follow from the turntable function of Rhein-Main airport, there are not enough aircraft positions at the terminal. Additional passenger planes have to be positioned in far-away tarmac areas. Tarmac buses are used to transport passengers from these planes to the terminal which has three bus stops equipped to this end with 18 gates.

Among the structurally most interesting buildings of the Frankfurt terminal are the four adjoining departure lounges with a semicircular layout, spanning 4000 square metres pillar-free each, much to the benefit of clarity and the smooth flow of traffic. The roof of the lounge ascending towards the sides is supported at the lowest point by a pylon from which the main girders beam out to the external supports. These load bearing members consist of prestressed trapezoid hollow girders spanning up to 55 metres. They are 3 metres high and are widest at the top at a width of 1.40 metres. These hollow girders which are accessible and passable from the roof, are also used as exhaust air ventilation ducts; in addition, they contain cables and other utility piping. Suspended glazing was chosen for the Northern facade of the departure lounges, of which the panes are 2 metres wide and up to 11 metres high. This facade, impressive in its modern design, is reinforced with vertical aluminium glazing bars.

Basically, the entire terminal is subdivided into four levels. Level 2 which is situated 4.53 metres above the ground and tarmac level, is reserved to the passengers and the pertaining check-in facilities of the airlines and authorities as well as shops and service installations. Level 1 (tarmac level) accommodates operating services and installations of the airlines and the airport authority inasfar as these are involved in the servicing of the aircraft. This level does, however, also house the arrival area and baggage claim, travel agencies, car hire firms, shops and restaurants as well as the meeting point underneath the departure lounges. Level O which is identical with the first basement level, is reserved to utility installations. In addition, in the area where it protrudes beyond the lounges, this level serves as a distributing channel leading to the underground car park and the airport train station. This area, called "Underneath the Airport", provides ample space for large supermarkets and leisure activities. The stream of visitors is guided to level 3 on a route completely separate from the passenger traffic. On level 3 there are also the lookout terraces of the central pier finger B which comprise a surface of 32000 square metres. Furthermore, there is a continuous gallery in the departure lounges.

Upon his arrival in the departure lounges, the traveller is immediately struck by the large flight information boards with electromechanical indication which list, in the sequence of their scheduled departure time, all flights leaving at least within the next two hours. From these boards the passenger is informed at which counter he is expected to check in and register his baggage. The gate from which the flight is leaving as well as possible delays are equally indicated here. The same kind of indicator boards are found in the waiting lounges and at the piers.

In the departure lounges there are 217 counters connected with the automatic baggage conveyor system. Baggage registration is, on principle, not reserved to specific flights so as to enable the traveller to check in at any one counter of his airline. Latecomers can register their baggage at the gate. Assembly lounges of up to 400 square metres in size are available there, where passengers stay until their plane is ready for boarding.

Whilst customs barriers are permanently installed at pier fingers B and C, customs and passport control is carried out, in the case of international flights departing from finger A, in a decentralised position at the gate where the appropriate facilities are available. This ensures optimum use of aircraft positions and avoids problems with so-called "switch flights" (plane arriving from a domestic airport, continuing flight abroad, or vice-versa). It has turned out to be more practical for pier finger A, on the other hand, to centralise security control stipulated to avert a danger from outside – these checks did not yet enter into consideration when the terminal was planned and built.

In order to shorten the way for passengers between fingers A and B, an approximately 300 metre-long tunnel was built underneath the tarmac, equipped with conveyor bands. A particular feature in pier finger A is a transit corridor on level 3 via which all gates presently used for international flights are interconnected without the transit passenger having to subject himself to customs and passport control. This transit level, again, is linked up with the transit tunnel underneath the tarmac. Passengers in transit from one international flight to another benefit considerably from this arrangement, particularly if they originate from countries who are subject to a visa.

For the comfort of passengers, there are conveyor bands in the pier fingers of an overall length of 1700 metres as well as a number of lifts, particularly because special baggage caddies are available which can be transported on escalators without any problem to get from one level to the other.

Since it is impossible to provide passenger and service information to an international public in several languages, a system of pictogrammes was developed in Frankfurt. The top row shows the signs for airport, departure, arrival, transit and waiting lounge.

A small part of the electronically controlled baggage conveyor system which makes it possible for Frankfurt as the only large airport to keep within a transit period of only 45 minutes.

An extensive pictogramme system aids orientation. On principle, all indications are given in German and in English, the aeronautics language. The signs are lit and colour-coded. All installations relevant to air traffic operation appear on a blue background, whereas green indicates services and white commercial facilities.

The technical equipment of the Rhein-Main terminal are numerous. The utility installations alone are immense if one considers the fact that the cubical content (including the underground car park) amounts to 2.8 million cubic metres. The electronically controlled baggage conveyor system which automatically sorts the suitcases of departing and transit passengers and transports them to the aircraft positions at a speed of 2.5 metres/second, is unique. The conveyor bands which run in tunnels around the pier fingers, boast a total length of almost 40000 metres. 12500 electric motors and magnetic drives as well as 760 switches have been installed in this system. The cost for this plant amounted to 118 million Deutschmarks. Owing to its baggage conveyor and sorting system, Rhein-Main airport is the world's only airport in a position to guarantee a transit time of only 45 minutes.

"Jumbo Station" – A city in its own right

Between the departure lounges and the corridors which interconnect all three of the pier fingers at their roof, rises a 250 metre long, eight-storey office building, adjacent to a six-storey administration section built in the centre line of the terminal. The closing stone of this complex which bridges the waiting lounge B for domestic flights is the control tower. These office buildings house not only the offices of the Federal Aviation Authority (Bundesanstalt für Flugsicherung), the German weather service, representatives of the airlines, central control desks for the technical installations, the offices of the airport authority and a great number of other companies, but also some public service installations. Among these are the airport clinics which has at its disposal two operating theatres, a fully equipped X-ray department, a lab and even several sick-rooms. In addition, there are a dental surgery, the premises of a police station, bank branch offices, social services of the churches, VIP lounges and facilities for taking care of children travelling unaccompanied as well as handicaped passengers. These facilities are within easy reach from the domestic waiting room B.

The terminal complex provides room for more than 100 shops and service installations offering almost anything one could wish for. Furthermore, there are nearly two dozens of restaurants of all kinds, three cinemas, a supermarket, a discotheque and even a fashion house. On the gallery of the departure lounges, the exhibitions of the Airport Gallery change every couple of weeks. All this makes the terminal a shopping as well as a communication centre. It forms a city in its own right which is frequented daily by up to 66000 passengers and thousands of visitors and people coming to meet arriving passengers, and in which more than 8000 people have a working place. The only thing that is missing is a residential population, although

there are 1600 guest beds and multiple conference facilities available in the hotel situated in front of departure lounge C. Frequently, conference participants arrive by plane from all over Europe in the morning and are back home again already in the evening.

Multi-level connection with road traffic

The capacity of an airport does not only depend on its runways or terminal, but also on the efficiency of the traffic installations on the land side. In accordance with the vertical division of the terminal, the approach is on two levels. The elevated road in front of the departure lounges is 22.25 metres wide so that, apart from a holding strip for taxis and buses, oblique short-term parking bays could additionally be provided between the four lanes. There is a similar lay-out on level 1 in front of the arrival lounges which have an adjacent bus terminal. Partly stilted roads directly link up the terminal with the Frankfurt motorway junction.

Because road traffic installations cannot absorb the capacity increase of the airport, in spite of generous expansion and development, the Frankfurt airport railway was inaugurated along with the terminal in 1972, being the first one of its kind. The Federal Railways are of the opinion that an airport with an annual capacity of 10 million arriving and departing passengers can no longer perform satisfactorily without a connection with a means of short-distance rail transport. For once, it provides a link between the passenger terminal and the centre of Frankfurt (travelling time is 12 minutes), but also connects it with the cities of Mainz and Wiesbaden. From these main stations it is possible to travel directly to any large city in the Federal Republic of Germany. Also, long-distance trains are increasingly routed via Rhein-Main airport. Already in the summer of 1975, an average of 15500 travellers made use of the airport train every day. 56% of these were air passengers.

The central control desk of the automatic, electronically controlled baggage conveyor and sorting system at Frankfurt airport.

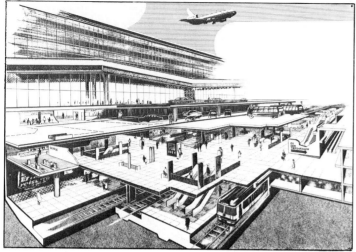

Perspective cross-section through the subterrranean traffic link-up installations. On the second basement level is the Frankfurt am Main–airport station which is part of the Federal Railways system. The first basement level is a juncture between terminal and train platforms as well as underground car park which stretches to the right of the station.

Top right: The land side of the Frankfurt passenger terminal with the approach roads on different levels leading to departures and arrivals as well as one of two pedestrian overpasses which channel the stream of visitors and, simultaneously, provide direct access to an airport hotel. Twelve metres below this area there is the subterranean station of the airport train.

A dense network of elevated roads link up the terminal with the road system. At the very right in the picture the Cologne-Nuremberg motorway. The ten-storey building in the right-hand third of the photograph houses a hotel which was built on the triplestorey underground car park with 6000 bays.

Two of the three platforms of the subterranean stations are 410 metre long and, thus, suited for accommodating even the longest of trains with fifteen coaches.

The subterranean station of the airport railway forms one inseparable and uniform traffic installation with the terminal. The trains stop immediately before the departure lounge at 12 metres below ground level. With a length of 410 metres each, two out of the three platforms are sufficiently long for the longest trains. Via escalators the traveller has access to the departure lounges which are three levels higher. Suitcases registered at the original station can be transmitted to the check-in counters of the airlines. The building cost for the airport railway amounting to about 100 million Deutschmarks were borne in equal shares by the Federal Government and the airport management company, Flughafen AG.

In order to accommodate stationary traffic, a parking garage for 1000 cars and an underground car park for 6000 vehicles were built directly next to the terminal in addition to the parking facilities for more than 30000 employees. This triple-storey underground car park extends over 527 metres between the Cologne-Würzburg motorway and the subterranean airport railway station. The underground garage building measures 9.15 metres in height and, due to topographical conditions, it is between 88 and 122 metres wide. The individual storeys are subdivided into 32 compartments each. Without this subdivision it would be near-impossible for the motorist, in view of the 2000 bays on one level, to orient himself. Another additional aid to the user lies in the fact that the parking ticket with the imprinted compartment number is not collected at the cashier's, but only at the exit barrier. The car park operation is controlled by micro-processors. Access and exit is via ramps and spindles with a 22 metre external diameter. There are sixteen elevator and stairs systems connecting the individual parking levels and level O with the terminal. The design of the building is such that the addition of a superstructure at a later stage is possible. Already, the ten-storey Sheraton airport hotel has been built above the underground car park.

Cologne/Bonn: A "drive-in" airport with decentralised processing

On the occasion of the inauguration of the new Cologne/Bonn airport terminal on 20 March 1970, the then Federal President, Dr. Gustav Heinemann, remarked: "Airports are the visiting cards of a country". This holds especially true for the Cologne/Bonn airport, less so because of its passenger turnover, but rather because of the state visitors arriving here. It was not only a purposeful, but, from an architectural point of view, also a remarkable reception complex that was built in the moorland of the Wahner Heide at the end of the Sixties. The present airport of the Federal capital was built by the Royal Air Force after the Second World War and passed on to civilian management in 1957. It is situated at 14 kilometre's distance from Cologne and 22 kilometres from Bonn. The airport management company was determined to make use in the plans for the new terminal of all the experience gained with previously built installations. For instance, it was tried to keep the distance between the parking lot and the reception building to an acceptable minimum; to avoid congestion on the approach roads; to ensure a clear lay-out of buildings and facilities; to avoid having to change level several times within the terminal and passengers being subject to adverse weather conditions on their way between the processing building and the tarmac or them being squeezed into crowded tarmac buses. In designing the new Cologne/Bonn terminal building, the aim was to achieve a substantial reduction of the ground times and a maximum flexibility as regards utilization of the premises. The result is a drive-in airport with a strictly decentralised processing. Based on the conviction that a central check-in hall cannot fundamentally improve passenger processing, the component functions of processing were bundled and concentrated in the immediate vicinity of the relevant aircraft. This decentralisation of operation holds many advantages for an airport of this size.

The reception section consists of a horseshoe – shaped main building from which project two star-shaped pier fingers accessible via two short passage ways. It is possible to double the number of pier heads, once the present maximum annual capacity of 3 million passengers is reached. Each one of the six processing units of a pier head is independent, i.e., it is equipped with all the necessary installations. These even comprise an individual dutyfree shop so as to enable passengers travelling abroad to shop dutyfree. For the purpose of processing a wide-body aircraft, two units can be drawn and operate together.

The main building which links up the pier heads accommodates all facilities which do not relate immediately to passenger processing. These are information desks and ticket counters, shops, restaurants, a post office, a travel agency and bank counters. Shape and design of the main building are such as to bring car and aircraft together as closely as possible. The approach to the terminal complex is via two levels: the upper one for departing and the bottom one for arriving passengers. Accordingly, the baggage claim is also to be found at ground level. The centre of the land side installation is a car park which, in its completed stage, will offer room for 2000 cars on three parking decks.

Because of the decentralisation of processing, passengers can still be admitted shortly before departure. Of course, the passenger is, on principle, obliged to transport his baggage to the gate himself at Cologne/Bonn airport. But in view of the limited distances this does not present a problem, and all the more so because baggage conveyor bands have been installed in the connecting passage between main building and pier finger head. It is particularly advantageous that the reception area is laid out in such a clear way.

The Düsseldorf architect Paul Schneider-Esleben has arranged the three structural tracts of the main building in steps ascending like a pyramid, as the space requirements diminish with every further level in proportion with their utilization. This adds greatly to the aesthetic attractiveness of the terminal which, moreover, is linked up with the motorway and trunk road system through a generously designed rapid transit road.

The terminal of Cologne/Bonn airport with both its star-shaped finger heads. In the background of the right-hand side picture one sees the Rhine river and at 14 kilometre's distance the city of Cologne. Bonn is 22 kilometres away.

A Boeing 707 being processed at Cologne/Bonn airport.

A detailed view of the ceiling and roof design at the pier finger heads.

Departure level in the main building of the Cologne/Bonn terminal.

Hanover-Langenhagen: A terminal with compact elements

After the passengers having had to put up with provisional check-in facilities for 21 years, the Hanover-Langenhagen Flughafen GmbH opened a new terminal in April 1973. Its capacity is for 4 million passengers per year. The processing facilities had to be laid out in such a way that 20000 passengers can be dealt with on peak days and even twice this number of travellers when the fair is being held.

A planning commission which was appointed as early as 1967 developed the "Hanover System", as the new design principle is called, on which the new terminal is based. Planning was determined by three prerogatives: Firstly, the distance between public transport facilities and planes should be as short as possible. Secondly, passengers must be able to find their way inside the terminal without the slightest problem. And the final premise was that passengers and their baggage be processed in decentralised positions. In fact, the tasks which had been set equalled those in Cologne/Bonn. They were, however, solved in a unique manner. The distance from the approach road to the aircraft averages less than 100 metres. Passengers can easily understand the sequence of procedure. The terminal consists of two so-called compact elements with six gates each and an interposed middle building. These buildings are arranged around a loop in the access road which, in this area, widens into a 70 metre-wide approach with 350 short-term parking bays, taxi stands and bus stops. On the other side of the 220 metre-long approach there is a four-storey parking garage with 1632 bays. The approach is divided into two levels, the departure level being 5.50 metres above ground level.

The lay-out of the compact elements is that of triangles with the corners having been cut off; the sides are more than 85 metres long. Upon entering the lounge passengers have full visual control of the interior. The information board specifies to which gate the traveller is expected to report. Each gate is equipped with a booking desk, four check-in counters and, immediately behind, a waiting lounge where taxfree goods can be purchased also. The piers have transit counters so that passengers have access to the waiting lounge without a boarding pass. In the case of international flights it is here that passport control takes place as well. During planning, the processing steps had been simulated on models on a 1:1 scale. The baggage is transported from the counters to the tarmac level via a short conveyor band from where it is brought to the aircraft, whilst passengers board via passenger ramps. A diversion of baggage, therefore, is virtually ruled out. The procedures followed on the arrivals level situated underneath, with the baggage claim bands and customs control, are equally simple. In Hanover, it is also possible to draw together the facilities of two gates for the purpose of processing a jumbo jet. On the apron side of the building, there is a distributing passage shielded off from the waiting lounges in order to separate domestic from international traffic.

If necessary, the terminal can be expanded by adding further compact elements. In that case, however, transit passengers would have to cover longer distances – but their number is limited in Hanover anyway.

In Hanover-Langenhagen, both the compact elements with six gates each, are connected by a middle building.

The parking garage with 1632 bays is situated directly in front of the terminal.

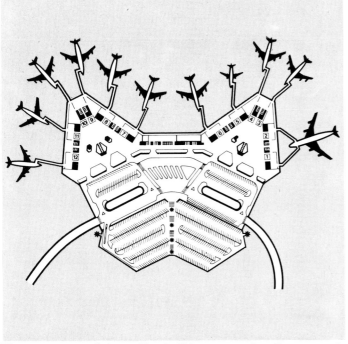

The arrangement of the parking facilities ensures that distances to the planes are short.

Departure lounge in one of the compact elements of the terminal.

In 1977, the second building stage of a terminal was put into operation in Düsseldorf for which the foundation stone had been laid in 1969. Since that moment, the old installations are no longer used except for the processing of charter flights.

As early as the Fifties, the first planning research work had been carried out for new processing facilities. A project study from the year 1952 provided for a long linear terminal between the two parallel runways. In another study, it was subsequently proposed to build a semi-circle structure with subterranean approach and exit roads. After weighing all advantages and disadvantages against each other, a combined system was chosen which allows both for central and decentralised processing. Being an incontestable advantage of decentralised installations, a drive-in arrangement could be put into practice whereby the passenger arriving by car or public transport reaches very near the check-in positions. This combined system is particularly advantageous for airports with few transit passengers, as is the case with Düsseldorf, but which boast a considerable number of switch flights. The terminal concept had to live up to the following requirements: As many aircraft as possible are to be processed at the building itself so that passengers may board or disembark without crossing the tarmac via passenger ramps. Apart from central installations, in particular with regard to baggage handling, decentralised processing facilities at the gate had been demanded. The traffic streams of departing, arriving and transit passengers are to be processed with as little overlapping as possible. Further conditions were minimum level differences and no long walks. An additional goal was to largely include the land-side traffic link-up into the building function and to be able to make further use of the existing old processing facilities.

The terminal built on this basis consists of a 250 metre-long, bent central building (70 metres wide on the groundfloor, 35 metres at the upper storey) and, in the completed stage, three pier fingers of varying length and width. The central pier with 9 processing positions is 183 metres long and 33 metres wide. As in Frankfurt it is designated B and serves for processing scheduled flights other than those carried out by Lufthansa. The 35 metre-high control tower projects beyond the finger head. From this position there is a clear view of the entire tarmac and the runways. Pier A which is 230 metres long and 45 metres wide follows, with a slight bend, in line with the central building. It has eleven aircraft positions and is used by Lufthansa. It is planned to build pier C for the processing of charter flights on the other flank of the central building homologous to the centre line of the terminal by the mid-Eighties. It will be designed particularly for the use of wide-body aircraft. If required, two processing units including their waiting lounges can be drawn together in both the existing pier installations for processing wide-body jets.

Departing as well as arriving traffic takes place on the first floor of the pier fingers. On the second floor there is a gallery for transit passen-

The new terminal of Düsseldorf-Lohausen airport allows for central as well as decentralised processing. Below a ground plan of the departure level and pier C which is still in the planning stage.

A metropolitan railway train pulls into the subterranean station which was opened in October 1975.

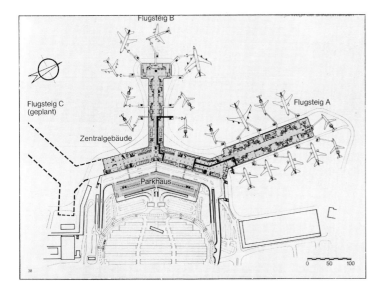

153

gers. In the central building the ground floor is used for arrivals, the first floor for departures and the floor above for transit passengers between domestic and international flights.

A parking garage with nine parking levels in a staggered arrangement accommodating more than 1100 cars, has been included in the main building on the land side. From the garage there are two bridges leading across the departures approach road to the roof of the main building where more parking facilities have been provided. All facilities for stationary traffic can be expanded substantially in the future. For example, there are three parking decks being planned with 1000 bays each within the circle road leading to the terminal.

Düsseldorf is the second airport in the Federal Republic of Germany featuring a railway connection. Since October 1975, metropolitan railway trains stop at a subterranean station in front of the parking garage. The number of passengers does, however, fall short almost by a tenth power of the results achieved by the Frankfurt airport railway.

Processing of two wide-body aircraft at pier B

Berlin-Tegel: Pier ring with approach road to the counter

For West-Berlin, air traffic takes on a special importance. During the Berlin airlift in 1948/49 a runway had been built on the Jungfernheide heathland near Tegel in less than one hundred days. This runway was then the longest in Europe with 2400 metres length. In 1960, Air France started its scheduled flights to Berlin-Tegel. Six years later, the entire charter traffic was concentrated in this airport as the Tempelhof central airport could no longer cope with all air traffic. With the number of passengers soaring, the Berlin Senate decided in 1964 to expand the airport which is located 8 kilometres from the city centre. An international competition to raise ideas resulted in 68 designs being submitted. After careful scrutiny of the structural, functional, operational and financial consequences the first prize was awarded by the jury to the Hamburg team of architects Gerkan, Marg and Nickels. The official inauguration was in 1974.

Since more than 90 per cent of all flights to and from Berlin take less than one hour's flying time, it was one of the major tasks to ensure a favourable ratio between flying and ground time. Hence, the processing counters and the approach were positioned closer to one another than in any other existing terminal in the Federal Republic of Germany. The distance is a mere 20 to 30 metres.

The master development plan for Berlin-Tegel provides for two circular processing installations interlinked by a central building and designed for a total annual capacity of 10 million passengers. So far, the Western one of the two pier rings and the central building have been built, the latter housing airline sales offices, shops, a post office, restaurants and the administration.

The exterior walls of the hexagonal pier ring are 120 metres long. At a developed surface of 28000 square metres, the cubical content of the building is 270000 cubic metres. 14 aircraft up to the size of the Boeing 707 or DC-8 can be positioned at the pier. There are two possibilities to combine two processing units for processing of widebody planes. 3.80 metres below the tarmac level there is a technical level. The operation premises of the airlines and the airport management company are situated on the ground floor. Inside the pier ring, parking facilities for about 1000 cars were created on this level. Later, it will be possible to create a parking garage with a maximum of six storeys. The first parking deck is already available.

Arriving as well as departing passengers are processed in decentralised positions on the approach road level which is 4.35 metres above ground level. It is here, in the interior of the pier ring loop that cars, taxis and buses approach. In addition, there are short-term parking bays. Each of the 14 aircraft positions features installations for the processing of passengers and their luggage. Immediately behind the counters, there are 200 square-metre waiting lounges from where passages lead to the passenger ramps. A passage runs along the land side of the building linking up all processing units. A special foot bridge was created inside the building for transit passengers. From the pier ring roof (12 metres above ground level), visitors have a good view in all directions. At the inner corners of the hexagon there are staircase towers.

Berlin-Tegel is connected to the urban motorway via a road network comprising several lanes and free of intersections. Already upon reaching the airport grounds, an electronic indicator board provides information on departures and arrivals within the next hour and a half. The processing positions are clearly emphasized. Further information is given along the approach road which crosses under a taxiway and the central building of the terminal before it leads into the interior of the pier ring. Design and advance information make Berlin-Tegel a real drive-in airport.

In Berlin-Tegel airport, passengers drive up in front of the counters. Additional parking decks may be built in the interior of the pier ring.

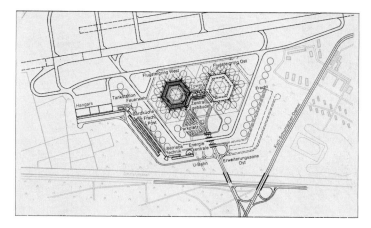

The master development plan of the Berlin-Tegel airport provides for the construction of a second pier ring in the future.

View from the tarmac onto the pier ring and the central building.

For wide-body aircraft, any two processing units can be combined, in which case there are also two passenger ramps available.

When the weather is sunny, the bar support structure of the glass roof makes Berlin-Tegel particularly attractive because of the light and shade effects in the double-storey hall.

Before reaching the terminal, indicator boards inform the motorist on the processing positions of individual flights.

A corridor running around the pier rings on the land-side interconnects all processing units.

There is no future for Munich-Riem airport.

In the processing installations of Munich-Riem airport, the assembly areas of the domestic departures lounge are arranged after the linear principle. At the entrance, the airline detaches the relevant flight coupon from the ticket. Passengers stay in the call room until they can board. They are transported to the plane by tarmac buses. The assembly areas are similarly arranged in the departure lounges at Stuttgart and Hamburg airports.

Munich II: A new airport is being created

Munich-Riem airport which since 1935 handles the air traffic of the Bavarian capital, has no future. With only one runway of 2800 metres length, it is not always possible to operate punctually and consistently. Each time the runway is closed, in the event of an incident, maintenance or repair works, or even snow clearing, diversions, cancellations or delays ensue, which have a chain-reaction effect on the entire air traffic. There is no scope for the construction of a second runway. In addition, the main flight direction from Munich-Riem airport leads forcedly over a densely populated residential area subjecting tens of thousands of people to a considerable noise strain every day.

Already in 1960 it was demanded, after a crash of an aircraft which had taken off from Riem in the urban area, to shift the airport to another location. In 1963, a commission was appointed with the task of finding an appropriate location for the projected large-scale airport. After extensive investigations of twenty possible positions, a 23 square-kilometre area in the Erdinger Moos was selected for the new airport. The distance to the city centre is 28.5 kilometres. As soon as flight operations commence at Munich II, the old Riem airport will have to be closed. During several years up till 1974, the documentation required for the plan finalisation procedure was gathered together. The expertises alone fill some 25 arch lever files. About 27000 objections from amongst the population were lodged against the plans, followed by lengthy hearings. In 1979 the final planning decision was taken which is to enable the construction works in the Erdinger Moos to begin. But the citizens from this region to the North of Munich are determined to make full use of legal recourse to prevent or at least delay the building of the new airport. Opposed to this is the standpoint of a pressure group of Munich citizens who demand, with no less vigour, that Munich II be built and Riem closed as soon as possible.

Munich II is the only international airport which is presently being planned as a complete new airport installation entirely from scratch. The plans provide for two 4000 metre runways running from East to West at a distance of 2300 metres and are staggered by 1500 metres. There will be an additional runway of 2500 metres length for general air traffic. The approach and take-off areas in the extended runway axis lead across a sparsely populated region.

The master development plan allows for a linear, step by step development of the main function in line with traffic volume which will be reflected in extensions built after the building-block method. Individual space has been allocated to passenger terminal, cargo handling, hangars, operating area and fuel depot, allowing for an unimpeded expansion of all installations. With the chosen configuration of the runway system it was obvious to arrange the structural parts principally between the two main runways. Maximising the experience gained in recent years with other new passenger facilities, the passenger processing complex is conceived as a drive-in terminal with decentralised processing at the gate. Munich II will be the first airport to have included in its planning right from the start the connection to a means of mass transport, i.e., the metropolitan railways. The terminal consists of two linear processing "shafts" arranged at a right angle to the runways, and a central building in the middle, the ground plan of the installation, thus, taking the shape of the letter H. The central building, which is 195 metres long, 80 metres wide and up to 25 metres high, forms the link between the two processing shafts and is, at the same time, the point of focus for the entire passenger area. It is here that the subterranean station for the metropolitan railway is built and it is also from here that the internal transportation will leave which is indispensible given the size of the installation at a later building stage. The central building will house, among other things, restaurants, shops, counters of car hire firms and banks, a post office, travel agencies and conference facilities.

The 600 metre-long and between 30 and 50 metre-wide processing shafts are made up from three modules containing all the facilities necessary for processing and which, as entirely independent, fully operational units, constitute, as it were, an airport within the airport. The capacity of each processing module has been estimated at 2.5 million passengers annually. With five modules, an annual capacity of 12 million passengers is, therefore, planned for in the first building stage. In building-block fashion, other modules may be added at the end of the processing shafts, thus, ensuring a high degree of flexibility.

For the passengers coming to the airport by car, Munich II will be the airport of short distances. On the land side, cars pull up on the departure level (first floor) immediately in front of the gate in the proximity of which it is intended to build short and long-term parking facilities. The arrival area and baggage claim are also situated on the first floor.

Before reaching the terminal, the motorist will be provided with drive-in information. The travelling time on the metropolitan railway between the Munich city centre and the new airport will be 35 minutes. Inclusive of building land purchase, building cost for Munich II have been estimated to be 2500 million Deutschmarks. It is expected that eventually 8000 people will work at the new airport. For comparison's sake: Riem airport employs 5000 and Frankfurt Rhein-Main 30000 people.

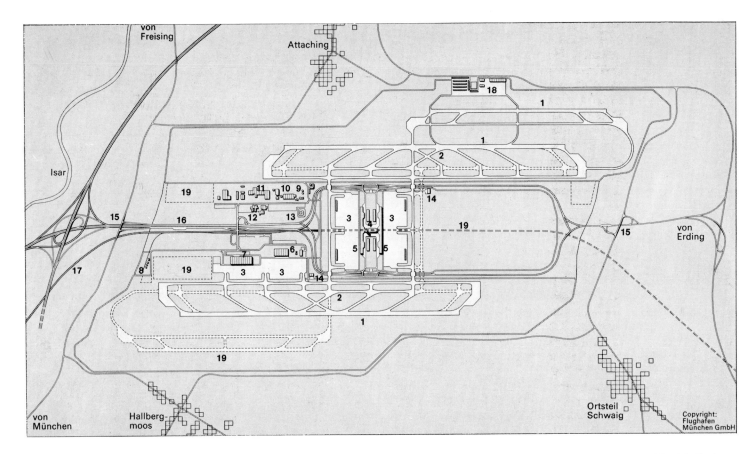

Ground utilization and function plan of the projected Munich II airport depicting the first building stage: Runways (1); taxiways (2); tarmac area (3); central building (4); passenger terminal (5); air cargo and airmail (6); wharf (7); fuel depot and refuelling services (8, 9); board services (10); technical services (11); administration building with canteen (12); look-out hill for visitors (13); fire brigades (14); main approach roads (15); drive-in information (16); metropolitan railway (17); general air cargo (18); expansion possibilities (19).

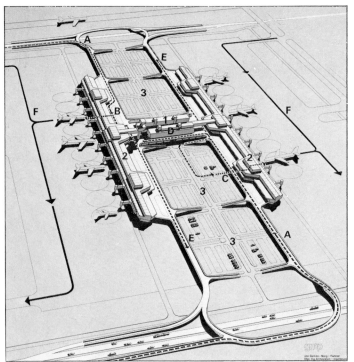

Terminal planning for the first building stage of Munich II: Approach (A); distance to be covered by passenger from approach road to aircraft (B); distance to be covered by passenger from parking lot to aircraft (C); access road to central building (D); exit (E); aircraft taxiway (F); central building with metropolitan railway station (1), processing building with gates (2), parking (3).

160

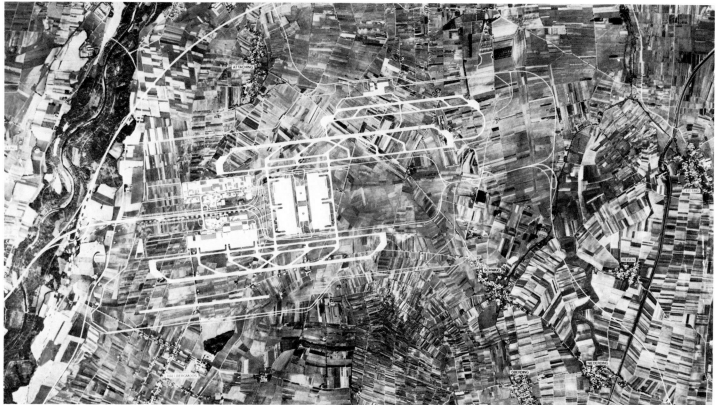

This aereal view reveals how the planned Munich II airport which is to take over from Riem, blends into the landscape.

Cross-section through the central building with metropolitan railway station, main lounge and stops for the inter-airport transport system (FIV).

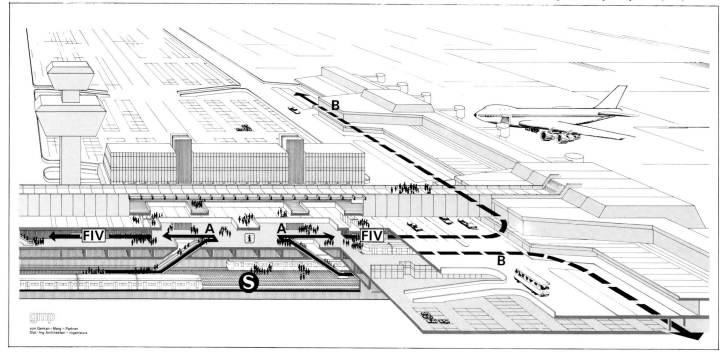

gmp
von Gerkan – Marg · Partner
Dipl.-Ing. Architekten · Ingenieure

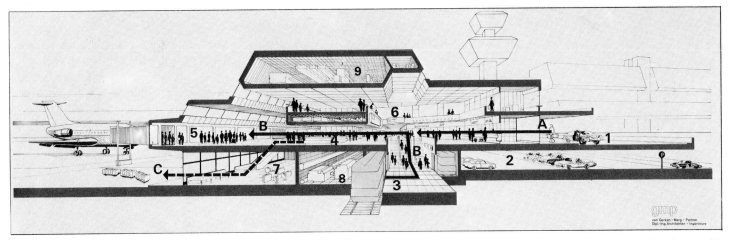

Cross-section through one of the planned passenger processing buildings: Passenger route from approach road (A), respectively, from inter-airport transport system (FIV) (B) to aircraft, baggage routing (C), approach road (1), parking lot (2), FIV stop (3), counter (4), waiting lounge (5), connecting level (6), baggage room (7), supply tunnel (8), supply and exhaust air ventilation (9).

Model of the passenger terminal planned for Munich II airport.

The impressive structure of the bearing trestles of the aircraft maintenance hall V at Frankfurt, arranged at the sides of the hangar.

Besides passenger terminals, airports require cargo handling installations, aircraft maintenance halls and a multitude of other technical operations, installations for the handling of airmail and control towers for air traffic security – buildings the design and construction of which defy the imaginativeness of architects and civil engineers. Hangar V which is the centre piece of the extensive Lufthansa base installations at Frankfurt airport, are a masterpiece of civil engineering. The Concrete Society of London who came to Frankfurt with two chartered planes specifically for this purpose, spoke of "one of the most interesting buildings to have been built recently anywhere in the world". The hangar, terminated in 1970, with its unique suspended roof structure, is held to be the largest aircraft maintenance hangar in the world. This 321 metre-long and 102 (at four pockets 112) metre-deep building can simultaneously accommodate six jumbo jets or a fleet of fourteen Boeings 707. In the construction of the hall (floor area 28300 square metres) new technologies have been invented due to its enormous dimensions.

According to the requirements set out by Lufthansa, the hall had to span without supports an effective area of 270 metres length and 100 metres depth. Only at the gate front and at the rear wall the designers had the possibility to place one middle support each. With a maximum deformation of the roof bearing structure, a clear height of 22 metres must remain below the crane runways. On the other hand, the height of the building was restricted by air traffic control to 34 metres. In its function as employer, the Flughafen Frankfurt/ Main AG invited tenders for a public design and prize competition under which it received 40 entries. Ulrich Finsterwalder's prestressed concrete design with a suspended roof turned out to be the most economical proposal.

The main structural members of the hangar are anchoring trestles with their counterweights, the middle girder frame and the tension bands. The roof – it is not only a spatial closing element but, at the same time, a supporting one, too – consists of ten lightweight concrete tension bands, each of which is 7.50 metres wide and only 8.5 centimetres thick, which span between the trestles and the middle girder over a length of twice 135 metres. Between these tension bands there are 3 metre-wide skylights. The tension bands sag in the middle by about 10 metres. To each tension band belongs a tieback consisting of five prestressing steel bars cast into a plastic coat. The tieback pierces the tension band approximately at the quarter points and is monolithically combined with the concrete structure at these piercing points, at the middle girder and at the trestles. It is the tieback's functions to regulate the deformation of the roof caused by crane load, wind and unilateral load because of snow. The tieback is not required for reasons of stability.

The total horizontal tension of the roof amounts to 8500 tons. It is led into the framework-like trestle structures and spread over the foundation soil by the first together with the vertical loads. Unlike what is normally the case, the tensile force is not anchored in the ground or absorbed by large abutments in the ground. Rather the required counterweight is borne by the anchoring trestles. The great horizontal tension of the roof is diverted in such a way that the struts of the trestles are only compressed. From this follows the characteristic shape of the trestles and, thus, of the entire maintenance hangar. Each of the trestles which stand out at 34 metres height, carries a dead weight of 1000 tons of heavy weight concrete. The 102 metre-long prestressed concrete middle girder which serves as a bearing for the tension bands, rests on two supports with a cross-section of 5.00 by 2.50 metres. The middle girder is 10.50 metres high and 7.60 metres wide and designed as a hollow box with transverse diaphragm.

The special design of the hangar offers the possibility to a, theoretically speaking, unlimited expansion of the hall at the gate front side. The entire apron side of the hangar is closed off by a gate installation consisting of 8 sections which can be opened up to the maximum clear width of 135 metres at any given point. The clear height amounts to 21.50 metres. Each gate weighs about 100 tons.

At the Northern side of the maintenance hall there are built-in operation rooms, offices, stock rooms and sanitary installations. Some 63 kilometres of heating piping have been encased in the concrete floor tiles. There are six passable canals running below the hall floor accommodating the utility piping. Dozens of dispense points for the supply of electricity on board, nitrogen, compressed air as well as warm and cold water for the purpose of washing and de-icing the air-

Tarmac view and longitudinal section of the 321 metre-long aircraft maintenance hangar V at Frankfurt airport. It accommodates six jumbo jets of the Boeing 747 type.

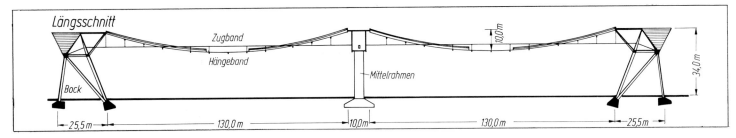

The lateral anchoring trestles with a dead weight of 1000 tons absorb the horizontal tension of the suspension roof.

During a strike, two dozens of passenger aircraft of all sizes were parked here.

Almost the entire reception hall and the forecourt of Frankfurt main station could fit into the "jumbo maintenance hall".

This double-nave wharf hangar with its cantilever roof was built in Frankfurt on the threshold of the yet age.

craft have been installed. Fire extinguishing installations based on powder and foam have been placed in the floor as well as on the side walls and middle columns.

Already at the end of the Fifties, i.e., at the beginning of the jet age, hangar III had been built at Frankfurt airport which, from an engineering point of view, was an extraordinary structure. Based on the experience gained in the United States, a double-nave wharf hall was created the roofs of which cantilevered from a triple-storey middle building towards the gates. The middle section, housing workshops, stock rooms and offices, is 172 metres long and 22 metres wide. At the longitudinal sides of this building adjoin the two halls which are 167 metres long and 55 metres deep each of which provides space for three long-distance jets of the Boeing 707 type.

The clear height of the halls is 15.60 metres at the outside and 10 metres inside. Both halls are covered by curved roofs consisting of individual cantilevering concrete shells which, on an average, are no more than 8 to 12 centimetres thick. The pressure-bearing members of the roofs resting on the middle section are held at the outer edge by steel ropes anchored above the middle section with stressing heads on concrete frames. Each one of the two roofs require 96 steel ropes which consist of fourty veins each and have a diameter of 7 centimetres. Six ropes carry one shell. Skylights have been arranged between these shells. Due to its optical impression, this individualistic building has come to be popularly known as "butterfly hall". As regards the cantilever structure, this wharf hall could not be matched, at the time, by any other single-shell concrete roof. Since the front edge of the shell rises and sags as a consequence of changes in temperature and load – an overhead crane with a hoisting capacity of 5 tons is suspended from the roof –, and this by as much as 90 centimetres (including a 20 per cent security margin), the building was equipped with a corresponding telescoping gate front.

One of the air cargo handling installations at the new Frankfurt cargo centre.

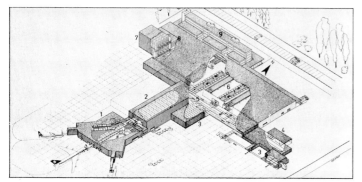

Lufthansa is presently building this air cargo terminal at Frankfurt, with electronically controlled conveyor and storage systems.

Modern air cargo facilities at Stuttgart-Echterdingen airport.

Special air cargo terminals

Over the past two decades, air cargo traffic has experienced even bigger growth rates than passenger traffic, and it is most likely that freight transport will one day outstrip the transport capacity of passengers in aviation. One single jumbo cargo plane can take about 100 tons of cargo. Even when used in passenger traffic, a Boeing 747 carries, as an additional load, almost as large a cargo as a mere cargo plane of the Boeing 707 C type – 30 tons.

Lest the increasing cargo volume has a negative bearing on performance, the decisive criteria of which are speed and reliability, modern airfreight facilities are being created which, as regards their dimensions, are no second to the passenger terminals. With these complexes, too, a differentiation is made between the land and the air side, the loading platforms for the lorries and, on the other side, the loading positions for cargo planes. In addition to the handling and storage areas, it is necessary to have extensive office space for the cargo departments of carriers, shipping agencies and customs in the closest proximity possible. This is why the new air cargo building at Stuttgart-Echterdingen airport provides about 6250 square metres of office space further to a 7600 square metres handling and storage area.

At Frankfurt, Europe's most important air cargo handling airport, a new cargo centre is presently being built on an area of more than one square kilometre which, after completion of the first building stage in 1981 (invested capital: 420 million Deutschmarks), will have a handling capacity of 1.5 million tons. The new Lufthansa cargo terminal which alone will employ 1200 people, comprises 20 700 square metres of storage surface and 18 500 square metres of office space. Conveyor and storage systems are electronically monitored and the handling steps will be mechanized to a large extent. A later building stage provides for a pier extension where cargo planes will dock.

Amongst the eleven airmail handling centres of the Federal German Mail, Frankfurt airport is by far the largest one. The airmail volume handled there achieves 80000 tons per year. On an average, about 500 employees process 780000 letters and 4300 parcels every day. The airmail handling centre is not only a junction between surface and air traffic, but also a transshipment station between international airlines and schedules. There is a daily turnover of 950 transit airmail bags.

The new building of the airmail handling centre which is a reinforced concrete skeleton structure built from prefabricated units with an effective area of 21000 square metres, was put into operation in 1977. It consists of two hall storeys (each one with a clear height of 6.50 metres) with two intermediate floors and a basement. The colour design of the facades is exemplary. Light grey prefabricated concrete members, orange-coloured enameled sheet-metal coverings and canopies contrast with the matt-black aluminium strutting between light glass panes.

In the age of the jet, aircraft noise has developed into a serious problem everywhere, particularly since residential areas have come to border closer and closer on the airport grounds.

Since 1961, Lufthansa is using a noise protection hall at its Hamburg wharf for the test runs of aircraft that have been overhauled. This hall measures 100 metres in length and 60 metres, on an average, in width. At the three sides of the hall wich are closed, the noise sensation is reduced to 1 or 2 per cent of the initial level. Due to exhaust gas generation, the fourth side needs to be kept open, but the stepped and angled walls and the acoustic lining of the hall reduce the noise escaping towards the tarmac to such an extent that it comes down to an acceptable level in the closest residential area which is two kilometres away. The hall accommodates jets up to the size of a Boeing 707.

In order to shield off a neighbouring town against the noise emanating from aircraft taxying on the ground under their own power, a 15 metre-high and – provisionally – 2000 metre-long noise protection wall was built at Frankfurt airport from prefabricated concrete units.

The Frankfurt airmail handling centre boasts a destination-controlled parcel sorting installation and container conveying facilities.

This 15 metre-high noise protection wall was built at Rhein-Main airport.

Noise protection hangars at the Lufthansa wharf facilities in Hamburg.

167

Control towers

From the pulpit on the upper floor of the control tower, air traffic controllers of the airport traffic control authority direct flight operations on the runways as well as taxiways. The position of the tower, therefore, must ensure a good view onto the runways, approach path, circuit and apron areas. No other building on the airport grounds should be higher than the control tower. On the other hand, the restrictions related to construction height stipulated by the Law on Air Traffic also applies to the tower. In addition, the controllers want to see the approaching aircraft because of the contrast against the sky. Hence, the compromise formula: As high as necessary, as low as possible. As a rule, modern control towers in the Federal Republic of Germany are about 40 metres high. At Berlin-Tegel airport, however, it reaches a height of 48 metres. To avoid light reflection, the window panes of the pulpit are slanted towards the inside by 15°.

Radar installations

Large-scale surveillance radar installations for flight course supervision by the air traffic control are installed on top of 40 metre-high reinforced concrete towers at topographically exposed locations. They can pick up aircraft cruising at a distance of 270 kilometres and at an altitude of 22 000 metres. With nine such installations, the Federal territory is at least doubly covered by radar. Two reflectors of 14.5 metres width and 9 metres height each are mounted back to back. The total weight of the aerial installation amounts to 55 tons. By engaging further electric motors, the speed remains constant even in the event of storm squalls.

The stability and vibration strength standards set for the towers are extremely high. The reinforced concrete structures are given a curtain wall facade so as to prevent the tower from slanting minimally due to one-sided thermal expansion. Although this might not strike the eye, it would impair the functioning of the radar installation immediately owing to the required extreme angle accuracy.

The control tower at Hanover airport with a sixteen-sided tower shaft.

Radar installations with Janus antenna at Mittersberg in the Oberpfalz region.

These two pictures show the history of aviation in its early days along with the relevant architecture: The airship hall built in Hamburg-Fuhlsbüttel in 1912 (160 metres long, 50 metres wide) was blown up after the First World War. LZ 129 "Hindenburg", in front of the hangar at Rhein-Main in 1936.

BIBLIOGRAPHY

Aral-Verkehrstaschenbuch 1978/79, Bochum 1978

Architekten- und Ingenieur-Verein zu Berlin (Editor), Weber, Klaus Konrad, Güttler, Peter and Ahmadi, Ditta (Editorship): Berlin und seine Bauten, Section X, Volume B: Anlagen und Bauten für den Verkehr – Städtischer Nahverkehr, Berlin, Munich, Düsseldorf 1979

BAUL, WILLI: Technische Sehenswürdigkeit in Deutschland (ADAC-Reiseführer), 3 volumes, Munich 1976–78

BEYER, E., THUL, H.: Hochstraßen, Planung – Ausführung – Beispiele, Düsseldorf 1967

BLANKENSHIP, EDWARD G.: Der Flughafen: Architektur, Urbane Integration, Ökologie. Stuttgart 1974

BONATZ, PAUL and LEONHARDT, FRITZ: Brücken, Königstein im Taunus 1965

BONATZ, PAUL: Leben und Bauen, Stuttgart 1950

BONGARTZ, NORBERT, DÜBBERS, PETER, WERNER, FRANK: Paul Bonatz 1877–1956, Stuttgart 1977

Bundesminister für Forschung und Technologie: Neue Ideen für Transport und Verkehr, Bonn 1979

Bundesminister für Raumordnung, Bauwesen und Städtebau (Editor): Siedlungsstrukturelle Folgen der Einrichtung verkehrsberuhigter Zonen in Kernbereichen, Bonn 1978

Bundesminister für Raumordnung, Bauwesen und Städtebau (Editor): Verkehrsberuhigung – Ein Beitrag zur Stadterneuerung, Bonn 1979

Bundesminister für Verkehr (Editor): Deutsche Autobahnen im Luftbild, Konstanz 1971

Bundesminister für Verkehr (Editor): HAFRABA Bundesautobahn Hansestädte – Frankfurt – Basel, Rückblick auf 30 Jahre Autobahnbau, Wiesbaden – Berlin 1962

Bundesminister für Verkehr und ADAC (Editor): Sicherheit für den Fußgänger – Verkehrsberuhigung, Bonn/Munich no date

Bundesminister für Verkehr (Editor): Die Verkehrswege in der Bundesrepublik Deutschland, Munich 1964

Bundesminister für Verkehr (Editor): Verkehr in Zahlen 1978, revised by Heinz Enderlein, Deutsches Institut für Wirtschaftsforschung, Bonn 1978

Bundesminister für Verkehr (Editor): Die Vogelfluglinie, Neumünster 1963

Bundesminister für Verkehr (Editor): Die Vogelfluglinie – Planung und Bau der Verkehrsanlagen in der Bundesrepublik Deutschland, Neumünster 1963

Bundesverband der Deutschen Zementindustrie (Editor): Straßenbau heute, Issue No. 1 Betondecken, Düsseldorf 1979

CENTRE GEORGES POMPIDOU: Le temps des gares, Paris 1978

CONIN, HELMUT: Gelandet in Berlin, Zur Geschichte der Berliner Flughäfen, Berlin 1974

DANIELEWSKI, GERD: Wo der Fußgänger König ist – Neue Wege der Cityplanung, Düsseldorf 1974

Deutscher Beton-Verein E.V.: Verschiedene Jahrgänge der Betontage Wiesbaden

Deutsche Beton-Verein E.V.: Welt des Betons, Wiesbaden no date

Deutsche Bundesbahn (Editor): Neue Hochbauten der Deutschen Bundesbahn, Frankfurt am Main/Bonn 1962

Deutscher Industrie- und Handelstag (Editor): Einkaufs-Magnet Fußgängerzone, Bonn 1979

Deutscher Rat für Landespflege (Editor): Landschaft und Moselbau, Bad Godesberg 1966

Deutscher Städtetag, Verband öffentlicher Verkehrsbetriebe (Editor): Öffentlicher Personennahverkehr, Investitionen - Bauleistungen - Erfolge 1967–1976, Cologne 1978

DIERKSMEIER, THEODOR: 25 Jahre Hochbau bei der Deutschen Bundesbahn, Offprint from "Die Bundesbahn" 3/1973, Düsseldorf

DIERKSMEIER, THEODOR: Neue Hochbauten der Deutschen Bundesbahn, Offprint from "Die Bauverwaltung" Issue No. 9/1964, Düsseldorf

DÜTEMEYER, KASPAR: 100 Jahre zur Wahrung der Rheinschiffahrtsinteressen eingetragener Verein, Duisburg-Ruhrort 1977

EINWÄCHTER, HELMUT: Die Frankfurter Häfen im Wandel der Anforderungen, Frankfurt 1976

Fachausschuß Straßenverkehr München 1965 (Editor): Straßenverkehr – Eine Dokumentation der Abteilung Straßenverkehr der Internationalen Verkehrsausstellung Munich 1965, Munich 1967

FARENHOLTZ, CHRISTIAN, WILLEKE, RAINER and HARTENSTEIN, WOLFGANG: Innerstädtischer Verkehr heute und morgen, Frankfurt 1971

FLIEGER, HEINZ: Bauen für die Zukunft, Düsseldorf 1970

FÖHL, AXEL: Technische Denkmale im Rheinland, Cologne 1976

FRANKE, FRIEDRICH: Flughafen Köln/Bonn, Cologne 1970

GÖÖCK, ROLAND: Post, Dokumentation über das Post- und Fernmeldewesen, Gütersloh 1965

GROSSHEIMANN, KARL-JOSEF and BÖHLER, KARL: Kraftwerksbau an der Mosel, Offprint from "Energiewirtschaftliche Tagesfragen", Essen 1961

HAASS, ELMAR (Editor-in-Chief): DB Report 79, Darmstadt 1979

HEINERSDORFF, RICHARD: Die Große Welt der Eisenbahn, Munich 1976

HITZER, HANS: Die Straße, Vom Trampelpfad zur Autobahn, Lebensadern von der Urzeit bis heute, Munich 1971

KAFTAN, KURT: Der Kampf um die Autobahnen. Geschichte der Autobahnen in Deutschland 1907–1935, Berlin 1955

KLASS, GERT VON: Weit spannt sich der Bogen 1865–1965. 100 Jahre Dyckerhoff & Widmann, Wiesbaden 1965

LAMPRECHT, HEINZ-OTTO: opus caementitium, Düsseldorf 1968

LEONHARDT, FRITZ: Bauen als Umweltzerstörung. Eine Herausforderung an uns alle, Lecture in print-form, Stuttgart 1975

LEONHARDT, FRITZ: Ingenieurbau – Bauingenieure gestalten die Umwelt, Darmstadt 1974

LEONHARDT, FRITZ: Zur Geschichte des Brückenbaus, in: Brücken der Welt, edited by Oto Bihaltji-Merin, Wiesbaden no date

LOHMER, GERD: Brückenästhetik – Brücken aus der Sicht des Architekten, published in: Der Deutsche Baumeister 3/1973

LORENZ, HANS: Trassierung und Gestaltung von Straßen und Autobahnen, Wiesbaden and Berlin 1971

MARSCHALL, KURZAK, HARALD, LINDE, RÜDIGER: Stadt und Verkehr, published in the Serial Publication Straßenverkehr des ADAC, Munich no date

MEYER-MARWITZ, BERNHARD: Großer Hamburg Spiegel, Hamburg 1978

MÜLLER, KARLHANS/SKARYD, MILAN: Airport der Zukunft, Terminal Mitte, Frankfurt 1972

MÜLLER, KARLHANS: Cockpit - Tower - Sicherheit, Luftverkehr der Jumbo-Zeit, Reutlingen 1977

NAGEL, S. and LINKE, S.: Bauten des Verkehrswesens, Gütersloh/Düsseldorf 1973

NECKAR AG UND WASSER- UND SCHIFFAHRTSDIREKTION STUTTGART (Editor): Der Neckar zwischen Mannheim und Plochingen, Stuttgart 1971

NOWARRA, HEINZ J.: 60 Jahre Deutsche Verkehrsflughäfen, Mainz 1969

OEHM, E. (Editor): Stadtautobahnen - Planung, Bau, Betrieb, Wiesbaden 1973

No Author: Berlin - die Stadt der Wasserstraßen und Häfen, Berlin 1968

No Author: Die Reichsautobahnen, Grundsätzliches über Gestaltung und Baudurchführung, Berlin 1936

Portland-Zementwerke Heidelberg AG (Editor): Beton im Straßenbau, Heidelberg no date

RELLS, KARL J.: 100 x Luftverkehr, Mannheim 1978

Rhein-Main-Donau AG: Kulturlandschaft und Wasserbau, Munich 1978

RÖTTCHER, HUGO: Empfangsgebäude der Personenbahnhöfe, Berlin 1933

SCHADENDORF, WULF: Das Jahrhundert der Eisenbahn, Frankfurt am Main/ Bonn 1965

SCHAECHTERLE, KARL and LEONHARDT, FRITZ: Die Gestaltung der Brücken, Berlin 1937

SCHIERK, HANS-FRIED and SCHMIDT, NORBERT: Die Schwebebahn in Wuppertal, Cologne 1976

Senator für Bau- und Wohnungswesen in Berlin (Editor): Fußgängerbrücken in Berlin, Berlin 1976

SIGNON, HELMUT: Brücken in Köln am Rhein, Cologne 1966

SILL, O. (Editor): Parkbauten - Handbuch für Planung, Bau und Betrieb von Park- und Garagenbauten, Wiesbaden 1979

Stadt Köln (Editor): Zur Einweihung der neuen Köln-Deutzer Brücke 16. Oktober 1948, Cologne no date

STEINMAN, DAVID B.: Brücken für die Ewigkeit, Düsseldorf 1957

TAMMS, FRIEDRICH and WORTMANN, WILHELM: Städtebau - Umweltgestaltung: Erfahrungen und Gedanken, Darmstadt 1973

TAMMS, FRIEDRICH: Verkehrsarchitektur, Dortmund 1977

TAMMS, FRIEDRICH: Von Menschen, Städten und Brücken, Düsseldorf - Vienna 1974

Verband der Automobilindustrie e.V. (Editor): Planen für die menschliche Stadt - Die Rolle des Automobils, Frankfurt 1973

Verband der Automobilindustrie e.V. (Editor): Stadtverkehr und Lärm, Frankfurt 1978

Various Authors: Der Ausbau der Mosel, Trier 1966

Various Authors: Vom Caementum zum Spannbeton, Beiträge zur Geschichte des Betons, 3 volumes, Wiesbaden and Berlin 1964-1965

Various Authors: Festschrift Ulrich Finsterwalder - 50 Years of Dywidag, Karlsruhe 1973

Various Authors: 75 Jahre Züblin-Bau 1898-1973, Stuttgart 1973

Various Authors: 100 Jahre elektrische Eisenbahn, edited by Bundesbahn-Ausbesserungswerk Munich-Freimann, Starnberg 1979

Various Authors: Internationales Congress Centrum Berlin, festschrift on the occasion of the inauguration 2 April 1979, Berlin 1979

Wasser- und Schiffahrtsverwaltung des Bundes (Editor): Elbe-Seitenkanal, Natur und Technik, Hamburg 1976

Wayss & Freytag AG 100 Jahre, Frankfurt am Main 1975

WERNER, ERNST: Die Eisenbahn über die Wupper bei Müngsten, Cologne 1975

WERNER, AXEL: Unsere Städte, Entwicklung - gegenwärtige Situation - Entwicklungstendenzen, no place 1978

WITTFOHT, HANS: Triumph der Spannweiten. Vom Holzsteg zur Spannbetonbrücke, Düsseldorf 1972

PHOTOGRAPHS AND ILLUSTRATIONS

Release endorsement for aerial views in brackets.